Labour Law in Japan

Labour Law in Japan

Third Edition

Tadashi A. Hanami
Fumito Komiya
Ryuichi Yamakawa
Chikako Kanki

This book was originally published as a monograph in the International Encyclopaedia of Laws/Labour Law and Industrial Relations.

Founding Editor: Roger Blanpain
General Editor: Frank Hendrickx
Volume Editor: Frank Hendrickx

Wolters Kluwer

Published by:
Kluwer Law International B.V.
PO Box 316
2400 AH Alphen aan den Rijn
The Netherlands
E-mail: lrs-sales@wolterskluwer.com
Website: www.wolterskluwer.com/en/solutions/kluwerlawinternational

Sold and distributed by:
Wolters Kluwer Legal & Regulatory U.S.
920 Links Avenue
Landisville, PA 17538
United States of America
E-mail: customer.service@wolterskluwer.com

ISBN 978-94-035-3719-1

e-Book: ISBN 978-94-035-3729-0
web-PDF: ISBN 978-94-035-3739-9

This title is available on www.kluwerlawonline.com

The Authors

Prof. Dr Tadashi A. Hanami was born in 1930. He was a professor of law at Sophia University in Tokyo from 1966 to 2000. He was also the Chairperson of the Central Labour Relations Commission of Japan from 1998 to 2000. As an internationally known labour law specialist, he published numerous books and articles on labour law and industrial relations, not only in Japanese but also in English. The publication project of this book was also initiated by Professor Hanami. He passed away in 2021.

Prof. Dr Fumito Komiya was born in 1948. He became a Bachelor of Law in 1972, a Master of Law in 1978 and a Doctor of Law in 1992, at Hokkaido University. He was also awarded a Master's Degree (LLM) from the University of California (Berkeley) in 1984 and a PhD from the University of London (LSE) in 1997. He was a Professor of Law at Hokkaigakuen University in Sapporo, Hokkaido from 1997 to 2011, and then at Senshu University in Tokyo until 2019. He was a visiting scholar at the University of California (Berkeley) in 1984 and at the University of Michigan in 1987, a visiting professor at the Catholic University of Leuven in Belgium during 1995–1996, and an overseas fellow at Churchill College, Cambridge University in 2009. He was a commissioner of the Civil Service Commission, Hokkaido Prefectural Government between 1998 and 2008. He is the author of several books in Japanese and a number of articles in Japanese and English on labour law.

The Authors

Prof. Dr Ryuichi Yamakawa, born in 1958, graduated from the University of Tokyo in 1982. He received an LLM from the University of Washington (Seattle) in the United States in 1991, as well as a PhD (Law) from the University of Tokyo in 2000. He has taught labour law at Musashi University, University of Tsukuba, Keio University, University of Tokyo, where he retired and became a Professor Emeritus in 2023, and Meiji University, where he currently belongs. He has been a member of the Labour Policy Council since 2005. In addition, he was the chairperson of the Central Labour Relations Commission in Japan from 2017 to 2019. He has written a number of books and articles in Japanese as well as in English regarding labour law.

Prof. Dr Chikako Kanki was born in 1977. She obtained her Bachelor of Health Sciences in 2000, Bachelor of Laws in 2003, Master of Laws in 2005, and Doctor of Laws in 2010 from the University of Tokyo. She served as a JSPS Research Fellow (PD) in 2008, then as a Global COE Specially Appointed Researcher at the University of Tokyo in 2011 and became a Visiting Researcher at the University of British Columbia in 2012. She was an associate professor at Rikkyo University from 2013 to 2020, then transferred to the University of Tokyo, where she has been a professor since 2023. She has been a public member of the Tokyo Labour Relations Commission since 2023, and a member of the Labour Policy Council since 2024. She has written several books in Japanese on labour law and numerous articles in Japanese and English.

Table of Contents

Table of Contents

List of Abbreviations

ACALM	Act on Comprehensively Advancing Labour Measures, etc.
ADR	Alternative Dispute Resolution
CCP	Code of Civil Procedure
CFLA	Child and Family Care Leave Act
Churitsu-roren	Federation of Independent Unions of Japan
CLRC	Central Labour Relations Commission
Domei	Japanese Confederation of Labour
DPEPA	Disabled Person's Employment Promotion Act
EEOA	Equal Employment Opportunity Act
EIA	Employment Insurance Act
ESA	Employment Security Act
EPI	Employee's Pension Insurance
GDP	Gross Domestic Product
GNP	Gross National Product
ICO	Immigration Control Office
ICRRA	Immigration Control and Refugee Recognition Act
Keidanren	Japan Federation of Economic Organization
Keizaidoyukai	Japan Association of Corporate Executive
LCA	Labour Contract Act
LDP	Liberal Democratic Party
APRILD	Act on Promoting the Resolution of Individual Labour Disputes
LPELRA	Local Public Enterprise Labour Relations Act
LRAA	Labour Relations Adjustment Act
LRC	Labour Relations Commission
LSIO	Labour Standards Inspection Office

List of Abbreviations

LSA	Labour Standards Act
LTA	Labour Tribunal Act
MWA	Minimum Wages Act
MWC	Minimum Wages Council
NCSA	National Civil Servant Act
Nikkeiren	Japan Federation of Employers' Association
NLRA	National Labour Relations Act
NPI	National Pension Insurance
OJT	On the Job Training
OPESA	Older Person's Employment Stabilization Act
PESO	Public Employment Security Office
PLRC	Prefectural Labour Relations Commission
PLB	Prefectural Labour Bureau
PWA	Part-time Work Act
PFEA	Part-time and Fixed-term Employment Act
QC	Quality Circle
Rengo	Japanese Trade Union Confederation
RH	*Rodo Hanrei* (Labour Law Reports)
RHS	*Rodo Keizai Hanrei Sokuho* (Quick Labour Law Reports)
SKS	*Saikosaibansho Keijisaibanreishu* (Supreme Court Reports on Criminal Cases)
SMS	*Saikosaibansho Minjisaibanreishu* (Supreme Court Reports on Civil Cases)
SWPA	Security of Wage Payment Act
TITA	Technical Intern Trainees Act
TUA	Trade Union Act
UCPA	Unfair Competition Prevention Act
WACIA	Workers' Accident Compensation Insurance Act
WDA	Worker Dispatching Act
Zenrokyo	National Trade Union Council
Zenroren	National Confederation of Trade Unions

General Introduction

Chapter 1. General Background

§1. Geography and Population

1. Japan is a long, narrow archipelago extending 3,800 kilometres (2,369 miles) north to south which consists of four major islands – Hokkaido, Honshu, Shikoku, and Kyushu – and about 3,900 smaller adjacent islands. Japan's total land area is about one-twenty-fifth that of the United States, one-ninth that of India, and one and a half times that of the United Kingdom. Japan occupies less than 0.3% of the world's land area.

2. The climate of Japan varies considerably from place to place although it is comparatively mild in most areas. The most southern area, the Okinawa islands, is in the subtropical zone, while the most northern area, northern Hokkaido, is in the sub-arctic zone. Most areas have four clearly distinct seasons.

3. Japan's population was 124,352,000 in October 2023. The population has decreased by 2.7% since 2005. This is due to a falling birth rate which will rapidly lead to Japan becoming an ageing society. The ratio of people aged 65 or over to the whole population rose from 15.1% in 1996 to 29.1% in 2023. The population is rather unevenly spread among different regions. Tokyo is the prefecture with the largest population, 14.08 million. Tokyo is the only prefecture where the population increased during the period of 2022–2023. The second largest prefecture is Osaka in the western part of Japan, the population of which is 8.76 million.

4. Being an archipelago at a fair distance from the Chinese continent, Japan has been fairly independent of foreign influence in terms of politics and culture. Japan Before industrialization, Japan was traditionally a rice-farming society and people struggled to control the land for the cultivation of rice. It is often said among Japanese that the planting and harvesting of rice encouraged the society to organize in tightly knit communities with strong family relationships. Any disagreements would have threatened the communal approach to the host of activities required for the survival of each community. This might be reflected in the present Japanese style of management and conflict resolution.

5. Most Japanese believe that they are homogeneous and unique. This may be due to Japan's geographical location and three centuries of national isolation in recent times. Also, Japan diplomatically closed itself off from the rest of the world for more than 250 years during the Edo era, although it stopped such policy shortly before the Meiji Restoration in 1868 and began its industrialization. All Japanese can understand the national standard version of their language although there are a lot of dialect forms. The average educational level of the Japanese is very high. Japan has no minority greater than 1% which is different by virtue of religion or ethnicity. There are about 254,000 Koreans in 2023 who have a special status of residence under immigration law and are culturally assimilated into Japanese society.[1] Most Japanese are followers of both Shinto and Buddhism although there are one million Christians. The Japanese have also been influenced by Confucian ethics, especially in their social behaviour.

§2. The Political System

6. The political modernization of Japan started in 1868, the year of the *Meiji* Restoration. The Constitution of the Empire of Great Japan (1889) established a kind of constitutional monarchy, and provided for a *Diet* of elected representatives, a bill of rights (though under the 'reservation of the law') and an independent judiciary. In comparison with the state of affairs before the Restoration, this was definitely a step forward in the direction of modernization. However, the Constitution itself was quite conservative, mainly because of the imperial retention of comprehensive prerogative powers. The draftsmen of the Constitution envisaged a strong bureaucracy consisting of civil and military branches, with prestige and honours emanating from the semi-divine emperor. The Diet was not to be allowed any direct control over the executive power, and even in matters of legislation and finance its authority was to be limited by the imperial prerogatives. Thus, the development of party politics in a democratic sense was hardly to be expected in pre-war Japan and was destined to be suffocated under military rule after the 1930s.

7. Under the Constitution of Japan of 1946, drafted during the Allied occupation with a view to the democratization of Japan after World War II, the emperorship was retained but only as a 'symbol of the State and the unity of the people' (Const. Article 1). The executive supremacy contemplated by the old Constitution was replaced by legislative supremacy. The constitutional position of the judiciary was elevated by including administrative matters in its jurisdiction which were outside it under the Meiji Constitution. Thus, the new Constitution allocated the legislative power to the Diet (Article 41), the executive power to the Cabinet (Article 65) and the judicial power to the Supreme Court and lower courts (Article 76). The Diet consists of the House of Representatives and the House of Councillors (Article 42) which are elected by all the people. The Prime Minister at the head of the Cabinet who is designated from among the members of the Diet by a resolution of the Diet

1. *Homu-sho* (Ministry of Justice), *Zairyu Gaikoku-jin Tokei* (Statistics on Foreigners Residing in Japan), 2023. There are also 11,450 aborigines in 2023 who are called Ainu. *See* Hokkaido Kankyo Seikatsubu (Department of Environment and Lifestyle of Hokkaido), Hokkaido Utari Seikatsu Jittaichosa Hokoku (Report on the Survey of Life of Utari in Hokkaido), 2023.

(Article 67). Thus, the Prime Minister is not directly elected by Japanese citizens. The Prime Minister appoints the other Cabinet members, i.e., Ministers of State (Article 68). Where the House of Representatives either passes a no-confidence resolution or rejects a confidence resolution, the Cabinet must resign *en masse* unless it dissolves the House of Representatives within ten days. The Cabinet has the power to designate the Chief Justice of the Supreme Court and to appoint other Supreme Court Justices and lower court judges. However, the appointment of Justices is not only subject to popular review by the voters at the first general election of the members of the House of Representatives after such appointment but also subject to popular review at the first general election after a lapse of ten years (Article 79). The Courts have the authority to determine the constitutionality of any law passed by the Diet (Article 81), while the *Diet* has the power to set up an impeachment court composed of the members of the Diet for the purpose of trying those judges against whom removal proceedings have been instituted (Article 64).

8. Under the Constitution, human rights, with some additions, are enumerated and are to be guaranteed by the judiciary. As befits the constitution of a 20th-century industrial state, the Constitution imposes not only the negative duty to refrain from violating human rights and fundamental freedoms but also the positive duty to promote the economic and social welfare of its citizens. That is, it provides not only for such classical liberties as freedom of thought, conscience (Article 19), religion (Article 20), assembly and association (Article 21), freedom to choose residence and occupation (Article 22) and academic freedom (Article 23) as well as equality under the law (Article 14); but also such rights as the right to maintain a wholesome and cultured standard of living (Article 25), the right to work (Article 27) and the workers' right to organize, to bargain and act collectively (Article 28).

9. Under the new Constitution, the Japanese people enjoy complete freedom to organize and participate in political parties and other political organizations including pressure groups and trade unions. However, political development in post-war Japan has been characterized by one distinguishing feature: the continuous rule of the conservative parties, except for one short period of socialist government during 1947–1948. After that, the conservative parties took the government again, and the government ruled by the conservative parties has continued since then. However, the opposition parties including left-wing parties took the government for the period of 1993–1996 and 2009–2012. In recent years, although the largest conservative party (Liberal Democratic Party (LDP)) has largely retained its power, small political parties, both liberal and conservative, have increased.

§3. The Economy

10. Japan is ranked fourth in terms of gross domestic product (GDP) in the world in 2023, next to the United States, China and Germany. The 2023 GDP (at current prices) stood at USD 4,219 billion, which was around 16% of the American GDP for the same year. Japanese gross national product (GNP) per capita in 2023 (i.e., USD 46,707) was around 56.5% of the US (i.e., USD 82,715) (*see* Table 1).

Although the Japanese GDP per capita became the second largest in the world in 1993, it has since then been gradually shrinking. In 2023, it was ranked in 38th place.

Table 1 Gross Domestic Product (at Current Prices) and Real Economic Growth Rates

	GDP (USD Billion) in 2023	*Per Capita GDP (USD)*			*Real Economic Growth Rates*		
		2021	*2022*	*2023*	*2021*	*2022*	*2023*
USA	27,720	71,258	77,980	82,715	2.7	1.2	1.7
China	17,758	12,572	12,643	12,597	8.4	3.0	5.2
Germany	4,527	52,301	49,725	53,565	3.7	1.4	-0.3
Japan	4,219	42,917	46,102	46,707	2.7	1.2	1.7
India	3,567	2,250	2,366	2,497	9.7	7.0	7.8
UK	3,382	46,731	46,103	49,648	8.6	4.8	0.3
France	3,052	45,361	42,581	46,305	6.9	2.6	0.9

Source: IMF 'World Economic Outlook Database'.

11. At the end of World War II, Japan lost all of its overseas territories. Production facilities had also suffered heavy damage. About one-third of the national wealth accumulated as a result of industrialization since the Meiji Restoration was lost. The combination of the Japanese people's efforts towards recovery and a relatively favourable international setting, including American assistance, enabled the Japanese economy to reach its pre-war level in less than ten years. After that, the economy continued to grow with a surprisingly rapid average annual growth rate of 9.7% between 1956 and 1970. Accordingly, Japan had by 1966 attained the second-highest-ranking GDP in the free world. However, the dollar crisis (in 1971) and the first oil crisis (in 1973) brought this rapid economic growth to an end; the annual growth rate was negative (-0.5) in 1974 for the first time. Around this time, Japan entered into a period of low economic growth. Thus, the average annual growth rate was 3.4% in the period 1974–1978. Furthermore, the second oil crisis of 1978 was hard on the Japanese economy. However, in response to this, Japanese enterprises made an effort to invest with a view to reducing the use of fuel and materials per product. They were also successful in improving productivity and in keeping the growth of wage levels within the level of improved productivity. As a result, despite the oil crisis, the Japanese economy has not suffered as much as other advanced countries such as the US, the UK and France; the average annual growth rate was 3.9% during the period 1980–1990. Accordingly, Japan surpassed the United States in terms of GDP per capita. However, Japan suffered a long structural depression for three years after the collapse of the 'bubble' economy in 1990. The real economic growth rate has drastically declined since 1991 when the rate was 4.0%; it declined to 1.1% in 1992 and 0.1% in 1993.[2] About three decades later, the growth rate has only slightly improved since then. In 2008, the Japanese economy was again badly affected by the world financial market crisis that erupted because of the collapse of the US subprime mortgage market. As a result, the real economic growth rate fell to -5.5% in 2009. In 2011, a huge earthquake hit eastern Japan, resulting in a decrease in real economic growth by 0.6%. Then, Japan's economy suffered again as a result of COVID-19. In 2020, the real economic growth rate fell to -4.2%. After that, however, Japan's economy has been slowly recovering. Its real economic growth rate in 2023 was 1.7%.

§4. Labour Force

12. Japan's labour force in 2022 numbered 69,020,000, of which 1,794,500 or 2.6% were totally unemployed.[3] Unemployment rose to the highest 5.5% both in 2002 following economic decline due to the burst of the 'bubble' economy and in 2010 after the Lehman shock. Since then, against the background of the recovery of Japan's economy as well as the decrease in working age population, Japan's unemployment rate has been considerably low.

13. The distribution of the labour force has constantly shifted from primary and secondary industries to tertiary industries (*see* Table 2). In 2020, 73.4% of the total employed persons were engaged in the tertiary industry, 23.4% in the secondary industry and only 3.3% in the primary industry.

Table 2 Change in the Industrial Distribution of the Employed (000)

Year	*1975*	*1985*	*1995*	*2005*	*2015*	*2020*
Primary industry	7,347 (13.8%)	6,102 (9.3)	3,820 (6.0)	2,981 (4.8)	2,222 (3.8)	1,963 (3.3)
Secondary industry	18,106 (34.1%)	19,334 (33.1)	20,247 (31.6)	15,957 (25.9)	13,921 (23.6)	13,259 (23.4)
Tertiary industry	27,521 (51.8%)	33,444 (57.3)	39,642 (61.8)	41,425 (67.2)	39,615 (67.2)	40,679 (73.4)
Total	53,141 (100.0%)	58,357 (100.0)	64,142 (100.0)	61,530 (100.0)	58,919 (100.0)	57,643 (100.0)

Source: Ministry of Internal Affairs and Communications, *National Census in Japan.*

2. Economic Planning Agency, *Heisei – Kunenban Keizai Hakusho* (White Paper on Economy), 1997.
3. Statistics Bureau, Ministry of Internal Affairs and Communications, *Rodo Ryoku Chosa* (Survey on Labour Force), 2023.

14. The percentage of employees among the gainfully employed has constantly increased (*see* Table 3). It increased from about 42.4% in 1955 to about 89.1% in 2020. In contrast, during the same period, the percentage of self-employed and unpaid family workers decreased from about 25.1% to 7.8% and from 31.4% to 2.1%, respectively.

Table 3 Employment Status of the Gainfully Employed: 1955–2012 (000)

Year	*Total (A)*	*Self-Employed*	*Unpaid Family Workers*	*Employees (B)*	*Percentage of Employees in the Labour Force (B)÷(A)×100*
1955	40,900	10,280	12,840	17,780	42.4
1965	47,300	9,390	9,150	28,760	60.8
1975	52,230	9,390	6,280	36,460	69.8
1985	58,070	9,160	5,590	43,130	74.3
1995	64,570	7,840	3,970	52,630	81.6
2005	63,560	6,500	2,820	53,930	84.8
2020	67,400	5,270	1,400	60,050	89.1

Source: Ministry of Internal Affairs and Communications, *Annual Report on the Labour Force Survey.*

15. The labour force participation rates by age group and sex are to be found in Table 4. The average labour force participation rate in 2012 was 59.1%. The rate constantly decreased from 1965 to 1975, but it rose in a gradual curve until 1992. This was due to the increase in women's labour force participation rate. It reached 50.7% in 1992, but since then it gradually decreased and was down to 48.2% in 2012. This stagnation of the women's labour force participation rate is mainly due to the economic depression which began in the early 1990s. The labour participation rate of those between 15 and 19 years constantly decreased to around 175% level in recent years. In the period 1965–1985, the labour participation rate of women aged 25–34 was significantly lower than that of women in other age groups. This indicates that many women aged 25–34 had the burden of childcare and could not remain employed. In 1985, however, women aged 30–39 had a lower labour participation rate than women aged 25–34. This is mainly due to an upward trend in women's marriage age. More importantly, the participation rate of women aged 30–39 in 2012 was much higher than that of women aged 30–39 either in 1965 or 1985.

Table 4 Labour Force Participation by Age Group (%)

Year and Age Group		*Total*	*Male*	*Female*
1965 Aged	15–19	36.1	36.3	35.8
	20–24	78.0	85.8	70.2

Year and Age Group		*Total*	*Male*	*Female*
	25–29	72.6	96.8	49.0
	30–34	74.1	97.0	51.1
	35–39	78.2	97.1	59.6
	40–54	76.8	96.3	60.2
	55–59	68.9	90.0	49.8
	60–64	61.0	82.8	39.8
	65–	37.1	56.3	21.6
	Total	65.7	81.7	50.6
1985 Aged	15–19	17.9	17.3	16.6
	20–24	71.1	70.1	71.9
	25–29	75.2	95.7	54.1
	30–34	73.8	97.2	50.6
	35–39	78.8	97.6	60.0
	40–54	81.2	96.5	65.8
	55–59	70.0	90.3	51.0
	60–64	53.7	72.5	38.5
	65–	24.3	37.0	15.5
	Total	63.0	78.1	48.7
2005 Aged	15–19	16.3	16.2	16.5
	20–24	69.3	68.6	69.8
	25–29	84.4	93.6	74.9
	30–34	79.7	96.4	62.7
	35–39	80.0	97.0	63.0
	40–44	84.0	97.0	71.0
	45–49	85.3	96.7	73.9
	50–54	82.2	95.7	68.8
	55–59	76.7	93.6	60.0
	60–64	54.7	70.3	40.1
	65–	19.8	29.4	12.7
Total		60.4	73.3	48.4
2020 Aged	15–19	19.2	18.0	20.4
	20–24	75.0	74.6	75.4
	25–29	90.3	94.4	85.9

Year and Age Group	*Total*	*Male*	*Female*
30–34	86.9	95.6	77.8
35–39	86.1	96.0	76.0
40–44	87.8	95.8	79.4
45–49	88.5	95.6	81.0
50–54	87.6	95.4	80.0
55–59	84.1	93.9	74.3
60–64	73.1	85.3	61.0
65–	25.5	35.1	18.2
Total	62.0	71.4	53.2

Source: Ministry of Internal Affairs and Communications, *Annual Report on the Labour Force Survey.*

16. The average labour force participation rate of those aged 55–59 gradually increased since 1965 and reached 84.1% in 2020. The rate of those aged 60–64 increased to 73.1% in 2020, a considerable increase from 54.7% in 2005, due to the introduction of the legal obligation to provide for continuing employment until age 65. The rate of those aged 65 and older, however, has gradually decreased since 1965. It was 37.1% in 1965 and 19.8% in 2005, although it has begun to increase again in recent years. It was 25.5% in 2020 (Table 4). However, these percentages seem exceptionally high in comparison with other advanced countries, especially European countries (Table 5). Japan has reasons to encourage labour force participation rate among those aged 60 and older. First, the Japanese population is ageing faster than in any other country (Table 6), and Japan will face a serious labour shortage in the near future. Second, as the proportion of elderly persons increases, it will be difficult to maintain the social security fund levels without elderly people's contribution.

Table 5 Older (Age 65 Plus) Workers' Labour Force Participation Rate in Six Countries (%) in 2020

Japan	25.5
US	19.4
UK	10.8
Germany	7.5
France	3.4

Source: Databook of International Labour Statistics 2024 (JILPT).

Table 6 Estimated Population after the Year of 2020 (%)

Year	*Aged 0–14*	*Aged 15–64*	*Aged 65 and Older*
2030	11.3	59.2	29.6
2040	11.0	55.8	33.2
2050	10.8	53.6	35.7

Source: Management and Co-ordination Agency, *Statistics of Japan*, 2004.

17. The racial and ethnic composition of the Japanese people is monolithic in nature and has existed for centuries without any significant racial mixture. Therefore, it can be said that racial discrimination in employment has not been a big social problem. In the pre-war period, however, there were a fairly significant number of foreign workers, mostly Koreans and Chinese, and therefore they were sometimes discriminated against as distinct minority groups both in employment and in society in general. Since World War II, the government has adopted a very strict policy preventing an influx of foreign workers into the Japanese labour market. Therefore, any problems of discrimination in employment are mostly encountered by women and trade union activity. Nevertheless, it should be pointed out that social segregation of minority groups exists, especially Korean, Ainu, and probably more importantly, Buraku people who, though they are racially Japanese, have been differently treated since long before the Tokugawa era, for social and religious reasons; however, the issue of their employment has not often been contested in the courts. The thing is only that the fact has not often been disputed in law. Since Japan has begun to relax the preventive policy regarding foreign workers in recent years, it is likely that racial discrimination will be taken more seriously (*see* Part I, Chapter 1, section 2 X).

§5. Wage Disparity

18. Table 7 shows how families were distributed according to their income in 1998, 2011 and 2022. The average income of the lowest quarter of families was 2.58 million yen in 1998, 2.10 million yen in 2011 and 1.90 million yen in 2022. while that of the highest quarter of families was respectively 9.37 million yen in 1998, 8.06 million yen in 7.97 million yen in 2022. The median incomes were 5.44 million yen in 1998, 4.23 million yen in 2011 and 4.05 million yen in 2022. These figures show a great shrinkage in the scale of Japanese family incomes as a whole. However, it is also noticeable that the income disparity between the families of the highest and lowest quarters has remained at almost the same level through the above period.

19. The wage disparity in Japan is neither small nor large in comparison with other major advanced countries (*see* Table 8). The most peculiar factor of such wage disparity is found between the sizes of enterprises. There is a large difference in working conditions including wages, according to the size of enterprise (*see* Table 9). In 2022, employees working in small enterprises with less than thirty employees received only about 54% of the amount of wages received by those working in enterprises with 1,000 or more employees. The amount of wages of employees of enterprises with less than 499 but more than 100 was around 75% of that of those in enterprises with more than 1000 employees. The reason for lower wages in smaller companies can be partly explained by several factors such as their employees' level of education and experience, length of services, working patterns, etc. However, it can also be partly explained by the long-term relationship between smaller and larger companies. In Japan, smaller companies are most often identified either as child companies or subcontractors of larger companies. This may also explain the low internal production rate of big manufacturing companies in Japan. The father companies most often demand their child companies and subcontractors to lower the prices of production or services in transactions by using their superior position against them. Then, smaller companies keep their labour costs lower to meet such demand. In recent years, however, the wage disparity has slowly been reducing.

Table 7 Average Income per Household and Household Member by Quartile Group (JPY 10,000)

Year	*1998*	*2011*	*2022*
Quartile group			
1	258	210	190
2	450	354	325
3	650	525	500
4	937	806	797
Median	544	423	405

Source: Ministry of Health Labour and Welfare, Comprehensive Survey of Living Conditions.

Table 8 Wage Disparity in Major Countries in 2001–2007 (D9/D1 Measure)

Small		*In-Between*		*Large*	
Sweden	2.30	Japan	3.01	Poland	4.05
Finland	2.43	Australia	3.10	Hungary	4.37
Switzerland	2.58	Germany	3.14	US	4.75
Netherlands	2.91	Spain	3.53		
France	2.95	UK	3.57		

Note: D1 and D9 refer to the upper earnings limits of, respectively, the first and ninth deciles of employees ranked in order of their earnings from lowest to highest.
Source: ILO, Global Wage Report 2008–2009.

Table 9 Wage Difference Index by Size of Enterprise (Total Cash Payment)

Year	*Enterprises Employing 1,000 or More Employees*	*500–999*	*100–499*	*30–99*	*5–29*
2002	100.0	88.7	76.3	63.0	54.2
2012	100.0	92.1	81.4	71.3	61.8
2022	100.0	86.3	75.4	64.9	54.2

Source: Ministry of Health, Labour and Welfare, *Maitsuki Kinro Tokei Chosa* (Monthly Labour Statistics Survey).

20. Wage disparity among full-time employees is also caused by wage disparity between male and female employees. In 2023, the average annual salary of female employees was 74.8% of that of male employees. In particular, female employees aged 50–54 earned only 68.4% of the average salary of male employees of the same age. However, these figures are slightly improved since those figures in 1993 were 61.6% and 51.2%, respectively. There is also a rather large wage disparity between regular employees and non-regular employees. Non-regular employees earn much less than regular employees. In 2023, the average monthly wages of male regular employees was 70.1% of that of male regular employees, and the average monthly wages of female non-regular employees was only 56.0% of that of male regular employees.[4]

§6. Social and Cultural Values

21. It is widely held that Japanese behaviour is greatly influenced by Confucian ethics, which were introduced into Japan from China in the sixth century. The Confucian system had been taught to the samurai class before it was widely propagated to the common people in the Meiji era. The object of Confucian ethics is to provide familial love to all people. It consists of five virtues; *jin, gi, rei, chi*, and *shin. Jin* is the ultimate object of Confucianism, that is, to completely understand human love. To achieve *jin*, one is said to need *ko* (respect for one's parents), *tei* (respect for one's brothers and seniors), and *wa* (to be in harmony with others). *Gi* is to do justice; *rei* is to observe social and moral norms; *chi* is to be intelligent; and *shin* is not to tell lies. However, since its introduction, Confucianism has been adapted to prevailing Japanese political situations. Professor Morishima's study indicates that Japanese Confucianism has a somewhat patriotic tinge. Above all, *chu* is more respected than *jin. Chu* in the Japanese context means that one should be loyal to one's lord. Before the end of World War II, the wealth and military strength of Japan were backed up by Confucian ethics.[5] After the war, although the Japanese political

4. Ministry of Health, Labour and Welfare, *Maitsuki Kinro Tokei Chosa* (Monthly Labour Statistics Survey), 2024.
5. M. Morishima, *Why Has Japan 'Succeeded'?* (TBS Britannica 1984).

system and philosophy changed radically to a democratic one, it seems that certain features of Confucian ethics still remain as Japanese social and cultural values. For example, the following features of Japanese society seem somewhat related to Confucian ethics: respect for seniors, respect for harmony with others, loyalty to one's own group and organization, diligence, shyness, mutual dependence, politeness and so on.

22. It is certain that harmony is very important in Japanese society, including the workplace. It is sometimes said that Japanese workplaces resemble rural society. Many systems and practices in the workplace are helpful for maintaining harmony there. Recreation meetings, group excursions or drinking parties for employees are often organized at the suggestion of supervisors or managers, in every type of workplace. Japanese companies ordinarily adopt a decision-making system known as the *ringi* system. Under this system, an employee in the lowest position usually writes a proposal, which is passed on to his supervisor and then to higher managers, one after another, for their comments and acceptance. By the time the proposal reaches the top managers for approval, it has already been seen by a number of other people. Since employees at every level have been involved in the decision-making process, once the decision is made, it is easy to carry out. In most official meetings, the decision is also made unanimously. This is because a peculiar strategy (*nemawashi*) is taken by those concerned before the official meeting. *Nemawashi* means that those concerned unofficially discuss a matter to pave the way for approval at an official meeting.

23. There is also a very insightful view on Japanese behaviour, namely the theory of *amae* as proposed by Dr T. Doi, a leading Japanese psychiatrist. 'The Japanese term *amae* refers primarily to the feelings that all normal infants at the breast harbour toward the mother – dependence, the desire to be passively loved, the unwillingness to be separated from the mother-child circle.' According to Dr Doi, in a Japanese person, these feelings are somehow prolonged and diffused throughout his adult life, so that they come to shape, to a far greater extent than in adults in the West, his whole attitude to other people and to reality. On the personal level, within his own intimate circle, he seeks relationships that allow him to presume familiarity. The assurance of another person's goodwill permits a certain degree of self-indulgence and a corresponding degree of indifference to the claims of the other person as a separate individual. Such a relationship implies a considerable blurring of the distinction between subject and object. In other words, in a society governed by *amae*, personal relationships do not exist between the self and others. The self exists only in relation to the existence of others. The theory of *amae* may well explain the prevailing character of Japanese human relationships, including those in the workplace. For example, most Japanese do not like others to presume too much upon their goodwill, but they expect to be able to presume upon others. Dr Doi argues that this is one of the reasons why the idea of privacy did not traditionally develop in Japan. Little value is attributed to the individual's private realm as distinct from the group. This has a bearing on the fact that the Western idea of freedom has been slow to take root in Japan. There is also a serious dearth of the type of public spirit that transcends both individual and group. This has its origins in the fact that the Japanese divide their lives into inner and outer sectors, each with its own distinct standards of behaviour; no one is conscious of the slightest oddity in this discrepancy. Therefore, the private and the public are often confused.[6]

24. The *amae* relationship may be seen in the way commercial contracts are made. Japanese tend to believe that the text of the contract should be as simple as possible and that any problem which may arise will be resolved by mutual consultation in good faith. This is the case to a greater extent in the conclusion of collective agreements between the employer and the union. In other words, most Japanese, especially those in some special relationship, usually expect to be taken care of by the other. Furthermore, the other is expected to respond even to unstated needs. In workplaces, the employer is supposed to be aware of his employees' discontent even when this is not made explicit; on the other hand, the employees assume that their employer is making an effort to understand them and therefore rarely take corrective action. However, when the employees find that the employer is completely ignoring their interests, sudden upheavals may be the result. One may find here something resembling the Japanese respect for the benevolent and virtuous, yet also autocratic, rulers of the Samurai era.

6. T. Doi, *The Anatomy of Dependence* (Kodansha International 1973).

Chapter 2. Definitions and Notions

25. Social law or social legislation in Japan consists of labour law on the one hand and social security law on the other hand. Labour law is defined as the law directly and indirectly regulating employment relations to protect workers with regard to their employment and working conditions. It is generally held that labour law has three different domains: individual labour law (employment relations law), collective labour law (industrial relations law) and labour market law. Social security law is not easy to define in an uncontroversial way. However, it can be defined as the law aiming to promote the general standard of living of all the people by ensuring that the State shall prevent, and provide relief for all people from, various types of accidents or risks in the workplace. Accordingly, it can be said that the law concerning unemployment benefits belongs to the domain of labour law as well as social security law. Some legislation which had been regarded as a part of labour law – such as workmen's compensation – has extended its protection to cover accidents on the way to work. Also, protection which had hitherto been given only to employees is now often extended to cover non-employed workers.

§1. Labour Law

26. Theoretically speaking, labour laws of Japan, like in many other countries, can be divided into individual labour law, collective labour law, and labour market law. In reality, there are a large number of statutory labour laws in each category. For example, the most important statutes among individual labour laws are the Labour Standards Act (LSA) and the Labour Contract Act (LCA). Similarly, the most important statute in collective labour law is the Trade Union Act (TUA), which was enacted in 1945 shortly after World War II ended and dramatically revised in 1949. Recently, the fourth category of labour law, i.e., labour dispute resolution law is beginning to be recognized. The Labour Tribunal Act (LTA) is one of the statutes that is classified as labour dispute resolution law. In most cases, the statutes in the domain of labour law do not use the term 'employees', but 'workers'. Moreover, the definition of 'workers' is not exactly the same in all the statutes. The LSA defines 'workers' as those who are employed at an enterprise or place of business and receive wages therefrom (LSA, Article 9). On the other hand, the Labour Union Act defines 'workers' as those who live on their wages, salaries or other similar remuneration (LUL, Article 3). The 'workers' defined in the LSA are considered to be those who provide labour in a position of subordination. Thus, labour law does not apply to independent labour such as that done by the self-employed. The distinction is fundamentally based on the civil law distinction between a contract of employment (contract of service) on the one hand and a contract of commission or trust (contract of service) on the other hand. So, work done, for instance, by a carpenter will be covered by labour law if he is employed by a construction company to do it, whereas the same work will be not covered by labour law if he merely works under a contract with a customer. Whether or not a person is a 'worker' in the LSA depends on whether he is substantially in the position of subordination to an employer and not on the token form of the contract. In fact, the LSA uses the terminology 'labour contracts' instead of 'contracts of employment' to express the contracts to which the Act applies. In determining whether a person is in the position of subordination, the courts have generally taken account of whether he is free to decide to refuse work and whether he is subject to the other party's instruction and control on when, where and how to work[7] (for details, *see* Part 1,§2 VIII).

27. The definition of 'workers' in LSA is shared by many statutes relating to individual labour law such as the Minimum Wages Act, the Equal Employment Opportunity Act (EEOA), the Industrial Safety and Health Act, the Workers' Accident Compensation Insurance Act (WACIA). Moreover, the LCA which was enacted in 2007 to provide the basic rules for employment contracts in order to prevent individual employment disputes also adopts basically the same definition of 'workers' as in the LSA.

28. Meanwhile, the number of self-employed in Japan's labour market is becoming larger and larger in recent years. Some of such persons' bargaining power vis-à-vis is considerably weaker than the other parties in their transactions, particularly when they do business with large corporations. While there is a continuing to apply labour law protections under the LSA and the LCA based on objective facts rather than contractual formality, there has been a growing demand for additional protection for such persons even where they are not entitled to the legal protection as 'workers' under LSA and the LCA. a so-called Freelance Protection Act (The Act on Ensuring Proper Transactions Involving Specified Entrusted Business Operators) was enacted in 2023. This act has a hybrid nature of the individual labour law and the economic law for the protection of small-size businesses. (For details, *see* Part I, Chapter 1, §2. VIII.)

29. In contrast to these statutes, 'workers' as defined under the TUA are not necessarily presently employed. Moreover, the moneys they receive are not necessarily limited to wages. Therefore, the unemployed who receive unemployment benefits and the self-employed who are in a similar situation to employees, for example, those who are paid for processing goods under the other party's everyday instruction may be 'workers' according to the TUA, although they are not 'workers' in the LSA's terms. However, this difference is understandable if one takes account of the different purposes of these two statutes. The LSA purports to establish the minimum standards of working conditions for employed workers (employees) while the TUA purports to promote collective bargaining in order to strengthen the bargaining power of workers (*see* Part II Chapter 1, section 2). However, there is no doubt that persons who are intended to be such main objects of the TUA are employees.

7. Rodokijunho-Kenkyukai (the Research and Advisory Committee of the Labour Standards Law), *A Report on Employment Contracts* (Ministry of Labour 1985).

30. Between 2011 and 2012, the Supreme Court decided important cases[8] in which the central issue was which workers might fall under the definition of 'workers' in the TUA: especially, whether a union whose members were employed under contract for services in form could make a petition for a remedial order of the Labour Relations Commission (LRC) under the TUA. Reaching these decisions, the Court applied almost identical criteria. One of these cases was that of the Victor Service-Engineering Company, in which independent contractors made a contract for services to repair audio equipment; the union demanded collective bargaining rights to consider working conditions. The lower courts held that these contractors were not 'workers' as defined by TUA, Article 3, and therefore that the union was not entitled to a remedial order of the LRC. However, the Court overturned this judgment and remanded the case to the high court. The Supreme Court stated as follows: (i) these contractors were incorporated into the work organization of the company to maintain production; (ii) the company unilaterally determined the contractual terms and conditions; (iii) the commission paid these contractors substantial remuneration for their work; (iv) these contractors could not in practice refuse the company's request to go to the customers' premises to repair; (v) the contractors' time and place of work were largely controlled by the company.

31. The term 'employer' does not always mean one party to a contract of employment to which the employee is the other party. Moreover, the usage of the term 'employer' is not unified in the LSA and TUA. The LSA defined the 'employer' as 'the owner (proprietor) or manager of the enterprise or any other person who acts on behalf of the owner of the enterprise in matters concerning the workers of the enterprise'. This is because the law intends to make the actual person who has violated the law punishable. Therefore, the LSA also makes the proprietor of the enterprise subject to a fine for the conduct of the person who violates the LSA as the employer except in certain cases. In comparison, the TUA does not have a special provision defining the 'employer'. However, it is generally held that the 'employer' under the TUA includes two different concepts of employers as follows:

1. The one party to a labour contract to which the concerned worker was, is or becomes the other party.
2. The proprietor has the power of control over or strong influence on industrial relations with regard to the concerned workers so that such proprietor can substantially be deemed as the proprietor as a party to the labour contract.

I. Individual Labour Law

32. Individual labour law is the law regulating employment relations between individual employers and employees. It has its constitutional basis in Article 27,

8. The *New National Theatre* case, the Supreme Court in 2011, SMS, Vol. 65, No. 3, p.943; the *INAX Maintenance Company* case, the Supreme Court in 2011, RH, No. 1026, p. 27; the *Victor Service-Engineering Company* case, the Supreme Court in 2012, RH, No. 1043, p. 5.

section 2 of the Constitution of Japan, which provides that standards for wages, hours, rest and other working conditions shall be fixed by law. Apart from this constitutional requirement, individual relations between employers and employees are governed by the civil law rules on contracts of employment, although these rules are modified considerably by labour law principles in order to protect employees and improve their working conditions.

33. Individual labour law is, therefore, concerned with the following subjects:

- the different categories of employees: blue-collar versus white-collar, private versus public, regular versus non-regular;
- the individual contract of employment: form and content, the legal capacity to conclude a contract;
- the rights and duties of the parties in the course of the employment relationship;
- working time, rest, holidays, annual vacation, balancing of work and private life and so on;
- remuneration including minimum wages;
- the rules concerning incapacity to work due to illness, an accident at work, health and safety at work and so on;
- job security;
- protection against discrimination and harassment;
- competition by former employees; and
- settlement of individual disputes.

II. Collective Labour Law

34. Collective labour law is the law regulating industrial relations in which the trade union or workers' organization is a main actor in addition to the employee and the employer. It has its constitutional basis in Article 28 of the Constitution which guarantees workers the right to organize, bargain and act collectively. Since these workers' rights are regarded as fundamental human rights which are inviolable and cannot be infringed by legislation, all laws which promote them can be seen as confirmation and materialization of the constitutional position. Thus, for instance, the provisions of the TUA of 1949 which provide legal protection for the unions and their rights to act (including the rights to bargain and to strike), and which give normative legal effect to any collective agreements, are regarded as confirming the constitutional principle. In other words, more or less the same legal effects would stem directly from the above-mentioned constitutional provisions, at least insofar as their substance is concerned. At the same time, if the law was ever amended in the future so as to deny these constitutional guarantees, such an amendment would be deemed unconstitutional and declared null and void by the courts.

35. Collective labour law is concerned with collective labour relations, which includes the following subjects:

- trade union freedom or the right to organize;

- relationship between trade unions and employers or their associations at plant, enterprise, industrial or national level;
- collective bargaining and collective agreements;
- collective actions, including strikes and lock-outs; and
- protection from unfair labour practices and resolution of labour disputes.

III. Labour Market Law

36. Labour market law is the law regulating the labour market. It purports to establish a fair labour market. Labour market law has its constitutional basis in Article 27, section 1 of the Constitution, which provides that all people shall have the right to work. It is in comparatively recent years that labour market law received recognition as an independent domain of labour law. It was previously thought that labour market law was included in individual labour law. However, the aim and function of labour market law are very different from those of individual labour law. Moreover, there are considerable needs to be met in developing laws concerning the labour market, for example, an increase in the number of gainfully employed persons, a decrease in unemployment and a decline in the gap between labour demand and supply. One of the most important statutes in the labour market law is the Employment Security Act (ESA) which establishes public employment agencies. Public employment agencies (its nickname is 'hello work') not only provide employment placement services for jobseekers and companies in need of workers but also administer the payment of unemployment insurance. The Act also regulates private employment agencies through a licensing system and regulation of their conduct such as fees and handling of private information of jobseekers. Another important statute is the Employment Insurance Act (EIA). In addition to establishing an unemployment insurance system as stated below, this Act also provides for various public subsidies for the purpose of improving the labour market. The Employment Adjustment Subsidy can be granted to employers who avoid economic dismissals in the case of business slowdown through such measures as training or temporary shutdown with certain allowances for employees.

37. Labour market law is concerned with the following subjects:

- establishment of public employment placement services and regulation of private employment agencies;
- promotion and stabilization of employment, especially of disabled workers, young, middle-aged and older workers and workers in depressed areas and industries;
- establishment and improvement of the market for certain types of employees such as dispatched workers, part-time workers and so on;
- development of workers' vocational abilities;
- unemployment insurance;
- unemployment insurance belongs to the system of social insurance and can be regarded as one of the elements of social security.

In this monograph, although an independent chapter will not be allocated to labour market law, some of the above subjects will be addressed in the discussion of individual labour law.

IV. Legal Nature

38. Japanese labour law can be regarded, in general, as having an imperative nature that constitutes public order, since both individual and collective labour laws have their constitutional foundation in the respective provisions of the Constitution which guarantee workers' rights as fundamental human rights. The Constitution regards these fundamental rights as inviolable by agreement of the parties; as long, that is, as they aim to protect the workers in view of their unequal position in relation to the employers. In individual labour law, most of the provisions of the LSA provide minimum standards for working conditions. Individual as well as collective agreements setting lower standards are null and void (Article 13), and employers can be punished by fines or imprisonment for violating most of the provisions of LSA. In collective labour law, the TUA admits the superiority of collective bargaining by giving normative legal effect to collective agreements. This means that any individual contract which contravenes the provisions of a collective agreement is null and void (Article 16). Also, any agreement, including a collective one, which infringes the fundamental human rights of workers as guaranteed by the Constitution is null and void, since such constitutional guarantees are interpreted as having established public order with respect to workers' rights. For instance, so-called yellow-dog contracts in which an employee promises to refrain from joining a union or to secede from a union as a condition of employment, or which allow the dismissal of an employee because of union activities or union membership, are interpreted as being null and void (TUA, Article 7).

39. At the same time, the TUA prohibits as unfair labour practices the employer's discriminatory treatment of his employees because of their union membership or union activities, his refusal to bargain collectively and any interference by him in the formation or administration of trade unions. The LRCs will investigate the case at the request of the union or the workers, and can accordingly issue orders which may include an order to reinstate a worker, to bargain in good faith or to cease and desist from interference. All these orders are enforceable with administrative or criminal sanctions. Thus, the jurisdictions of the Courts and the LRCs overlap when unfair labour practices take the form of legal action, as in the case of dismissal. The Courts have only generally agreed that there is, in fact, no real overlap. The Courts judge only the legal nature of the employer's action and declare whether or not it is illegal and therefore null and void, while the Commissions estimate the case from the administrative point of view to protect and encourage union activities and order the appropriate measures without paying any attention to, or even touching on, the legal effect of the action (for a more detailed description, *see* Part II Chapter 7).

40. As we have already stated, the constitutional guarantees of the rights of workers are regarded as fundamental human rights and thus constitute public policy.

This assertion, which has been overwhelmingly supported by almost all labour law scholars, has raised the difficult legal problem of the constitutionality of certain provisions to restrict the right to organize, to bargain and especially to strike in the public sector. More fundamentally, this problem poses the general question of how far workers' rights should be restricted in order to protect public welfare and convenience and whether the restriction should be applied only in emergencies or should be permitted, for instance, merely to protect or promote government finances. Such problems will be discussed in detail in their relevant sections later in this monograph, especially in Part II Chapter 6, section 6.

V. Governing Law in Transnational Labour and Employment Relations

41. In cases relating to transnational labour and employment relations, an important issue arises regarding conflict of laws, i.e., which country's law shall be applied as governing law.[9] As long as the cases can be resolved through the application of private law, this issue is resolved under the rules of each country by the courts of that country if they have jurisdiction over the cases in question. These rules are generally called 'private international law' or 'choice-of-law rules'. However, labour and employment laws often have the nature of public law. The geographical scope of applicability regarding public law is usually determined unilaterally through the interpretation of each statute regardless of choice-of-law rules. In other words, there are two approaches to determining the applicability of law in a transnational setting: the choice-of-law approach and the approach to determine the geographical reach of statutes.

42. As regards the choice-of-law approach, Japan's courts currently apply 'the General Act Regarding the Application of Law' enacted in 2004 to determine the governing law. This Act provides for a special rule for employment contracts to resolve such issues as the validity of dismissals under the Labor Contract Law. This new rule is basically similar to the EC's Rome I Regulation. Under this Act, the parties to an employment contract are, in principle, allowed to choose the law to be applied to the employment contract by their agreement (the principle of party autonomy). However, Article 12, paragraph 1 of this Act provides for a special rule that limits the party autonomy: if the law to be applied by the choice of law by the parties is a law other than the law of the place most closely related to the employment contract in question, and if the employee notifies to the employer that a specific mandatory provision of the law of the place most closely related should be applied, that mandatory provision shall also be applied. With respect to the employment contract the law of the place where the service is performed is presumed to be the law of the closest relationship as a general rule. If the place where the labour is provided cannot be specified, the law of the place of business where the worker is employed is presumed to be the law of the closest relationship (paragraph 2 of

9. *See* Ryuichi Yamakawa, *Transnational Dimension of Japanese Labor and Employment Laws: New Choice-of-Law Rules and Determination of Geographical Reach* , 31(2) Comparative Labor Law and Policy Journal (2010).

Article 12). Thus, when a German citizen is working at a branch office of a New York company located in Japan, the issue regarding the validity of his/her dismissal will be determined under Article 16 of Japan's LCA, which provides for the doctrine prohibiting abusive dismissal as a mandatory law, if the employee notifies the employer of the application of this provision. Meanwhile, if the parties have not chosen the applicable law, the law of the place most closely related to the contract in question should be the governing law. As regards the employment contract, the same rule as provided under paragraph 2 applies, and, in general, the law of the place of performance should be the law of the closest relationship with the employment contract.

43. On the one hand, the approach to determine the geographical reach of statutes should be applied to labour statutes that have been traditionally classified as public law. For example, the applicability of the Labor Standards Act and the TUA is determined by defining their geographical reach by way of statutory interpretation, since these Acts have a nature of public law enforced by administrative agencies. Since the Labor Standards Act is intended to apply to the 'enterprise' or place of business (Article 9), the Act is interpreted to be applied where the enterprise in which the workers are employed is located in Japan. It is to be noted, however, that since the LSA also has the nature of private law as it regulates rights and obligations under the employment contract, there is a view that the aforementioned choice-of-law rule applies to such issues as the payment of overtime wages. On the other hand, the Labor Union Act has no explicit provisions regarding its geographical scope. However, it is generally understood that the Act should be applied to cases where collective labour relations exist in Japan, as the Act is intended to regulate collective labour relations according to Japan's labour policy.

§2. Social Security Law

44. The social security system is roughly divided into four categories: social insurance, social assistance, social welfare and child allowance (social allowance). Social insurance is financed by contributions from employers and employees or the self-employed, plus a government subsidy. Social insurance for most private employees is administered by the Ministry of Health, Labour and Welfare. Social assistance is jointly financed by the national government and the local government and is administered by the local Welfare Offices. The social security system in general is complicated by its division into various categories according to the status of the insured person and the nature of the accident, and these – for mainly historical reasons – are administered by different agencies and provide unequal benefits for beneficiaries.

45. Social insurance is basically divided into an occupational scheme for employees of public and private institutions and a scheme for all those without employment status, which includes the self-employed, students and so on. The occupational scheme for employees of private institutions is divided into Health

Insurance, Seamen's Insurance, Day Labourers' Health Insurance, Employees' Pension Insurance, Workers' Accident Compensation Insurance and Employment Insurance. The non-occupational scheme includes National Health Insurance and National Pension. There is a non-divided social insurance which is Nursing Care Insurance which covers all insured persons older than 40 in need of care enacted in 1997.

46. In most occupational insurance schemes, the cost of the benefits is covered by contributions from employees, employers and the government in roughly equal shares. With regard to Workers' Accident Compensation, the contributions are paid by the employer and the government alone. In some social security programmes for those other than employees, contributions are collected from the insured persons, but the Government finances the whole cost of most programmes. The administrative costs of all the social security programmes are taken care of by the national government, with subsidies from local government in some cases.

47. The following are short comments on major insurance legislation:

1. Employment Insurance Act: this law is intended to prevent unemployment, stabilize employment conditions, increase employment opportunities, develop and improve worker potential and promote the welfare of workers. The law provides not only unemployment benefits for employees but also various subsidies for employers (for the details of this subject, *see* Part I, Chapter 5, §7 and §10).
2. Workers' Accident Compensation Insurance Act: the purpose of this law is to grant necessary insurance benefits to workers in order to give them prompt and equitable protection against injury, disease, physical disability or death resulting from employment or commuting and to promote rehabilitation of workers who have suffered injury or contracted a disease resulting from employment or commuting, to assist workers and their survivors and to secure proper working conditions. The LSA provides that when a worker suffers an injury, illness or death resulting from employment, the employer must furnish compensation: medical compensation, compensation for lost time, compensation for discontinuance, compensation for disabilities, survivors' compensation, compensation in instalments, and funeral expenses. The WACIA was enacted at the same time as LSA to establish a workers' compensation insurance system which secures certain enterprises' compensation obligations for workers' accidents under LSA. After a number of revisions, the WACIA became the principal law of workers' accident law. The law covers not only workers' injury or illness in the course of duty but also workers' accidents occurring on the way to and from work.
3. National Pension Insurance (NPI) and Employee's Pension Insurance (EPI): employees in private enterprises are covered by both the NPI and EPI. They are entitled to the specially provided earnings related to old-age employees' pension benefits under the EPI and fixed-rate old-age employees' pension benefits. The minimum qualifying period is ten years. Formerly, the payable age of these pension benefits was 60. However, the payable age of the fixed-rate

pension benefits under the NPI is 65. Also, the payable age of the specially provided earnings-related old-age employees' pension benefits under the EPI is gradually being raised, finishing in 2025.

4. Health Insurance Act: employees' illness and injury that is not work-related is covered by the Employees' Health Insurance Act while work-related cases are covered by the LSA and WACIA. The latter provides much more generous benefits. Under the Health Insurance Act, the insured person is entitled to medical services at any insurance medical care facility or medical institution. He or she pays 30% of the medical costs; dependents are granted the same medical care benefits as insured persons but the insured persons must pay basically 30% of the medical costs for them. When an insured person is unable to work while undergoing medical care, an amount equivalent to two-thirds of his or her daily standard wage is paid as an allowance for sickness or injury during a period of at most eighteen months in which he or she is unable to work, commencing three days after such incapacity.
5. Long-Term Care Insurance Act: this law which was enacted in 1997 provides for those aged 65 and older in need of care and those aged 40 and older who suffered from prescribed diseases with necessary nursing services. The insurance scheme is financed by the insured persons' contribution, national subsidy, prefectural subsidy and municipal subsidy. The ratio of these subsidies varies depending on the contents of benefits. The insurers are municipalities that make plans for and operate their own nursing care undertakings.

48. There are differences in the level of benefits provided for different categories of insured persons under the social insurance system. In general, the insurance scheme for employees provides better benefits than the one for non-employees, and the scheme for public employees provides better benefits than the one for private employees. One should also take into account the fact that most of the larger companies are providing additional benefits under the social security system for their employees as part of well-developed company welfare systems. However, because of an ageing population, these privileges are rapidly fading away.

Chapter 3. Historical Background

§1. Pre-World War II

49. Japan entered into industrialization during the Meiji era between 1868 and 1891. More precisely, it is considered that the Japanese industrial revolution began around the period of 1886–1890 during which time the total capital became four times as much as before, and that the revolution was completed soon after the victory in the war against Russia (1904–1905). During the Tokugawa era between 1603 and 1867, the employment relationship was mainly controlled by private contracts with a strong feudalistic tinge. Many of these contracts were for a fixed term, e.g., ten or twenty years. In some cases, the term was for life. Thus, some of these contracts could in fact be classified as contracts for bondage.

50. Every worker who entered into employment was obliged to be entered in his or her employer's family register. During the contractual term, only the employer could exercise the right to terminate the employment. If the employee was missing from his employment during the term of his contract, the person who was a surety for the employee was obliged to search for him and, if he failed in both refunding the employee's advances and taking him back to the employer, could be punished. This punishment was handcuffing, imprisonment, banishment, exile or even death in the first half of the Tokugawa era. Things changed under the Meiji Restoration. The Civil Code enacted in 1896 provided that, if no period of service had been fixed by the parties, either party could at any time give notice to the other party to terminate the contract. The Code enabled either party to terminate the contract at any time after the expiration of five years even if the period of the contract exceeded five years.

51. In the period of the above-mentioned industrial revolution, the munitions industry, mining industry, transport industry and textile industry developed by using workers like slaves. All kinds of evils flourished in the workplace, such as extremely low wages, extremely long working hours, child labour, de facto confinement of young female workers in spinning mills, concentration shacks for coal miners, and the frequent occurrence of industrial accidents. Under these circumstances, the first labour union distinguishable from a craft organization was established in 1897 although workers' sporadic disturbances had already begun in the 1870s. The government had oppressed the labour movement by applying criminal laws and police regulations, but two additional laws were enacted around 1900. The Public Order and Police Act of 1899 subjected to criminal punishment those who committed violent acts, threats or public defamation with the purpose of causing another person to join a group, or tempted or agitated another person to engage in a strike. The Administrative Enforcement Act of 1900 subjected to preventive custody those who harmed the public peace and order and provoked fear.

52. On the other hand, a project began inside the government to enact employment protection legislation in 1881 and started to survey working conditions in workplaces. Due to fierce opposition from employers, however, the enactment of a protective law faced considerable difficulties. Supporters of employment protection legislation managed to get the Factory Act passed in the Diet in 1911 and this came into enforcement in 1916. However, it concentrated mainly on providing protection for female and child workers, and even this protection was very limited. For instance, the maximum number of working hours per day for women and children was twelve (later to be made eleven by the Amendment of 1923) and the enforcement of the prohibition of night work was postponed for fifteen years after its introduction. The only protection provided for adult male workers was compensation for accidents at work. In addition to the Factory Act, a protective law for seamen and an order to protect miners (a ten-hour working day) were introduced.

53. It should be pointed out that before World War II the government made a persistent effort to introduce a trade union law. Depression after World War I activated the labour movement and the government had a bitter experience in selecting labour union representatives to the first ILO Congress in 1919. Therefore, the government concluded that it would be better to encourage the growth of moderate unions and to enact a trade union law. The first draft of the TUA was submitted to the Diet in 1921, and after that – for a few years – almost every session of the Diet had similar drafts pending but never passed due to strong opposition from employers who faced a severe business depression. In the end, the government's attempt to legislate a trade union law petered out in the House of Peers in 1931. Instead, in 1926, the Labour Dispute Mediation Act was passed. This law provided a mediation service for settling labour disputes, and in particular introduced a system of compulsory mediation for public utility work such as transportation. It also prohibited the inducement and instigation of acts of dispute during the mediation process. The beginning of the war against China in 1937, and then World War II, completely ruled out the possibility of any developments in labour law until the end of the war. In 1940, the military government ordered the unions to join the *Sangyo Hokoku Kai* (Industrial Association to Serve the State), which was the Japanese version of the *Arbeitsfront* of Nazi Germany.

54. The underdevelopment of labour law in pre-war Japan can be best explained by the weakness of the trade unions and the political parties which represented the working classes. The Japanese economy, to which industrialization came late, found it necessary to depend on cheap labour, longer working hours and other poor working conditions in order to compete with the already developed economies of the Western world. The ruling political forces represented the interests of employers, landowners and bureaucrats. The unions and the political parties which represented the working classes were not only weak but also suffered from repeated splits and confrontations between small internal factions. These splits in the union organizations caused by ideological commitment, as well as being characteristic of the pre-war union movement, still, to some extent, regulate the character of the union movement and, as a result, the character of industrial relations in Japan today.

55. The influence of organized labour in the pre-war period was very limited. The highest organization rate (the percentage of organized workers among the total number of employed persons) in pre-war Japan was 7.9% in 1931; the number of unions was 818 and the number of workers involved was 369,000. In addition to the small number of organized workers, the union organizations suffered from ideological strife between unions and especially between their leaders. In a social and political climate antagonistic towards the union movement, unionism tended to be associated with radical political movements, anarcho-syndicalism, socialism and communism. Serious confrontations and rivalry between these political groups brought about splits between the union organizations connected with the respective political factions. A split between the parties immediately resulted in a union split and vice versa. The ideological differences between the union organizations helped to weaken a union movement which was not very influential to begin with. Thus, taken together, the antagonistic social and political climate, the legal setting and the weakness of the unions' influence caused by their poor organization and splits between them hardly made for the development of sound trade unionism or indeed for the development of a modern labour law system based on such trade unionism. After World War II, the peculiar political situation created by the policy of the occupation forces meant that a modern labour law system was suddenly born. However, the characteristics of the pre-war labour movement were mostly inherited by the post-war union movement, and they prescribed its fundamental nature. These elements still cannot be neglected if we are to understand present-day Japanese industrial relations and labour law enforcement.

§2. Post-World War II

I. Enactment of Labour Laws

56. In the early stages after World War II, the Occupation Forces (GHQ – General Headquarters of the Allied Powers) pursued a policy of promotion of worker protection and trade unions in order to diminish pre-war quasi-feudalistic totalitarianism and to democratize society. Under such a policy, the *Romu Hosei Shingi Iinkai* (Council on Labour Law and Policy), which was established in the government, drafted a trade union bill. Although the draft was made on a new conceptual basis, the pre-war labour law bills were taken into consideration. The draft thereafter received only minor modification and became the trade union bill which was thereafter presented to the Diet and passed ten days later. The contents of the TUA of 1945 were greatly influenced by foreign laws; for instance, there was British influence on the provisions for immunity from civil and criminal liabilities of trade unions, German influence on those for the effects of collective bargaining agreement and American influence on the LRCs. In 1949, however, the TUA of 1945 was to some extent amended for the purpose of correcting the political inclination of the labour movement at that time, ensuring the independence and democracy of trade unions and preventing governmental intervention into the organization and operation of trade unions.

57. Due to the intensification of the confrontation between the United States and the Soviet Union and the Chinese Revolution, the United States radically changed its occupation policy on Japan. In February 1947, the political inclination of the labour movement reached its highest point. Following successful strikes of employees in the private sector for wage hikes, various unions of public employees demanded wage increases from the central and local governments. After their demands were rejected, the unions organized a united front and economic strife developed into a political movement to overthrow the cabinet. National labour organizations, the Japan Socialist Party, the Japan Communist Party and public employees organized an executive committee to overthrow the cabinet. A general strike was planned but had to be called off just before it went into operation because of an order of stoppage issued by MacArthur, SCAP. In 1948, Government Order No. 201 was issued in a letter from MacArthur provisionally denying collective bargaining rights to and prohibiting strikes by civil servants. This policy was followed by the National Civil Service Act amended in the same year. In 1950, the Local Civil Service Act was enacted whose fundamental contents were similar to those of the National Civil Service Act.

58. Besides the TUA, the Labour Relation Adjustment Act was promulgated in 1946 to establish procedures for dealing with collective labour disputes, regulate dispute acts in public utility enterprises and prohibit dispute acts by civil servants. In the same year, the new Constitution was adopted. It provided for the right to live (Article 25), the right to work (Article 27, paragraph 1) as well as the worker's right of organization, collective bargaining and collective action (Article 28). It also provided that standards for wages, hours, rest and other working conditions were to be fixed by law. To realize this constitutional provision, the LSA was promulgated in 1947. In the same year, the WACIA, the ESA, the Unemployment Allowance Act and the Unemployment Insurance Act were enacted. After the Korean War in the early 1950s, the Japanese economy started growing. The Vocational Training Act was enacted in 1958 to increase the skilled workforce in 1958. Japan's policy was to promote the employment of physically handicapped workers by enacting the Physically Disabled Persons' Act in 1960. Japan also promoted older workers' employment by enacting the Act of Special Measure and Middle-Aged and Older Persons in 1971. After the first oil crisis in 1973, Japan entered into a period of low economic growth. The Worker Dispatching Act (WDA) was enacted in 1985 to respond to the changing labour market. In the same year, the Equal Employment Act was enacted to secure equal opportunity and treatment between men and women in employment. In 1993, the Employment Management for Part-time Workers Act was enacted to ensure proper working conditions and improve employment management for part-time workers. Since the collapse of the bubble economy early in the 1990s, the Japanese economy has been deeply depressed and the number of individual labour disputes has very rapidly increased. This led Japan to enact the Resolution of Individual Labour-Related Disputes Act in 2001, the LTA in 2004 and the LCA in 2007.

II. The Formation of Enterprise Unionism

59. Just after the war, not only because of GHQ's policy of promotion of trade unions but also because the owners of businesses and high-ranking managers were in a weak position, having failed to achieve their goal, workers wishing to form unions faced no objections either from the government or from the employers. If there is no resistance to unionization, it is quite natural and most convenient for the workers to start their organizing efforts within the enterprises, where most workers already are. They need not go to the trouble of gathering somewhere in town after work, often in secret, in order to avoid the attention of the employers or even of the police, which has usually been the case with regard to the formation of unions in other countries. This is one of the historical reasons why, after World War II, unions were organized within enterprises. Another reason for this is that post-war unions inherited the features of unions before and during the war. After World War I, large companies started to form their own closed employment system which enabled them to retain regular workers until retirement. Trade unions, on the other hand, could not obtain the power to establish industry-wide standards, control wages and other working conditions because they were oppressed under criminal law as well as under the special law concerning trade unions. Therefore, immediately after the war, it was much easier for workers to form unions within enterprises than to form unions outside enterprises.

60. The peculiar historical situation immediately after the war only explains why enterprise unionism developed in the first place; but one may, with good reason, wonder why enterprise unionism still exists and functions. The answer is that it is still the most suitable type of union organization for protecting the interests of regular workers employed in larger enterprises. Under the life-time employment system prevailing among larger enterprises, the fate of regular employees depends on how much they can get from the particular enterprise in which they have been employed throughout their working lives. Since they do not expect to move from one enterprise to another, working conditions in other companies are of no concern to them. The standard wage level in a certain industry in a certain district would only be of concern to those workers who might eventually move within this sector – which happened to be the case in Western society when the craft unions were organized. Given that the worker expects to stay in a particular enterprise until retirement, he will prefer to be protected by the union which bargains exclusively with the employer about working conditions in the particular enterprise.

61. The economic dilapidation and confusion shortly after the war also provided fertile ground for the emergence of unionism. Thus, within three years of the end of the war, the unions were organizing more than six million workers, the organization rate having reached 55.8% in 1949. However, the organization rate has gradually been falling since then. Particularly, since 1950 when it was 46.2%, the rate has constantly been falling and in 2023, there were 22,789 unions organizing 9,938,000 workers, which is about 16.3% of all employed persons. Moreover, the organization rate in private sector alone was only 16.3%.[10] This constant decrease in the organization rate is mainly caused by the expansion of the tertiary industry, changes in employment structure due to technological innovation, an increase in the number of

10. Ministry of Health, Labour and Welfare, *Rodokumiai Kisochosa* (A Basic Survey on Trade Unions), 2023.

atypical employees, the collapse of socialism, the expansion of individualistic ideas into workers, etc. This low rate reflects today's reality of the powerless labour unions in Japan. Labour unions are losing their voice towards the employers as well as the government.

III. The Function of Enterprise Unions

62. In Japan, more than 90% of organized labour, are enterprise unions.[11] Thus today, with a few exceptions – including, most significantly, the Seamen's Union, as well as some general unions mainly organizing small shops and factories where the establishment of enterprise unionism is hardly to be expected on a district basis – the overwhelming majority of unions organize employees in a particular enterprise or in a particular plant. In these enterprise unions, being an employee of the particular enterprise is a prerequisite for union membership. Those who have lost the status of employee will also lose union membership unless the union challenges the legality of the dismissal.

63. Enterprise unions are often suspected, especially by Westerners, of being too dependent on management; and they are undoubtedly more cooperative, if not more loyal, than industrial unions. Their bargaining power must inevitably be limited by their natural tendency to consider the financial position of their own enterprise and the competitive situation with regard to rival companies since their very existence depends on the existence and well-being of the enterprise. Because an enterprise union normally limits its membership to regular employees in a particular enterprise, it is also comparatively easy for the union to share the employer's business information and therefore to flexibly bargain with the employer. Most enterprise unions organize all employees within a particular company irrespective of whether they are white-collar or blue-collar. Therefore, they are able to reduce wage differentials between white-collar and blue-collar employees. This results in achieving comparative equality in peoples' income as well as comparative equality in employees' wages.

64. As an enterprise union represents only employees in a particular enterprise, if an employee leaves his company, he automatically loses his membership rights. Most Japanese enterprise unions represent only the interests of regular workers employed in their enterprises. Many enterprise unions explicitly exclude non-regular workers such as part-time workers, seasonal workers, temporary workers, etc. This is understandable because under Japanese standard employment practice, standards and procedures of recruiting, hiring, training, and promoting non-regular workers are very different from those of regular workers. In a sense, the enterprise union's interests coincide with those of the enterprise.

11. Japan Institute of Labour, Labour-Management Relations in Japan, 1995.

IV. Industrial Unions and National Centres

65. Collective bargaining is mainly carried out at enterprise level; that is, between the employer and the union in the particular enterprise. However, most of the enterprise unions are affiliated with industrial federations. Industrial unions in Japan are mostly federations of enterprise unions in a certain industry. The only significant exception is the Seamen's Union, which organizes seamen regardless of the enterprise in which they work. Among the industrial federations in the private sector, the most important are those covering automobiles, electricity, construction, textiles, insurance, metal and engineering, information, electric power generation, steal and private railways. Among them, the three biggest are the UA *Zensen* (1,894,000 members in 2023), the Confederation of Japanese Automobile Workers' Unions (799,000) and the Japanese Federation of Electrical Machine Workers' Unions (565,000). Most of the unions in the public sector are organized on an enterprise basis, namely, one for each public corporation or government enterprise. However, there are some exceptions such as the All-Japan Prefectural and Municipal Workers' Union (717,000) and the Japanese Teachers' Union (200,000), both of which organize public employees.[12]

66. These industrial federations and some important enterprise unions, especially the larger ones in the public sector, are directly affiliated with the national centres. There are three major national centres; a large one and two smaller ones. The largest one is *Rengo* (the Japanese Trade Union Confederation), and the others are *Zenroren* (the National Confederation of Trade Unions) and *Zenrokyo* (National Trade Union Council). In 2023, *Rengo* covers 6,81,000 workers or 68.6% of the total union membership in Japan, while Zenroren and Zenrokyo organize 464,000 workers (4.7%) and 76,000 workers (0.8%) respectively. Besides these national centres, the Japanese Council of Metal Workers' Unions (IMF-JC), which was affiliated with the International Metalworkers' Federation in 1964, has been influential, especially in wage bargaining, since 1967. In 2023, it covered 2,007,000 workers or 20.2% of the total union membership.[13]

67. A significant difference between industrial unions in Western countries and industrial federations in Japan is that Western workers directly belong to industrial unions, while Japanese workers are indirectly covered by industrial federations through their enterprise unions. Thus, while industrial unions in Western countries collect union fees directly from all members and allocate these to the local union offices, the enterprise unions in Japan collect union fees and contribute less than 20% of those fees to industrial federations and national centres. Industrial federations do not have strong decision-making power since their decision often does not have the power to effectively bind their member unions. Even though the union federation or its officials sometimes participate in negotiations between their member union and the employer, the collective agreement will be mostly exclusively concluded between the member union and the employer. In practice, union federations

12. Ministry of Health, Labour and Welfare, *Rodokumiai Kisochosa* (*A Survey on Trade Unions*), 2023.
13. *Ibid.*

and national centres draw up general policies and coordinate and assist member unions in negotiations and consultations with employers.

V. History of Labour Politics and National Centres

68. Three national centres were established in 1947: *Sodomei* (the Japanese Confederation of Labour) which was related to the Japan Socialist Party; *Sanbetsu-kaigi* (the Congress of Industrial Unions of Japan) which was influenced by the Japan Communist Party and *Nichiro-kaigi* (the Japan Congress of Labour Unions) which was politically neutral. The Japan Communist Party took over the leadership in the overall labour movement until the suspension of a general strike in 1947. As a result of the democratization movement in 1948, a group of unions formed *Shin-sanbetsu* (National Federation of Industrial Organization) in 1949 and another group formed *Sohyo* (the General Council of Trade Unions of Japan) in 1950. *Sanbetsu-kaigi* was dissolved in 1958 and the influence of the Japan Communist Party was diminished. In 1950, the Japan Socialist Party split into the leftist Socialist Party and the rightist Socialist Party as a result of inter-party conflict concerning the Japan-US Security Treaty. There was a continuous conflict between rightists and leftists within *Sohyo.* When *Sohyo*'s action policy began to stress class strife ideology, a rightist group of unions left *Sohyo* and set up *Zenro* in 1954, which later developed into *Domei* (the Japan Confederation of Labour). In 1956, *Churitsu-roren* (the Federation of Independent Unions of Japan) was established as a national centre. Although the above-mentioned two socialist parties had by this time reunified, they split up again in 1959, a rightist group formed the Democratic Socialist Party, and *Domei*, which was established in 1964, became the supporting organization. After 1964, the four national centres, i.e., *Sohyo, Domei, Churitsu-roren* and *Shin-sanbetsu* led the Japanese labour movement until 1987. *Sohyo* especially made a significant contribution when it introduced *shunto* (the spring offensive) in 1956. *Shunto* is a tactic by which several unions in enterprises of more or less the same size or significance within a certain industry will coordinate their wage demands once a year, mostly in the late spring, arranging their schedule of bargaining with the individual employers and their strikes for the same period, all under the leadership of the industrial federations. The Japanese economy grew surprisingly rapidly from this time period to the beginning of the 1970s. In such a favourable economic situation, *Sohyo* had been gaining influence among the workers because of its success in getting higher wages through the spring offensive. However, the very results of economic development and higher wages started to work against the *Sohyo* leadership. The conspicuous features of the affluent society have made their radical ideology and slogans, and their emphasis on political activities, more or less obsolete. Around 1968, some industrial federations moved to unify themselves beyond their national centres. In 1978, the eyes of unions in the public sector were focused on the unification of the labour front for the following reasons: the slowdown of economic growth; the equilibrium of conservatives and reformists in the *Diet*; the *Sohyo*'s change in its policy; the unions' failure in the *shunto* of 1978. In 1982, the Japanese Private Sector Trade Union Council was set up, and in 1987 it developed into the Japanese Private Sector Trade Union Federation (the old

Rengo). At that time, *Domei* and *Churitsu-roren* were dissolved. *Sohyo* did not dissolve itself but most of its member unions in the private sector were affiliated. Finally, *Sohyo* and the old *Rengo* merged to establish the Japanese Trade Union Confederation (*Rengo*) in 1995. This made the *Rengo* the most powerful national centre, organizing around 6.8 million workers in 2023.

Chapter 4. Management Style and Employment Practices

§1. Lifetime Employment Practice as a Policy and Strategy

69. As mentioned above, large Japanese enterprises started to form employment practices which enabled them to retain regular workers until retirement. Such systems were required because of shortage of labour, rapid development of mechanization in factories and an expansion of the union movement. Under rapid economic growth after World War II, these practices, including lifetime employment, seniority-based wages and promotion and on-the-job training, became prevalent among larger companies. These practices (the traditional employment practices), although experiencing various changes in recent years, will be briefly described below since they have been important factors for the courts in making judgments in cases concerning employment.

70. Lifetime employment practice means that a company generally employs those who have just graduated from school, college and university and educates and trains them by transferring and promoting them within the company for its business needs. The employees generally continue to stay or to be retained in the same company typically until their company's mandatory retirement age. The lifetime employment practice is supported by seniority-based pay and promotion systems. Employees' wages and other benefits are regularly increased to reflect the length of their employment in the same company. Employees are generally promoted according to their years of service. An employee's training usually takes place on the job site (OJT). OJT necessarily accompanies transfer of employees among different workplaces and job reassignment.

71. There is also a peculiar management style which is related to traditional employment practices in Japan. In order to have stable shareholders, companies in general mutually hold other companies' shares. These shareholders are satisfied with long-term benefits reflected in the companies' stock prices as well as stability of management, and are not very concerned about their short-term dividends, except in case of a business crisis. Management of a company is not effectively checked through general meetings of stockholders, the board of directors and auditing officers. As a result, the top managers, including company presidents, most of whom come from inside the company, control the company without the shareholders' intervention. Because the top managers, including company presidents, are selected from among long-serving employees, and because they are generally free from shareholders' pressure, they tend to pay more attention to employees' interests than those of shareholders. The top managers are no more than higher-ranking employees and therefore their interests are most closely tied to those of employees. So long as the company is growing and its stock is rising, the stockholders do not intervene in the company's management unless a business crisis occurs. This helps to secure lifetime employment and seniority-based wage systems.

72. It has been said that the traditional employment practices in Japan have the following merits: under the lifetime employment practice, employees have more employment security; this may bring about employee loyalty; it also makes it easier for the employer to invest in the training and education of employees, as well as in research and development. Because labour mobility within a company or among related companies through transfer should be kept very high under the lifetime employment practice, functional flexibility of labour may be enhanced. Seniority-based wage and promotion systems may lead to equality of treatment among workers in the workplace. The level of wage may correspond to the average employee's life cycle. However, it has been increasingly asserted that traditional employment practices have the following disadvantages: the lifetime employment practice makes the top managers' responsibility unclear; it delays restructuring of the company and, therefore, damages the interests of shareholders. Once the employee leaves his company, it is very difficult for him or her to find employment elsewhere with equivalent positions and income. Therefore, it hampers labour mobility and therefore development of new industries. Frequent transfers of an employee, sometimes to distant workplaces and unfamiliar job contents, may adversely affect his or her private life and career development. Seniority-based wage and promotion systems may damage workers' incentives to work. Also, the traditional employment practices have made differentials of working conditions between regular employees and non-regular employees, since the seniority-based wage and promotion systems are closely related to working styles of regular employees.

§2. Recent Changes and Developments

73. The traditional employment practices became much less prevalent as economic growth began to slow down after the first oil crisis. Moreover, since the beginning of the long-term depression just after the collapse of the 'bubble economy' in the early 1990s, the voice of employers and business circles has become stronger and stronger, asserting that the traditional employment practices should be made more flexible because they are obstacles to Japanese competitiveness in the global economy. Many larger companies have gradually changed their recruitment system. They have started to hire more mid-career workers for managerial posts, to hire workers throughout the year instead of hiring new university graduates and school leavers once a year, and to recruit workers by occupation instead of recruiting them regardless of occupation. Companies have gradually been revising their wage systems from a seniority-based one to a performance-based one. Moreover, a majority of companies have introduced or plan to introduce annual salary systems in which the employer may exclude the length of the employee's service in determining an individual employee's wages (*see* Part I, Chapter 4, section 1). Technological innovation demand for high-value-added work has increasingly required workers to have sophisticated, professional and creative abilities. Therefore, OJT programmes became increasingly inadequate to meet the needs of companies and industries. In fact, 50.9% of employees participated in OJT during 1994. That figure included 61.7% of supervisory and managerial employees and 55.5% of professional and technical employees.[14] Workers' attitudes towards employment were also changing: more and more workers supported the idea of merit-based wages and promotion; workers' feeling that they belonged to their company had become diluted and young workers' willingness to change their jobs had become stronger. Although the percentage of employees changing jobs among the total number of employees was still rather small, it had slightly increased from 4.1% in 1981 to 4.6% in 2012, and 4.9% in 2023.[15]

74. In 1995, *Nikkeiren* (the Japan Federation of Employers' Association) issued a report on employment policy. They asserted that the optimal system to be adopted is one which flexibly copes with diversification of people's ideas and tastes and changes in the structure of industry. Whether people like it or not, mobility of employment will increase. Employees should be diversified into three different groups: those who develop their abilities and are employed over a long period of time under contracts of indefinite term, those who are employed for professional work under fixed-term contracts, and those who are flexibly employed in response to the demands of business under fixed-term contracts.[16] The report indicates that working conditions such as promotion, wage, bonus, welfare and retirement allowance should be decided in accordance with each group of employees. This report put forward the establishment of a new management style. The *White Paper on Labour 1996* also made proposals on the assumption of greater labour mobility and used the phrase 'long-term and stable employment' instead of the phrase previously used, 'lifetime employment'. The paper also indicated that efforts to minimize costs arising from labour mobility and suppress joblessness amidst labour mobility would be essential. In fact, there has been a noticeable trend for companies to restrict to lifetime employment and to increase the number of atypical employees for whom making employment adjustments is relatively easy. The percentage of lifetime employment workers is about 20% or less. In small and medium-sized companies, workers tend to frequently leave companies for personal reasons, company bankruptcy or business closings.

---

14. Ministry of Labour, *Minkan-kyoiku-kunren Jittai-chosa*, 1995.
15. Management and Co-ordination Agency (Ministry), *Report on the Special Survey of the Labour Force*, 1998, 2012 and 2023.
16. Nikkeiren, Shinjidai No Nihonteki Keiei, Tokyo: Nikkeiren, 1995.

Chapter 5. The Role of the Government

§1. The Autonomy of the Social Partners

75. The autonomy of the social partners has long been a major principle of Japanese industrial relations. In general, government leadership in the field of business is fairly strong, especially with regard to finance, exports, imports and industrial development, including the development of new technologies. Without such leadership, the rapid economic recovery after the war and the huge growth of the economy could not have been realized. The close relationship between industry and the government should not be overemphasized since the governmental industrial policy has often been opposed by industry even during periods of high economic growth. Many export-oriented industries which grew rapidly did not benefit from the governmental industrial policy. However, even today, the government considers that there are many industries under government regulation and protection, especially agriculture, financing, transportation and communication.[17] Accordingly, these two activities – regulation and protection – have been reviewed and discontinued under the deregulation policy of the government especially since 1994, several years after the collapse of the 'bubble' economy. For example, the reform of the financial system, the so-called Big Ban, started in April 1998 in order to establish a free, fair and global financial system. Even before the beginning of this reform project, many banks and securities companies went bankrupt.

76. In the field of employment and industrial relations, the government has always been very careful to refrain from intervention until the late 1980s. The only exceptions were labour inspection to enforce the minimum standards set by the LSA and other protective labour laws, as well as police intervention in criminal cases arising from labour disputes. The Japanese police have been very cautious in this respect because of their notorious record from the pre-war period. Today, since the industrial relations situation is rather calm, police intervention is not really conceivable. The government, however, has positively promoted labour and social policy to respond to structural changes in the industrial structure and labour market. In the process of forming such policy, the government has convened advisory study meetings and meetings of advisory councils. Through discussion in such meetings, the government establishes the opinion of the social partners and makes adjustments to their interests accordingly in policy-making. However, around the beginning of the 1990s, the government became eager to promote deregulation policy even in the field of employment and industrial relations. The Cabinet laid down three-year plans for promotion of deregulation in 1995 and 1998, and three-year plans for promotion of regulatory reform in 2001 and 2004. According to these plans, the laws concerning employment and industrial relations have been, are and will be deregulated to a large extent as described later. It should be noted that the reason why these deregulations and reforms have been realized almost as the Cabinet planned is partly because of the contemporary economic situation as well as the weakening of labour

17. K. Nakamura, *Going Global* 34 (Japan Times 1996).

unions. In fact, in the meetings of advisory councils prior to drawing up the bill for reformation, representatives of *Rengo*, the national biggest centre of labour unions seem not to have a strong voice. Governmental intervention grew a little stronger during the period when the Democratic Party took over the government. However, after the LDP returned to the position of the ruling party in 2012, the initiative for relaxing labour regulation started again.

§2. Government Institutions

I. The Ministry of Health, Labour and Welfare

77. The Ministry of Health, Labour and Welfare is the government institution which bears the most responsibility for individual and collective labour relations and some aspects of social security. The Ministry has several bureaux including Labour Standards, Employment Environment and Equal Employment, Children and Families, Employment Security, Human Resource Development, etc. At the local level, the Ministry has Prefectural Labour Bureaus (PLBs) in each prefecture. It also has Labour Standards Inspection Offices (LSIO) and Public Employment Security Offices (PESOs) in each district. With regard to social insurance, employment insurance and workers' compensation insurance were taken care of by the former Ministry of Labour, while most other sorts of social insurance were the responsibility of the former Ministry of Health and Welfare. Thus, the Ministry commands almost exclusive administrative authority in the field of labour relations.

II. Labour Inspection

78. The Labour Standards Bureau is responsible for labour inspection. Labour inspectors are national public employees as qualified specialists. They are authorized to inspect working places and other facilities, to examine records and documents, to interrogate employers and employees and to act as a judicial police officer with regard to violations of protective labour law. They also implement administrative guidance.

III. The Labour Relations Commission

79. There are two divisions of the LRC. The Central Labour Relations Commission (CLRC) located in Tokyo and the LRCs in each Prefecture cover labour relations in private industry and local public enterprises. The CLRC also deals with labour relations in Government enterprises. Formerly seamen's labour relations were dealt with by the Seamen's CLRC and the Seamen's Local LRC. However, they were abolished in 2008, and the LRC took over their jurisdiction over seamen's labour relations. The LRC has two functions which are of a very different nature; one is a quasi-judicial function with regard to unfair labour practice cases, and the other concerns labour dispute settlement through conciliation, mediation and arbitration. The former function only covers complaints about discriminatory treatment, refusal to bargain and interference in and dominance over union administration by the employers. Other complaints and disputes in the field of industrial relations will fall only under the jurisdiction of the ordinary courts since there is no labour court in Japan. (For a more detailed description of the functions of the LRCs, *see* Part II, Chapters 6, 7 and 8.)

IV. The Prefectural Bureaus of Labour Affairs

80. In addition to the Ministry of Health, Labour and Welfare, each prefectural government also has its own section of the labour policy bureau and labour policy offices, but their function is basically educational and consultative. Because of an increase in the number of individual labour disputes, many Prefectural bureaus of labour affairs have recently received an increasing number of requests from employees and employers for guidance on problems relating to dismissals, wages, working hours and so on (*see* Part II Chapter 8, section 3).

Chapter 6. Sources of Labour Law

§1. The Constitution

81. Articles 27 and 28 of the Constitution are regarded as being the most fundamental legal sources of labour law. Article 27, section 1, provides for the right to work, thus giving a constitutional basis to the legislation concerning security of employment – including public employment security agencies, unemployment insurance and vocational training. Section 2 of Article 27 provides a basis for protective labour law in general by requiring the fixing of standards of working conditions by law. Section 3 of the same article prohibits the exploitation of children, thus providing a basis for the legislative protection of child labour. Article 28 guarantees the right of workers to organize, bargain and act collectively, which gives a constitutional basis to legislation in the field of collective industrial relations. The fact that these Constitutional provisions guarantee the rights of workers – while at the same time, the Constitution provides that they should be defined by law 'in conformity with public welfare' – gives us good reason for interpreting the spirit of the Constitution so as to ensure fairly favourable treatment of workers as against employers. Thus, it is believed that the very nature of the Constitution provides a favourable atmosphere for labour law in Japan.

§2. Legislation

82. Most major labour law legislation was enacted shortly after World War II and amended later, to a certain degree. These statutes include the TUA, the Labour Relations Adjustment Act (LRAA) and the LSA, which are often called the three major labour laws. Important statutes in force are roughly classified below with regard to Constitutional provisions:

1. Relating to Article 27, section 1 – right to work: the ESA of 1947; the Employment Measures Act of 1966 (currently called the Act on Comprehensively Advancing Labor Measures, and Stabilizing the Employment of Workers, and Enriching Workers' Vocational Lives); the EIA of 1974; the Vocational Ability Development and Promotion Act of 1969; WDA of 1985; the Disabled Person's Employment Promotion Act (DPEPA) of 1960; the Older Person's Employment Stabilization Act (OPESA) of 1971; the Part-time Work Act (PWA) of 1993 (currently the Act on Improvement of Personnel Management and Conversion of Employment Status for Part-Time Workers and Fixed-Term Workers or Part-time and Fixed Term Employment Act); Child and Family Care Leave Act (CFLA) of 1995.
2. Relating to Article 27, section 2 – fixing minimum standards: the LSA of 1947; the Minimum Wages Act of 1959; the Security of Wage Payment Act (SWPA) of 1976; the WACIA; the Industrial Safety and Health Act of 1972; the EEOA of 1985; the LCA of 2007.
3. Relating to Article 27, section 3 – prohibition of child exploitation: the LSA of 1947 (Articles 56–64).

4. Relating to Article 28 – the right to organize, bargain and act collectively: the LRAA of 1946; the TUA of 1949.

83. All the laws listed above are applied generally to private employees and in part to public employees. Another group of laws covers only certain categories of employees; the most important laws in this group being the Seamen's Act of 1947, the Act on the Labour Relations of Specified Independent Administrative Agency of 2001, which became the Act on the Labour Relations of Administrative Executive Agencies in 2014, the National Civil Service Act of 1947 and the Local Civil Service Act of 1950, the Local Public Enterprises Labour Relations Act of 1952.

84. Apart from the above statutes enacted by Parliament, there are orders (ordinances), which the Cabinet, the Ministry of Health, Labour and Welfare and the CLRC issue based on the statutes. These subsidiary laws have a validity that is inferior to that of the statutes. The Ministry of Health, Labour and Welfare has issued numerous orders concerning the interpretation and implementation of each statute in the field of labour law. Of these, the most important are the Enforcement Ordinance of the LSA, the Ordinance of the Labour Standards for Women and many ordinances and rules regarding the Labour Safety and Health Act.

§3. Administrative Interpretation

85. The term 'Administrative interpretation' or 'Circular' means instructions which the upper levels of the ministries or agencies give to their subordinate administrative organs and officers with regard to interpretation and application of statutes and orders. These instructions are a mere administrative code binding on organs and officers within the ministries or agencies and are not binding on people as a matter of law. However, in the field of employment and labour relations, as administrative organs and officers rely on such administrative interpretation to discharge their duties under the workers' protection law, it often plays an important role in interpretation of the law before the courts interpret that law.

§4. Guidelines

86. Some recently enacted statutes provide for the authority of the Ministry of Health, Labour and Welfare to formulate administrative guidelines with respect to the measures which employers have to endeavour to take in order to achieve the statutory purposes. Typical examples are to be found in the present EEOA and the Part-time and Fixed-term Employment Act (PFEA). These guidelines themselves are not enforceable in law. However, the guidelines formulated by the Ministry of Health, Labour and Welfare on the basis of the EEOA provide examples of employers' measures prohibited as discriminatory.

§5. COLLECTIVE AGREEMENTS

87. Collective agreements between the union and the employer or employers' association have the force of autonomous legal norms in Japan. The TUA provides that every individual contract or work rule which contravenes the standard of working conditions established by the collective agreement is null and void, and replaced by relevant provisions of the collective agreement (Article 16). Since collective agreements may not run counter to imperative legal provisions, a collective agreement is the second strongest legal norm. It is an autonomous norm in the sense that it is created by private parties and is, in principle, binding only on those parties and their members. However, the TUA admits that it has a legally binding effect beyond this limitation under certain conditions. If three-quarters of the employees in a certain plant are covered by a collective agreement, the agreement is automatically extended to cover all the remaining employees in similar positions– at least as far as working conditions are concerned (Article 17). If the majority of workers of one kind in a certain locality come under the application of one collective agreement, it will be declared by the Minister of Labour or the Prefectural Governor to extend to the remaining workers of the same kind in the locality and their employers in accordance with the resolution of the LRC.

88. However, given the strong legal effect of collective agreements, one should not overestimate their function. First, it is often pointed out that, in general, Japanese collective agreements are both simple and vague, with fewer and less detailed provisions than Western ones. Thus, in Japanese industrial relations, most of the rules of behaviour and the concrete rights and obligations of both parties are actually decided by the power relationship between the union and the employer and also by the power structure at shop-floor level. Second, in Japan today, only a small percentage of employees are covered by collective agreements. Only 16.3% of all employees were organized in 2023 and about 4.7% of all unions did not conclude collective agreements in 2022. The details of the significance, formation, legal effect and termination of collective agreements will be fully discussed in Part II, Chapter 3.

§6. WORK RULES (SHUGYO-KISOKU)

89. Shugyo-kisoku also acquires the nature of legal norms in relation to individual contracts. *Shugyo-kisoku* is a set of work rules which is given a special legal status in law. The LSA requires the employer, continuously employing more than ten employees, to draw up *shugyo-kisoku* on specific items concerning conditions of employment (Article 89), to consult the opinion of a labour union organizing a majority of employees or a representative of a majority of employees (Article 90), to submit the *shugyo-kisoku* to administrative office (labour inspection office) along with the union's or the representative's opinion, and to inform the employees of it by displaying it or posting it in conspicuous places (Article 106).

90. Article 93 of the LSA, which was replaced by Article 12 of the LCA, previously provided that stipulating conditions inferior to those fixed in the work rules was null and void. In this case, conditions which became invalid are replaced by the standard fixed in the *shugyo-kisoku*. However, besides the legal effect given by Article 93, there has been controversy over whether stipulations of the *shugyo-kisoku* generally have normative effects or only constitute contractual terms of employment. In the *Shuhoku Bus* case, the Supreme Court held that the *shugyo-kisoku* had the nature of a legal norm as long as it provided reasonable working conditions. In that case, the employer amended the provision about mandatory retirement age so that the new retirement age might be applied to employees in chief or higher rank who had been excluded from application of the previous retirement age. As a result, an employee in a senior position was dismissed on the grounds that he had reached retirement age. The Supreme Court stated as follows:

91. In practice, *shugyo-kisoku* does not only have the nature of a social norm but it has also been recognized that it has the nature of a legal norm in the sense that there exists a prima facie custom between the employer and the employee that the working conditions should be based on the *shugyo-kisoku* as long as it provides reasonable working conditions. Therefore, the employees, irrespective of whether they are in fact aware of the existence of the *shugyo-kisoku* or its contents, or whether they have in fact agreed to them, the contents of the *shugyo-kisoku* are automatically applied to them. We think that the employer is usually not entitled to deprive the employees of their vested rights or to impose unfavourable working conditions by unilaterally forming or changing *shugyo-kisoku*. We think nevertheless that as long as the stipulations of *shugyo-kisoku* are reasonable, the employees are not entitled to refuse to comply with them on grounds of their disagreement since *shugyo-kisoku* makes it its principle to determine the terms and conditions of employment collectively and uniformly.[18]

92. This ruling has dual implications: one is that the contents of *shugyo-kisoku* are binding if they are reasonable. The other is that the employer is entitled to unilaterally vary those contents if such variation is reasonable. This ruling is very pragmatic but not quite comprehensible as a legal theory. A recent view of influence understands that the Supreme Court applied to *shugyo-kisoku* the legal theory which affirms the effect of standard covenants in a similar way as the contracts of life insurance, transportation, etc. on the conditions of the prior disclosure and reasonability of their contents. The Supreme Court held in a later case that the contents of *shugyo-kisoku* became those of an employment contract if those were reasonable. However, even if it is possible to apply the analogy of the legal theory of standard covenants to *shugyo-kisoku*, why should employees who refuse to agree with the variation of *shugyo-kisoku* be bound by it? Many academic views have been presented to answer this question. One says that employees have given an implied agreement to a reasonable variation at the time of making employment contracts. Another says that an employer has a right to vary terms and conditions according to

18. The *Shuhoku Bus* case, the Supreme Court in 1968, SMS, Vol. 22, No. 13, p. 3459.

certain requirements. None of these academic views are very successful in answering that question. However, since the *Shuhoku Bus* decision, the Supreme Court has affirmed this ruling many times and the ruling has been firmly established. Therefore, even though the general principle of the law of contract does not allow one party to unilaterally vary contractual provisions without the other party's consent, the employer may vary the contents of individual employment contracts by varying the *shugyo-kisoku* on the condition that the change is reasonable. Accordingly, in Japan today, because of the existence of *shugyo-kisoku* as well as collective agreements, the role of the individual contract is very limited. The role of shugyo-kisoku to vary an employment contract will be discussed in Part I, Chapter 1, section 5.

93. In cases following the *Shuhoku Bus* case, the Supreme Court has held that the courts should examine the contents and necessity of the amendment in order to determine whether or not the amendment of the *shugyo-kisoku* is reasonable.[19] Accordingly, the courts have generally taken account of the following factors: how much and what sorts of employees' disadvantage are caused by the amendment; how much business necessity there is for the amendment; whether the contents of the amended *shugyo-kisoku* are appropriate; whether any compensatory provision is given to employees in return for the amendment and other factors including the process of negotiating with a trade union, the attitude of other trade unions and employees and social circumstances in general. Where the amendment is made with regard to important working conditions such as wages and retirement allowances, the court has required a greater degree of business necessity for the amendment than in cases of less important working conditions.[20] One increasing trend is that, in determining the reasonableness of the contents of the amendment, the courts make much of the fact that the employer has negotiated and agreed on the amendment with a union organizing a vast majority of employees in the company except in a case where the amendment is so much disadvantageous to employees and therefore improper in its contents.[21] An increasing number of scholars are beginning to respect this established case law, pointing out that the Supreme Court struck a balance between the need for changes in working conditions through the continuous employment relationship and the need for the security of employment under the traditional long-term employment practice as well as the doctrine of abuse of right to dismissal: instead of protecting employees from arbitrary dismissal, the Court has given employers the right to change their employees' working conditions if the requirement is satisfied.

94. However, the above binding effect of the *shugyo-kisoku* on individual contracts in the workplace has remained in force supported only by decisions of the

19. The *Takeda System* case, the Supreme Court in 1983, RH, No. 418, p. 21.
20. The *Omagari Nokyo* case, the Supreme Court in 1988, SMS, Vol. 42, No. 2, p. 60; the *Michinoku Ginko* case, the Supreme Court in 2000, RH, No. 787, p. 6; the *Hakodate Shinkin* case, the Supreme Court in 2000, RH, No. 788, p. 17; *Ugo Ginko* case, the Supreme Court in 2000, RH, No. 788, p. 23.
21. The *Daiichi Kogata Hire* case, the Supreme Court in 1992, HJ, No. 1434, p. 133; *Daishi Ginko* case, the Supreme Court in 1998, RH, No. 710. p. 12; the *Michinoku Ginko* case, *supra.*

Supreme Court. It was necessary to clarify statutorily such effects in order to prevent disputes about working conditions between the employer and their employees. For this purpose, the LCA was enacted, several provisions of which concerned the binding effect of the *shugyo-kisoku*. Article 7 provides that where an employee and an employer conclude an employment contract, and the employer has informed the employee of the *shugyo-kisoku* stipulating reasonable working conditions, the content of the employment contract shall be based on those stipulated conditions of the *shugyo-kisoku*. Article 7 further provides that the above rule cannot apply to any part of an employment contract in which an employee and employer have agreed on working conditions that differ from the content of the *shugyo-kisoku*, except in cases that fall under Article 12. Article 12, the contents of which are the same as former Article 93 of the LSA provides that any working conditions agreed between the employee and employer inferior to those fixed in the *shugyo-kisoku* is null and void and that, in such case, working conditions which become invalid are replaced by the standards fixed in the *shugyo-kisoku*.

95. LCA provides for the binding effect of an employment contract under changes involving the *shugyo-kisoku*. Thus, Article 9 makes it clear as a contractual principle that the employer may not change, without making an agreement with the employee, any of the working conditions that constitute the content of the employment contract. However, this Article recognizes an important exception for this principle specified in Article 10. Incorporating the above-mentioned case law regarding *shugyo-kisoku* into the LSA, Article 10 specifies that if an employer informs the employee of changes in the *shugyo-kisoku* and if the change is reasonable in view of the extent of the disadvantage incurred by the employee, the need for changing the working conditions, the appropriateness of the contents of the changes on employment conditions, the state of negotiation with any labour union or the like, and any other circumstances pertaining to the change to the *shugyo-kisoku*, the working conditions which constitute the content of the employment contract shall be based on such changed *shugyo-kisoku*. It is to be noted that the term 'inform' does not mean that every employee does not have to notice and understand the contents of the *shugyo-kisoku. It suffices that the employer places the shugyo-kisoku* in a place where all employees can find and understand the *shugyo-kisoku* in such a manner as posting or distributing copies or making it freely accessible on the computer at the workplace.

§7. Labour Relations Practice

96. Opinions are divided as to whether or not labour relations practices (customs) in general are a source of law. However, past practice may have a significant legal effect in the following cases. First, a long-standing repetitive practice can be considered to have become part of the employment contract. Second, a long-standing repetitive practice can be used to clarify vague provisions of collective agreement and work rules. Third, the employer's exercise of his right in contradiction of a longstanding repetitive practice can be regarded as void because of an 'abuse of a right'. Fourth, the employer's conduct contradicting a long-standing repetitive practice between him and the labour union can constitute an unfair labour practice.

§8. Cases and Legal Theories

97. As Japan has adopted a continental (civil) law system instead of a common law system, the notion of binding precedent or *stare decisis* is unknown in Japan. In theory, no judge is bound by anything except the Constitution and the law, and he/she is free to decide independently according to his/her conscience. However, a lower court's decision which clearly conflicts with a previous decision of the Supreme Court will most probably be overruled if the case goes to the Supreme Court. For this reason, a lower court tends to follow judicial precedents, especially those of the Supreme Court. At the same time, case law is important because the legislation tends to be rather abstract, prescribing only the fundamental rules, and so case law is necessary to fill out the legislative provisions when new cases arise. It is clear, therefore, that for the study of law, the study of legal precedents is inevitable. In labour law, especially with its short history, case law has played a very important role. However, at the same time, this fact also leads to some confusion in the case of labour law. Both the theory and the practice of labour law are rather new and no significant established tradition exists, with the result that almost any legal argument can command respect. Younger judges often tend to adopt new theories, and this trend causes instability in the case law. As for legal theory, Japanese law, like most other modern legal systems, does not recognize it as a legal source. However, the judges pay considerable attention to the work of legal scholars. Quite a few reviews of court decisions are published in a number of legal journals and they are usually carefully considered by the judges. The orders and decisions of the LRCs have almost as much importance as decisions of the courts in the field of unfair labour practice cases.

§9. International Sources

98. The Constitution provides that treaties should be faithfully observed (Article 98(2)) and that they should be approved by the *Diet*, the highest organ of state power, in order to come into effect (Articles 61 and 73). However, the Constitution is silent on the question of whether a signed and ratified international treaty itself has the value of law at national level. Therefore, legal theories are divided on this point even for signed and ratified ILO Conventions. However, it is reasonable to assume that at least the ILO Conventions providing concrete norms should have the value of law at national level[22] or at least similarly respected. As of 2024, Japan has ratified 50 ILO Conventions (although Japan has denounced seven of them), including important ones on the Freedom of Association and the Protection of the Right to Organize and Bargain Collectively (No. 87), the Right to Organize and Bargain

22. T. Ariizumi, *Rodokijunho (Labour Standards Law)* 31–32 (Yuhikaku 1963).

Collectively (No. 98), Equal Remuneration (No. 100), Workers with Family Responsibilities (No. 156), Vocational Rehabilitation and Employment (Disabled Persons) Convention (No. 159), Private Employment Agencies Convention (No. 181), Worst Forms of Child Labour Convention (No. 182) and Promotional Framework for Occupational Safety Convention (No. 187).

Part I. The Individual Employment Relationship

Chapter 1. Formation and Variation of the Relationship

§1. The Means of Recruitment and Hiring

99. In Japan, employers recruit employees through various routes. The Japanese labour market is divided into two separate markets: one is a new graduate market and the other is a mid-career job seeker market. The new graduate market is peculiar to Japan. This is closely related to Japanese traditional employment practice which is described in Chapter 4. Enterprises generally hire a group of new graduates from universities, senior high schools, etc. immediately upon their graduation. The hiring process starts with a request for materials from the company. University students seek information on companies either from company brochures or the company's homepage. Some students start job-hunting activities during their junior year. Many companies hold a seminar for recruitment and then a written examination and interview with students. This process usually occurs between April and July and many companies start to send the successful students a letter promising employment from April of the following year. On the other hand, in the mid-career job-seeker market, the most common route for recruitment is the personal connection. For example, a survey found that mid-career jobseekers in metropolitan areas found their jobs through personal connections (31.1%), help-wanted ads in newspapers (11.4%), help-wanted ads in ad inserts (10.9%), free help-wanted magazine (9.5%), public employment placement agencies (8.8%), recruit information in internet sites (7.5%), paid help-wanted magazine (4.4%), private worker-dispatching undertakings (1.8%), company homepages (1.5%), employment placement agencies (1.5%), or by direct inquiry to the company (7.4%) or other means (4.4%).[23]

100. Since World War II, employment agencies have been monopolized by the government, which found that private employment agencies often worked as a means of intermediary exploitation resulting in long working hours, low wages and forced labour in an era of severe shortage of demand for labour. Thus, by 1997, the ESA of 1947 had not only prohibited labour supply projects but also prohibited fee-charging private employment placement services. It had excluded from prohibition those services arranging employment for persons engaged in certain occupations

23. Recruitment Works Institute, Working Persons Survey, 2007.

requiring special skills, which were conducted under licence from the Ministry of Health, Labour and Welfare. This regulation was in line with Part III of ILO Convention No. 96 (1949). Thus, occupations that were designated by the Enforcement Ordinance of ESA as those requiring special techniques were strictly limited. However, due to the rapid structural change in Japanese industry, employment and population, in 1977, the Enforcement Ordinance of ESA widened very much the scope of occupations permissible for fee-charging employment placement services. Namely, the operation of such services has been prohibited with regard to only certain occupations listed by the Ordinance. In 1999, the ESA was finally amended to be brought into line with ILO Convention No. 188, which was adopted in 1997 to replace ILO Convention No. 96. The law regarding employment placement and other related matters under the present ESA will be described below.

101. The ESA defines 'employment placement' as 'receiving applications for workers and for jobs and extending services to establish employment relationships between those seeking workers and those seeking jobs' (Article 4(1)). This definition of 'employment placement' has been broadly interpreted by the courts so that it may include out-placement as well as head-hunting.[24] Any person may engage in fee-charging private employment placement services except for arranging employment for workers engaged in certain occupations being likely to affect protection of workers such as port transport and construction work (Articles 30 and 32.11). The Ministry of Health, Labour and Welfare shall give a person a licence for a fee-charging employment placement service where he has sufficient financial resources, takes necessary measures to properly keep confidential personal information and secrets of those seeking workers and those seeking jobs, and is competent to conduct employment placement business (Article 31). However, a person is disqualified from obtaining such a licence in the following cases: where five years have not elapsed from the completion or invalidation of a certain penalty to which he was sentenced; where he has not been reinstated from a declaration of his or her incompetence, quasi-incompetence or bankruptcy; where five years have not elapsed from the date of the revocation of his previous licence; where he is a minor who is not competent to conduct business and to any minor's legal representative to whom the preceding cases apply; or where any entity which has juridical personality has been struck off and has not been reinstated. An entity which has a juridical personality is also disqualified if any of its executives fall into any of the above-stated categories (Article 32). It can be said that the new ESA liberalized fee-charging employment placement projects. However, the Law still requires people to obtain a licence from the Ministry of Health, Labour and Welfare if they intend to operate even a free employment placement service (Article 33) and the commissioning of recruitment (Article 36). However, the law excludes schools and universities from the obligation to obtain a licence to conduct a free employment placement service although they should notify the Ministry (Articles 33 and 33.2). Furthermore, the Law also provides for the protection of those seeking jobs. It requires both employment agencies (including employment placement agencies and persons being engaged in the

24. The *Tokyo Executive Search* case, the Supreme Court in 1994, 654 *Rodo Hanrei* (RH) No. 654, p. 6.

recruitment of workers) and those seeking workers to provide written particulars on working conditions for employment (Articles 5.3 and 32.13). It requires employment placement agencies to collect, maintain or use personal information only for proper business purposes (Article 5.4). It prohibits discrimination in employment placement, vocational guidance, or the like, on the grounds of race, nationality, creed, sex, social status, family origin, previous profession, membership of a trade union, etc. (Article 3). A fee-charging agency is required to appoint a person who deals with complaints from those seeking workers or jobs, administers personal information or deals with other matters (Article 32.14). The Minister is given the power to give instruction and advice to employment agencies and to recommend them to take corrective action (Article 48.2). In order to maintain their neutrality in labour disputes, the ESA also prohibits employment agencies from referring job applicants to a workplace in which there is a strike or lock-out (Articles 20, 34 and 42.2).

102. Although a fee-charging employment agency which conducts employment placement under a licence shall not collect any fees from jobseekers, it may receive registration fees (presently 690 yen) and service fees from those seeking workers. However, the service fees are limited to either the amount subject to the prescribed limit for those agencies offering only services of matching particular demand and supply or the amount reported to and authorized by the Ministry of Health, Labour and Welfare in advance for those agencies offering consulting, counselling, finding suitable workers and similar services as well as the basic matching service (Article 32.3). The maximum chargeable fee for matching services only is fixed at 10.5% of a worker's wages for six months where he has been employed for over six months. The ESA prohibits an employment placement agency from receiving any fees from those seeking jobs except in cases of entertainers or models.

103. The PESO, which the Employment Security Bureau of the Ministry of Health, Labour and Welfare operates, has generally played a more important role than private employment placement agencies. In 2013, the number of Employment Security Offices was 544 and the number of officers was about 11,300. In 2012, PESOs received about 8.98 million applications for workers and about 6.82 million applications for jobs. The number of matching services which PESOs actually provided was about 12.5 million. 2.16 million workers were hired through PESOs.[25] The PESOs not only provide employment placement services and vocational guidance but also provide employees with unemployment benefits and employers with various subsidies for the purpose of employment stabilization. Furthermore, they also help employees to have vocational training offered by the public vocational training facilities. Besides those Employment Security Offices, the Employment Security Bureau operates six job banks which register white-collar workers, whether employed or unemployed, and provide professional training services as well as employment placement.

---

25. Ministry of Health, Labour and Welfare, *Rodoshijo Nenpo* (Annual Report on Labour Market), 2012.

104. Private employment placement agencies took only a minor role in employment placement services until 1999. After the liberalization of fee-charging employment placement projects, the number of private employment placement agencies rapidly increased and reached 18,184 (17,315 fee-charging agencies and 869 free agencies) in 2012. In the same year, those agencies received about 4.10 million applications for workers and about 9.24 million applications for jobs. About 660,000 workers were hired through private employment placement agencies.[26]

§2. The Different Categories of Employees

I. Overview

105. In Japan today, the distinction between blue-collar and white-collar employees is almost irrelevant, at least legally speaking. The traditional distinction between these two categories, which had been important in terms of social status and also within enterprises in the pre-war period, is now fading away rapidly, partly because labour law does not recognize any distinction in its field of jurisdiction and partly because of the efforts of individual enterprises to abolish most of the differences in working conditions. Working people are broadly divided into employed workers (i.e.,, employees) and non-employed workers. Employees are divided into those who work full-time (full-time employees), those who work part-time (part-time employees) those who are employed for an indefinite term (indefinite term employees) and those who are employed for a fixed term (fixed term employees). Non-employed workers include not only independent workers and freelancers but also home workers, despatched workers and contractors' employees.

II. Regular Employees and Non-regular Employees

106. The most important distinction in Japanese daily employment relationships is now the one between regular employees and non-regular employees. Regular employees are those who are employed by the employer with a contract of indefinite duration and who are expected to stay in the enterprise for long. They are usually recruited on an annual basis from university and school leavers, although this practice of recruitment is now going through some changes (*see* Chapter 1, section 5). Non-regular employees can also be recruited fresh from school, but more often they have already worked in other enterprises. They are either employed for a definite or an indefinite term. However, even if they are employed for an indefinite term, neither of the parties expects that they will stay in the enterprise for long and they are not recognized as having permanent status. Quite often non-regular employees do stay in the enterprise for a considerable period of time, but they are the first to be dismissed whenever the enterprise has a labour surplus. They are often used as a kind of shock absorber to cope with normal business fluctuation since the regular

26. Ministry of Health, Labour and Welfare, *Shokugyo Shokai Jigyo Hokoku* (Report on Employment Placement Agencies), 2012.

employees who are employed for a lifetime are an inflexible labour force. Regular employees enjoy job security, guaranteed steady advancement in rank and wages, the required training for a given job and finally, a generous sum as a retirement allowance. Non-regular employees do not usually enjoy such privileges and often they are not even entitled to use company welfare facilities. Thus, non-regular employees are an essential ingredient of the lifetime employment system (the long-term employment system) but, in most cases, are second-class citizens compared with regular employees, being the last hired and the first fired. However, the precise situation of a non-regular employee also depends upon what type of non-regular employee he or she is. One can distinguish the following types of non-regular employees: part-time employees (or part-timers), daily workers, *arubaito* ('side-job workers'), dispatched workers, fixed-term employees, and short-term workers (including seasonal workers and contract employees). The proportions of these different categories of non-regular employees among the total number of employees in 2022 are listed in Table 10.

Table 10 Numbers and Proportions of Different Categories of Non-regular Employees in the Non-agricultural Sector in 2022 (10,000)

Categories of Employees	*Number*	*Proportion(%)*
Employees (excluding directors)	5,699	100
Regular employees	3,597	63.1
Non-regular employees	2,101	36.6
Part-time employees[a]	1,021	17.9
Arubait	453	8.0
Dispatched workers	149	2.6
Fixed term employees	283	5.0
Others	190	3.4

[a] These include genuine and non-genuine part-time employees, the definition of which will be given below.
Source: Ministry of Internal Affairs and Communications, Statistics Bureau, Annual Report on the Labour Force Survey.

III. Full-Time Employees and Part-Time Employees

107. Under the PWA of 1993, the term 'part-time employees' is defined as 'workers whose prescribed weekly work hours are less than regular employees employed in the same establishment'. However, the part-time employees so defined should be called 'genuine part-time employees' or 'short-time workers'. This is the first category of 'part-time employees'. The term 'part-time employees' in the actual practice sometimes includes workers who work the same, or almost the same, number of hours per week as regular full-time employees but who are nevertheless classified as part-time employees in the same establishment. Thus, there are not only 'genuine part-time employees' but also 'non-genuine part-time employees' (the second category). These non-genuine part-time employees are workers who merely do not have the status of regular full-time employees and are often described as 'quasi-part-timers'. The third category of 'part-time employees' which is often used for the statistics indicates workers working under thirty-five hours per week. These workers can be called 'statistical official part-time employees'. According to the 2019 survey, the total number of statistically official part-time employees is 31.1% of the total number of non-agricultural employees. However, the same survey in 1990 found that the total number of statistically official part-time employees was only 15.0% of the total number of non-agricultural employees in that year. Table 11 shows a rapid increase in the proportion of part-time jobs between 1990 and 2019.

Table 11 Changes in the Proportion of Part-Time Workers[a]

Year	*Proportion of Part-Time Workers (%)*
1990	15.0
1995	17.1
2000	19.8
2005	23.6
2010	26.1
2015	29.2
2019	31.1

Source: Management and Coordination Agency, Annual Labour Force Survey, 1990–2019.
[a] Workers working under thirty-five hours per week

108. The PWA was not enacted to provide for the rights and duties of part-time work but to provide for a legal base for guidelines governing part-time work and the employment management of part-timers as well as for the establishment of part-time work support centres which may offer employers and part-timers such services as provision of information and counselling and which may also conduct training projects for and research on part-time employees. However, it was amended in 2007 and 2014 to introduce some provisions to prohibit an employer from treating part-time employees less favourably. However, many provisions of the PWA still require an employer only to endeavour towards a balanced treatment between full-time and part-time employees. The problems of the PWA will be discussed in Part I, Chapter 7, section 5.

IV. Temporary Workers and Permanent Workers

109. The term 'temporary workers' means those who are employed under fixed-term contracts. 'Permanent workers' may be identical to 'regular workers' in many cases. However, this is not always the case. For example, there are many part-time employees who are employed under contracts of indefinite duration but are not considered to be regular workers. There are various types of workers who are often temporarily employed in seasonal projects or projects of a definite term, or during the busy period of business: 'seasonal workers', 'side-job workers' (*arubaito*), 'daily workers' and other temporary workers. Among them, 'daily workers' and 'side-job workers' are employed for a very short period on a daily basis. Most 'daily workers' work on a full-time basis but a few work on a part-time basis. Some 'side-job workers' work on a part-time basis. About 40% of these are students who attend schools, colleges or universities. Most temporary workers – other than 'daily workers' – are employed under fixed-term contracts of less than one year; for example, two or three months in many cases. However, except for those of 'seasonal workers', their terms of employment are often renewed many times. Workers who attained the company's mandatory retirement age are often re-employed by the same company as so-called *shokutaku* under one-year contracts and often expect to be retained by renewal for several years.

110. In 2012, several provisions were inserted into the LCA in order to regulate fixed-term employment contracts. One of those is a provision that entitles workers under fixed-term employment contracts the right to convert their contract into a contract for an indefinite term in order to promote stability in employment for workers under fixed-term contracts. As explained later (205-3), Article 18 of the LCA provides that workers who have renewed a fixed-term employment contract at least once in the past and who have been working for more than five years reserve the right, upon application, to convert the contract into an employment contract for an indefinite term. Another is the provision regarding the regulation on unreasonable differentiation of contractual terms between the contract with a terminal and the contract without such a date in the same workplace. Thus, Article 20 of the LCA provided that where the working conditions differ between the fixed-term employee and the non-fixed-term employee employed by the same employer, the difference should not be unreasonable having regards to the difference of job contents, responsibility, duty contents and the extent of changes in duty. This provision was removed from the LCA and is now replaced by Article 8 of the PFEA, Which also covers part-time employees (*see* Part 1, Chapter 6, section 5).

V. Contractor's Employees

111. 'Contractor's employees' are those employed by a company which concludes a 'contract for work' with another company. Under a 'contract for work', a company (the trustor company) undertakes specific, delimited pieces of work for another company (the trustee company) at the latter company's premises. To carry out this contract for work lawfully, the trustor company directs and supervises its own employees (i.e., contractor's employees) at the trustee company's premises because labour-supply projects are generally prohibited under the Employment Security Act (ESA) of 1947. In addition to Article 6 of the Labour Standards Act which prohibits, with penal sanction, third parties from engaging in intermediate exploitation by participating in the employment relationship, ESA in principle prohibits a fee-charging job placement service, recruitment on commission and labour-supply business. However, there is debate not only as to whether both companies violate the ESA's prohibition but also as to whether the employees of the trustor company may insist that they are in fact employed by the trustee company. According to the courts' decisions, the employees may win the case if they can prove that their employment contracts have been implicitly formed between them and the trustee company under certain circumstances: for example, in the case in which pay rates are substantially determined by the trustee company, that direction and supervision are substantially conducted by it, and that the decisions of the personnel management are substantially made by it.[27]

VI. Dispatched Workers

112. The term 'dispatched worker' refers to hired-out workers who are employed by an employer and sent to third-party users for the purpose of performing work for these third parties. The WDA of 1985 defined a 'dispatched worker' as a 'worker employed by one person to be engaged in work for another person under the direction of the latter, while maintaining their employment relationship with the former, but excluding cases where the former agrees with the latter that such worker or workers shall be employed by the latter'. 'Worker dispatching' is excluded from the 'worker supply' which is prohibited by the ESA only when it satisfies the requirements prescribed in the WDA. Two different types of worker-dispatching undertakings are recognized under the WDA: a 'specified worker-dispatching undertaking' and a 'general worker-dispatching undertaking'. The former is the undertaking which dispatches only workers regularly employed by it while the latter is any undertaking other than a specified worker-dispatching undertaking in which workers are only registered. However, a general worker-dispatching undertaking also must conclude a contract of employment with an employee whenever it intends to dispatch that employee. A person who intends to carry on a general worker-dispatching undertaking must obtain a licence for it from the Minister of Labour while a person who intends to carry out a specified worker-dispatching undertaking must submit to the Minister a notice containing the listed particulars listed in the WDA.

113. The WDA intends to regulate worker-dispatching business from the following viewpoints: to prevent the exploitation of dispatched workers, to regulate and clarify the working conditions of dispatched workers, to specify the parties responsible for the observance of labour protective regulations in dispatched employment and to prevent worker-dispatching undertakings from eroding the jobs of regular employees under lifetime employment systems.[1] Therefore, the WDA originally allowed worker-dispatching undertakings to conduct only certain types of work. Those types of work must be either work which requires special knowledge, skill or experience for expeditious and appropriate performance, or work which

27. For example, the *Saga TV* case, the Fukuoka High Court in 1983, RH, No. 410, p. 29.

requires special management of the workers because of the characteristics of the form of engagement or employment, and which Cabinet Order designated as being necessary for the expeditious and appropriate matching of labour demand and supply. In 1996, the number of types of work which worker-dispatching undertakings were allowed to conduct under Cabinet Order increased from sixteen to twenty-six. However, in 1999 when the ESA was amended in line with ILO Convention No. 188, the WDA was also amended to a great extent in order to abolish restrictions on permissible types of work. In 2003, some amendments were added to the WDA in order to further liberate worker-dispatching undertakings. Under the amended WDA, only port transport, construction, guard services, and medical services are listed as prohibited types of work (Article 4 and Cabinet Order). However, worker-dispatching undertakings are not totally liberated.

114. Worker-dispatching agencies for registration-type worker dispatching should obtain a license from the Minister of Health, Labour and Welfare even after the amendment. One prominent feature of the amendment is that the WDA treats dispatched work other than the above-described twenty-six types of work as temporary work in a strict sense. Therefore, except for the twenty-six types of work and some other work, a user company (client) is prohibited from receiving a dispatched worker continuously at the same post in the workplace for over the permissible period. The permissible period is either what is less than three years and fixed by a client after listening to the opinions of his employees' representative opinions or one year (Article 40.2). As a result of the recession that followed the so-called Lehman Shock in 2008, a number of dispatched workers lost their jobs. Thus, the WDA was amended in 2012 to strengthen the regulation. For example, it is now prohibited for worker dispatching firms from concluding employment contracts with dispatched workers for a certain short period, i.e., thirty days or less, except for certain types of jobs such as those which require special skills (Article 35.3).

115. However, soon after the LDP returned to the position of the ruling party, another development occurred in labour legislation including the WDA. In 2015, a significant amendment was made to the WDA. The amendment contains several important provisions that changed the contents of the current policies regarding worker dispatching. For example, the distinction between the twenty-six types of specialized works and other works regarding the permissible period of the reception of dispatched workers was abolished. Instead, the permissible period of three years for worker dispatching was set for individual dispatched workers regardless of their job contents. At the same time, the limitation on the reception of dispatched workers at the establishment level was introduced. However, this limitation can be relaxed so that the renewal of the worker-dispatching contract would be permissible under certain conditions such as the dispatching employer's notice to the majority union or the individual who represents the majority of workers who are employed by the dispatching employer. These limitations do not apply when a dispatched worker concludes employment contracts for an indefinite term with his/her employer, i.e., the worker dispatching company.

116. Where a client, who has received worker dispatching services from a dispatching agency continuously until the end of the permissible period (up to three years), intends to employ a worker in order to continue having the worker engaged in the work concerned, he must endeavour to employ without delay the dispatched worker who has engaged in the same work concerned continuously for the permissible period if the worker has notified the client of his desire to be employed (Article 40.3). Where the client has received a notice from a dispatching agency that it would no longer send the dispatched worker because the permissible period ends, but where the client intends to have a dispatched worker continuously after the expiration of that period, he must endeavour to offer without delay an employment contract to the person who is the dispatched worker concerned and wishes to be employed by the day before the first day after expiration of the permissible period (Article 40.4). However, this rule only imposes a public law sanction on the client and does not create the state of conclusion of an employment contract without parties' agreement.[28]

117. There have been many cases in which a worker who concluded a fixed-term employment contract in form with one company, was despatched by a company to another company to work under the latter's supervision. He was later terminated by the former after several renewals of that contract during the term or at its expiry due to termination of some kind of business contract between the former and the latter. He went to court against the latter to claim a judgment affirming his status as an employee in the latter. In such case, the worker often argues that as the business contract work contravenes several provisions of the WDA, it cannot be legitimized by the WDA as an exception from the ESA's prohibition of labour supply and therefore is void. However, the Supreme Court clearly rejected this argument in the *Panasonic Plasma Display* case.[29] The Court stated as follows:

118. Under the business contract for work, on the one hand, the contractor has the duty to complete work for the party ordering work, but on the other hand, he is exclusively given all right to instruct and supervise the worker. Accordingly, where the contractor does not instruct and supervise the worker and the party ordering work actually instructs and supervises him in his workplace, the contract cannot be regarded as a genuine business contract for work, even if it is called a business contract as a matter of form between the parties. In this case, if no other employment contract is concluded between the party ordering work and the worker, the relationship of the three parties should be regarded as one of worker-dispatching under the WDA (Article 2(1)). There is no room to interpret that the relationship falls under the category of 'labour supply' prohibited by the ESA. In the case before us, the appellant (the party ordering work) by actually instructing and supervising the appellee (the worker) was violating the provisions of the WDA. However, regarding factors such as the purport, the administrative nature of the WDA and the necessity of the worker. It should not be considered that even if the business contract

---

28. *Matsushita Plasma Display* case, the Osaka District Court in 2006, RH, No. 913, p. 49.
29. The *Panasonic Plasma Display* case, the Supreme Court in 2009, RH, No. 993, p. 5.

violates the provisions of the WDA, the employment contract between the contractor and the worker will be void merely for that reason. Then, for the relationship between the appellant and the appellee, it cannot be considered that there was in existence an implied agreement to conclude an employment contract between them because the appellant did neither play a part in hiring the appellee nor decided the amount of his wages. On the contrary, the contractor determined in large part how the work should be carried out, including reassignment of the worker.

119. Accordingly, where a business contract is determined as falling under the definition of a worker-dispatching contract, even if there is some violation in the WDA neither the business contract nor the employment contract between the contractor and his employee will be considered legitimate. However, some lower courts have held that if the party ordering work terminates the worker-dispatching contract before the expiry of its term, in bad faith, the employer's conduct will constitute a tort and make him liable for damages.[30]

120. Although the above provisions are enforced merely through administrative measures, the 2012 amendment of the WDA introduced a new provision that provided for a civil remedy for the violation of the WDA. When client companies engage in certain types of violation of the WDA such as the reception of dispatched workers for impermissible jobs or beyond the permissible period, or so-called disguised contracting, in which a client firm conducts direction and supervision with employees of a contracting firm without necessary procedures for worker dispatching, the client company shall be deemed to offer the dispatched worker for direct employment (Article 40.6). Thus, only if such dispatched worker accepts the offer of the client company, there shall be an employment contract between them. This article took effect on 1 October 2015.

121. The Minister can provide necessary instruction and advice to a client violating the rules provided by the WDA (Article 48(1)). Where the client still continues the violation or is feared to do so despite such guidance and advice, the Labour Minister can order the client to take the necessary corrective action (Article 49(1)). The Minister can also recommend the client to employ the dispatched worker if the worker wants to be employed at the client's workplace (Article 49.2(1)). Furthermore, the Minister can publicize the names of the companies which have not followed his recommendation (Article 49.2(2)). A worker-dispatching agency must not dispatch its worker after a client company has employed the worker continuously at the same post in the workplace over the permissible period (Article 35.2). An agency violating this rule can be penalized by fine (Article 61). There are also special provisions to require the client to offer or endeavour to offer an employment contract to dispatched worker (Articles 40–45).

30. For example, the *Mitsubishi Electric Company* case, the Nagoya High Court in 2013, RHS, No. 2174, p. 3.

122. To conduct worker dispatching, a contract for worker dispatching should be concluded between the employer who will dispatch workers and the client. The contract must contain the matters prescribed by WDA (Article 26). The maximum period of the contract is presently three years except in some cases (Article 2 and the Ministerial Ordinance). This is intended to prevent a client from using dispatched workers instead of employing regular workers. No client may cancel the contract on the grounds of a dispatched worker's nationality, creed, sex or social status or his or her having engaged in proper trade union activities, etc. (Article 27). An employer of a worker dispatching undertaking should clearly notify the worker of his intention to employ him or her as a dispatched worker before employment. Before newly assigning an employee who was not originally employed as a dispatched worker, the employer running a dispatching undertaking should clearly notify the worker of this intention and, where the worker was not originally employed as a dispatched worker, should obtain the worker's consent (Article 32). An employer of a dispatching undertaking should notify the workers of the dispatch work conditions in writing before conducting worker dispatching (Article 34 and the Ministerial Ordinance).

123. The WDA requires a worker-dispatching agency to provide educational training to dispatched workers employed thereby so that they can acquire the skills and knowledge necessary for work under a dispatching arrangement and in the case of dispatched workers employed without a fixed term, the agency must give consideration so that they can effectively exercise their abilities throughout their working lives (Article 30.2(1)). The WDA prohibits worker-dispatching agencies from creating unreasonable differences between the conditions, such as base pay and bonus pay conditions of dispatched workers employed thereby and the corresponding conditions of regular workers employed by the relevant client in consideration of the prescribed circumstances (Article 30.3(1)). It also prohibits worker-dispatching agencies from treating each condition of dispatched workers, such as base pay and bonuses, as disadvantageous compared with corresponding conditions of regular workers employed by the relevant client, when certain requirements are met (Article 30.3 (2)). However, Article 30.3 does not apply to the scope of dispatched workers whose treatment is as prescribed by a written agreement which is made between the worker-dispatching agency and the labour union consisting of a majority of the workers or with a person who represents a majority of the workers at the worker-dispatching agency in the case where such a labour union does not exist, where the agreement stipulates necessary conditions prescribed by Article 30.4.

124. The WDA requires the worker-dispatching agency to endeavour to promote the welfare of dispatched workers by taking measures necessary to secure employment, education and training opportunities, improve their working conditions and stabilize their employment (Article 30.7). The agency is also required to give due consideration to taking the necessary measures to ensure that a client observes the law (Article 31). On the other hand, the WDA requires the client to take the appropriate measures to ensure there is no violation of the stipulations of the worker-dispatching contract concerning working conditions (Article 39). The client is also required to take measures necessary for the proper performance of the dispatch work (Article 40(2)). With regard to statutory protection regarding working conditions, the worker dispatching agency is generally the responsible employer. However, there are many exceptions. As to the provisions of the LSA, the client as well as the dispatching agency is responsible for carrying out the duties imposed by the provisions concerning equal treatment, the prohibition of compulsory labour and the removal of apprenticeship abuses (Article 44(1)). Moreover, the following duties arising from the provisions of LSA are imposed only upon the client: the guarantee of time off for exercising civil rights, working hours, rest periods, rest days, night work, hazardous and toxic occupations, mine work and women's nursing time and menstrual leave. However, the duty to set forth the framework for flex-time, averaging working hours or overtime and holiday work, and the obligation to pay premium wages rests with the dispatching agency (Article 44(2)).

125. As to the provisions of the Industrial Safety and Health Act, the general responsibility for ensuring the safety and health of workers at the workplace is placed upon the client as well as the dispatching agency. The client also is responsible for the maintenance of sanitation at its workplace during the dispatch. The responsibility to establish systems for managing safety and take measures to prevent hazards and dangers to workers' health is solely imposed upon the client (Article 45). Clients are regarded as employers with regard to certain provisions of the EEOA (*see* Chapter 7, section 4), that is, those concerning sexual harassment and special arrangements of working hours and job assignments for pregnant employees (Article 47.2). A worker-dispatching agency must inform a client whether the dispatched worker is enrolled in social and labour insurance or not (Article 35(1)). An agency must take necessary measures to administer personal information properly, to keep dispatched workers' secrets (Article 7(1)), and to collect, keep and utilize personal information within a limit of what is necessary for business purposes (Article 24.3). The client is required to endeavour not to engage in actions for the purpose of identifying dispatched workers (Article 26.6). A worker-dispatching agency, its proxy and its employees are required not to reveal private information obtained in the course of performing their functions (Article 24.4). A dispatched worker can report to the Minister of Health, Labour and Welfare the fact that a worker-dispatching agency or client has violated provisions of the DDA or its administrative orders. Retaliatory action against the reporting worker is prohibited (Article 49.3). Employment Security Offices are to counsel a dispatched worker and provide necessary advice and other assistance (Article 52).

126. The 2003 amendments to WDA formally recognized 'job introduction dispatching'. It is defined as worker-dispatching which is the carrying out of job introductions or preparations for carrying out job introductions, by a person who has received the licence for a 'general worker-dispatching undertaking' or a person who has submitted the notice pursuant to 'specified worker-dispatching undertaking', in relation to the dispatched worker connected to that worker-dispatching and the client, having received a licence or given notice given pursuant to the provisions of the ESA and other laws, and includes dispatching pursuant to the job introduction where employment is agreed between that dispatched worker and that client before the provision of worker-dispatching service completes.

127. The number of dispatched workers can be determined on the basis of the reports submitted by worker-dispatching agencies to the Ministry of Health, Labour and Welfare in compliance with their statutory duty. According to such reports submitted by worker-dispatching firms to the Ministry, those agencies employed 1,560,000 dispatched workers in 2017 and 1,860,000 in 2022 (Table 12).

Table 12 Changes in the Number of Dispatched Workers (10,000)

Year	*Number of Dispatched Workers*
2017	156
2018	134
2019	157
2020	156
2021	169
2022	186

Source: Ministry of HLW, Rodousha Haken Jigyou Hokoku (Report on Workers Dispatching Undertakings), 2018–2023.

VII. Home Workers

128. The term 'home workers' is not identical to the term 'home-based workers'. The latter are defined broadly as workers undertaking work at home. Home workers are usually defined as those who, in response to manufacturers, traders, etc., are engaged in manufacturing or processing goods provided by them either alone or with the help of their families. The minimum wages and safety and health measures are regulated under the Industrial Home Work Act of 1970. The number of home workers is small and has gradually decreased since 1973. In 2014, it was only 117,000. Apart from home workers, there are an increasing number of home-based workers who work at home doing shorthand, translation, interpretation, word-processing, marketing, etc.[31] The number of these workers is estimated at about 970,000. The protection of home-based workers has recently become a subject of discussion. In addition to them, there are 3,110,000 employees who work at other than their ordinary workplace for more than eight hours per week. These workers and self-employed are called teleworkers.[32] It was said that Japan has been rather slow to develop telework in comparison with the United States and the European Union (EU) countries. This is partly due to the Japanese way of working, with its

31. Ministry of Public Management, Home Affairs, Post and Telecommunication, *Annual Report on the Labour Force Survey*, 2003.
32. Ministry of Land, Information and Transport, *Report on Teleworker*, 2003.

group rather than individual orientation. In recent years, however, there has been a considerable increase in the number of teleworkers. According to the survey by the Ministry of Land, Information and Transport, there were 9,300,000 teleworkers in 2012.[33]

VIII. 'Independent' Contractors and Freelancers and the Definition of 'Employee'

129. In Japan, the protection of individual labour statutes including the LSA, the Labour Contracts Act, etc. is limited to employees, that is 'a person who works by being employed by an employer and to whom wages are paid' (the LCA, Article 2). Thus, independent contractors and freelancers who work based on contracts other than employment contracts are not eligible for protection under individual labour law. Therefore, whether or not a worker falls under the category of employee has been considered one of the biggest issues in court. Courts have traditionally determined whether a person falls under the category of employee based on the following criteria:

1. Does he/she work under supervision?
   a. Does he/she have the freedom to accept or reject work requests, work instructions, etc.?
   b. Does he/she receive direction and supervision in carrying out his duties?
   c. Is his/her work restricted by time and location?
   d. Is it permissible to have someone else work on his/her behalf?
   e. How is his/her remuneration paid and calculated?
2. Supplementary criteria:
   a. burden of cost of machinery and equipment;
   b. amount of remuneration;
   c. exclusive service to one company; whether or not it is a business entity;
   d. burden of social insurance premiums;
   e. others.

130. In Europe, several countries have introduced a third category distinct from 'employee' and 'self-employed person', to extend the scope of protection for working persons by labour law. However, in 2023, Japan introduced legislation with economic and labour law perspective to protect a range of freelancers from unfair treatment by their contract partners. That is so-called the ('Freelance Protection Act' ('The Act on Ensuring Proper Transactions Involving Specified Entrusted Business Operators') of 2023. The person protected by this Act is a 'freelancer', who is a business person to whom work is entrusted, and is either an individual who has no employee or a corporation that has no officer other than a representative and has no employee. The Act provides for the following: (1) clarification of contract terms,

33. Ministry of Land, Information and Transport, *Report on Teleworkers*, 2012.

prohibition of unfair trade practices, advance notice and clear explanation of reasons for contract termination, prohibition of extremely low remuneration, ensuring payment of compensation; and (2) prevention of harassment, consideration for pregnancy, childbirth, childcare and nursing care, etc. If there is a fact in violation of the provisions of (1), the freelancer may report it to the Fair Trade Commission or the Commissioner of the Small and Medium-Sized Enterprise Agency and ask for appropriate measures to be taken. If there is a fact in violation of the provisions of (2), he or she may report it to the Minister of HLW and ask for appropriate measures to be taken.

IX. Private Employees and Public Employees

131. Another important distinction between categories of employees stems from the nature of the employer. The major distinction is between private and public, with the public sector itself divided into several categories. This distinction is of a much more legal nature, since for each of the different categories, different laws apply based on different principles – especially in connection with the right to organize, to bargain and to strike. The National Civil Service Act of 1947 (NCSA) and Local Civil Service Act of 1950 cover, respectively, national and local government employees and grant them well-protected civil servant status. However, both laws regulate employees' organizational activities in an identical way. For instance, the NCSA requires such organization to be registered with the National Personnel Authority (Article 108-3), does not grant the right to conclude a collective agreement after negotiations (Article 108-5) and prohibits it from going on strike, engaging in delaying tactics or other acts of dispute against the National government as an employer (Article 98(3)). On the other hand, the NCSA provides that the National Personnel Authority shall prepare and submit revision proposals for raising or lowering the amount of remuneration to the Diet and Cabinet when it finds it necessary to do so (Article 67). Previously, the National Enterprise Labour Relations Act (NELRA) of 1948 had covered labour relations in three government enterprises (i.e., the Postal Service, State-Owned Forests and Printing (of bank-notes, postage stamps, etc.) and Minting (coins)). However, the Postal Service was privatized in 2007. The Printing and Minting have been converted and semi-privatized into specified Independent Administrative Institutions and the State-Owned Forests have become a branch of the general government. The Independent Administrative Institution (IAI) is a newly designed legal body for governmental organizations established and regulated by the Basic Act on Independent Administrative Institutions (BAIAI of 1999). The employees of general IAIs lost civil servant status under the BAIAI. Accordingly, the Labour Relations Act concerning Specified Independent Administrative Institutions applies to specified independent administrative institutions. It does not recognize the right to strike of the employees of those institutions just as the NELRA did not. In 2015 the name of this law was changed to the Labour Relations Act concerning Administrative Executive Agencies as a result of the reorganization of independent administrative institutions.

X. Foreign Workers

132. Since World War II, the Japanese government has adopted a very restrictive policy towards the introduction of foreign workers into Japan and this policy remains essentially unchanged. Under the Immigration Control and Refugee Recognition Act (ICRRA) of 1951, foreigners coming to Japan could get a visa with a work permit only when the worker's special abilities are irreplaceable and the government grants him or her admission for this reason – for instance, a Chinese cook who is needed by a Chinese restaurant. However, the 1989 amendment to the ICRRA only expanded and increased the categories of professional or skilled jobs open to foreigners. Thus, under the amendment, foreigners can get a visa with a work permit where they are engaged in the following activities: investment and management, legal and accounting service, medical service, research, education, entertainment, activities requiring technologies or natural science, activities requiring knowledge of social science or thought or sensibility based on foreign culture and activities requiring special industrial skill. The amendment also expedited the examination procedures for issuing visas. Foreigners who come to Japan to study in universities, colleges, high schools or special schools can be engaged in work for four hours or less if they obtain a permit from the Ministry of Justice. Foreigners who are accepted as 'trainees' to learn skills or knowledge can receive practical business training for about two-thirds of the training period. The industrial training period is in principle one year or less and the trainee is not regarded as a worker. However, after the trainee has completed the training and demonstrated a satisfactory level of mastery of the skills taught, he or she can receive further training in practical business under the so-called technical internship program which was introduced in 1993. The total of the aforesaid training period and the period of practical skill training must be three years or less. The labour legislation will be applied during the period of 'practical skill training'. The 1989 amendment to the ICRRA also made it clear that any foreigner who is a child or grandchild of Japanese emigrants is entitled to legally work without any special profession or skill. It is illegal for foreign workers to be engaged in gainful work in Japan in violation of the above policy under the ICRRA of 1951.

133. As described above, Japanese policy towards foreign workers has changed somewhat in one decade. That is to say, Japan became only more willing to accept professional and skilled foreign workers while maintaining a policy of preventing unskilled foreign workers from entering its labour market with a few exceptions such as a child or grandchild of Japanese emigrants and skilled trainees. However, in March 2000, the Ministry of Justice issued the Second Basic Plan for Immigration Control which implied more willingness to accept foreign workers including unskilled ones. The plan stated as follows:

> Japan should seek the prosperity and stability of people's livelihood in a society more open to the international community. It is therefore necessary for Japan not only to create an environment for smooth exchanges of personnel but also to conduct smooth and proper immigration control to meet the need for the flexible use of manpower in response, in particular, to changes in industrial

> structure and corporate behaviour. Moreover, with the population rapidly aging, with less childbirth, and with the total population expected to begin decreasing in the 2000s, Japan is faced with the task of coping with the decreasing workforce and finding measures to cope with it.[34]

This plan indicates that the plan of immigration control will be necessarily connected with the ageing population in Japan. For example, the shortage of care workers will be an urgent problem.

134. The Basic Plan for Immigration Control issued by the Ministry of Justice in March 2005 made much of open acceptance of foreign nationals needed in Japanese society. The plan included the following statements concerning the acceptance of foreign nursing-care workers and the improvement of training and technical internship programmes:

> As for nursing-care workers who will be in growing demand due to the ageing of the population, consideration will be given to whether and how to accept foreign workers in the field while paying careful attention to the acceptance of such foreign nationals under economic partnership agreements with foreign countries and taking into account nursing-care jobs being created for Japanese workers.[35]

135. The training and technical internship programmes have widely spread throughout industries, including the manufacturing sector, as an increasing number of foreign nationals have been accepted for these programmes. In some cases, however, foreign trainees and technical interns are treated as low-cost workers. Some of the enterprises and other organizations accepting foreign trainees and technical interns, as well as these foreign nationals themselves and the foreign organizations sending them to Japan, have failed to fully understand the objectives of the programmes – 'training' as learning and 'technical internship' to master skills while under employment. In this respect, strict instructions to supervisors of foreign trainees and full notification to them of the program objectives will be given. Stringent examinations will be conducted through measures such as investigation of the training and internships in cooperation with the labour administration, if necessary. While taking into account protection of the foreign trainees and technical interns who have no reason to be blamed for any problems, the implementation of these programmes, according to their objectives, will be improved by taking measures such as prohibiting organizations who have engaged in inappropriate practices from accepting foreign trainees for three years.[36]

136. In response to the Basic Plan for Immigration Control of 2005, first the government introduced the foreign nursing care worker system in 2007. The government made an economic partnership agreement with Indonesia in 2007 and the

34. Ministry of Justice, *Basic Plan for Immigration Control*, March 2000.
35. *Ibid.*
36. Ministry of Justice, *Basic Plan for Immigration Control*, March 2005.

Philippines in 2008. The reason for this is double folds: On the one hand, Japan is a rapidly ageing society and the number of elderly people who need to have nursing care is rapidly increasing. On the other hand, care workers are badly paid even though it is heavy labour so the Japanese are short of hands. Second, the government amended the ICRRA in 2009 partly in order to enable labour laws such as the LSA and the Minimum Wage Act to apply to foreign trainees. This is because industrial trainers have not been treated as an employee and therefore labour law protection was not applied to them. As a result, there were many problems such as low remuneration, unpaid overtime work, confiscation of passports, forced labour, non-payment of social security contributions, etc. The ICRRA was amended to add two new statuses of residence, namely 'nursing care' in 2016 and 'specified skills' in 2018. By obtaining the 'nursing care' status, foreign students who have obtained a national qualification such as a certified care worker will be able to work in Japan. The 'specified skills' status will allow foreign workers having considerable skills to work in the prescribed jobs in certain specific industries that are difficult to fill within the domestic labour market. Foreign workers who are admitted under this system are called 'specified skilled' workers.

137. The Proper Technical Intern Training and Protection of Technical Intern Trainees Act (TITA) was enacted in 2016 in order to systematize the existing technical intern training system. The purpose of the TITA is, in conjunction with the ICRRA, to ensure the proper implementation of the training of, and protection of, technical intern trainees, and promote international cooperation through the transfer of skills, techniques, and knowledge to developing countries and other regions through human resource development (Article 1). The type of 'technical intern training' is divided into individual-enterprise-type and supervising-organization-type (Article 2(1)). In either type-training, during the first year, two months of classroom training in principle and practical training based on employment contracts are conducted, and at the end of the course, an examination equivalent to the basic level of the skill certification is held. For a trainee who has passed the above examination, further training based on employment contract is conducted to become proficient in specific skills, and at the end of the above two-year course, an examination equivalent to the higher level of the skill certification is held. For trainees who meet certain conditions and are recognized as excellent by the accepting enterprise or the accepting organization, the enterprise will be allowed to have further practical training based on employment contract after returning to their country of origin for a period of one month or more in principle.

138. Any Japanese individual or corporation shall prepare a plan relating to the implementation of technical intern training for each technical intern trainee and submit it to the Commissioner of the Immigration Services Agency and the Minister of Health, Labour and Welfare in order to be accredited as conforming to the prescribed requirements (Article 8). Any person seeking to conduct supervising business shall obtain a licence from a competent minister in accordance with the prescribed business categories (Article 23).

139. For the protection of technical intern trainees, the TITA has the following provisions.

1. A training supervisor (person engaging in the supervision) or its officers or employees must not force the technical intern trainees against their will through the use of assault, intimidation, confinement or other similar means (Article 46):
2. A training supervisor, etc. must not enter into a contract that stipulates penalties for or predetermines compensations for damage on the non-performance of a contract regarding technical intern training. They must not have a technical intern trainee, etc. into a savings contract incidental to the contract for technical intern training or enter into a contract assuming control of the savings of the trainee (Article 47).
3. A person associated with technical intern training (a person conducting technical intern training, training supervisor, or officer or employee thereof) must not retain the passport or residence cards and improperly restrict the freedom of the technical intern trainees to go out or their freedom in their personal lives (Article 48).

140. Any violation of the above provisions, the trainee may report the fact to the Commissioner of the Immigration Services Agency and the Minister of Health, Labour and Welfare. The implementing organization, etc. must not subject the trainee to disadvantageous treatment due to the trainee having given the above report.

On 14 June 2024, the TITA was drastically amended to change the legislative purpose of the Act and make the content in accordance with the purpose. The amended Act clarifies that the purpose is to secure human resources in specific industrial fields in Japan as well as to develop skills for admissible foreigners. Under the amended Act, the system of the 'Employment for Skill Development' will be established to achieve these purposes, the current status of residence called technical intern training will be abolished and a new status of residence called employment for skill development will be created. Accordingly, the amendment changed the name of the TITAN into the 'Act on the Employment for Skill Development.' In order for a company to accept a training worker, a training employment plan that specifies the following items must be approved: (1) the training employment period must be within three years, (2) the work, skills, Japanese language ability, other goals and contents, the system for the acceptance period, and the expenses paid by the foreign national during the sending period must the standards, and (3) others. Training workers can only move to another company in the following cases: (1) when there are unavoidable circumstances, and (2) when the work is within the same work category and certain requirements regarding the employment period, level of skills, etc., and the legality of the transfer are met.

141. In 2023, the number of foreigners staying in Japan was about 3.42 million or 2.75% of the total population of Japan.[37] Asian nationals accounted for about 85% of the total number of foreigners. About 280,000 Koreans have been permanent foreign residents since they and their parents lost their Japanese nationality after World War II. The number of foreigners who were reported to engage in working was about 2,300,000 in 2023.[38] Against the background of labour shortage in Japan, the number of foreigners who work in Japan is increasing, This figure includes the numbers of foreigners working in professional or technical fields, and technical interns as well as those who have permanent residence and status of residence for which there is no restriction on the contents of jobs, including descendants of Japanese nationals who emigrated to foreign countries such as Brazil in the past. The number of foreign workers who were discovered to illegally engage in gainful work and against whom the Immigration Control Office (ICO) initiated deportation procedures was 18,198 in 2023. It was estimated that the number of foreigners who illegally remained in Japan beyond their permitted period of stay was about 70,000 and most of them are assumed to be illegal workers. A typical illegal worker enters Japan on a tourist visa through a broker. However, if those who smuggled themselves into Japan were included, the number of illegal foreign workers would be greater than that of illegal residents.

142. The 2009 amendment to the ICRRA abolished the registration system for foreigners. Instead, the government continues to control the residence of foreigners through the residence card system administered by the Ministry of Justice. This new system took effect on 9 July 2012.

143. All labour laws are applicable to foreign workers whether their work is legal or illegal. However, for illegal foreign workers, it is in practice difficult to file a complaint about a violation of labour laws without risking compulsory expulsion. In fact, the Ministry of Health, Labour and Welfare has a policy to inform the ICO when a foreign worker is found to be working illegally. There is also difficulty in claiming compensation benefits and receiving medical treatment after returning to his or her country. However, in cases of industrial injury, the Ministry usually does not inform the ICO that the injured worker worked illegally. However, foreign entertainers, trainees, etc., are excluded from application of compensation for industrial injury under the WACIA. There are some cases where an illegal foreign worker went to court to claim compensation for an industrial accident in tort. For example, in the *Kaishin-sha* case where it was held that an illegal Chinese worker who suffered an industrial accident was entitled to his lost income at the Japanese income level for three years (i.e., the maximum duration permissible for a foreign worker to work in Japan) and his lost income thereafter at the Chinese income level.

---

37. Immigration Services Agency, Number of foreign residents as of the end of 2023 (https://www.moj.go.jp/isa/publications/press/13_00040.html?hl=en).
38. Ministry of Health, Labour and Welfare, Gaikokujin Koyo Todokede Jokyo Reiwa 5 Ne 10 Gatsu Matsu (Report of Employment of Foreigners)(https://www.mhlw.go.jp/content/11655000/001195785.pdf).

144. It has been disputed whether workers who are not Japanese nationals but have permanent foreign resident status are entitled to be promoted to managerial positions in local public offices. The Supreme Court has recently made a very important decision on such dispute in the *Tokyo Metropolitan Government* case. In this case, the plaintiff was a female local civil servant fifty-four years old who was born to a Korean father and Japanese mother and had lived in Japan. The Tokyo Metropolitan Government, the defendant rejected her request to take a screening test that could qualify her for promotion on the grounds that she does not have Japanese nationality. She has argued that the defendant violated the Constitution, Article 14 which guarantees equality under law. She won in the district court but was defeated in the appeal court and then appealed to the Supreme Court. However, the Court has rejected her appeal by majority votes (13 to 2). The Court has stated as follows: Special consideration should be given to a group of managerial local government civil servants who perform acts involving the exercise of public authority, such as directly forming residents' rights and obligations and defining the scope thereof, or making decisions concerning important local government measures or participate in such decisions. These employees are assumed to be Japanese nationals since Japan's sovereign power rests with Japanese people. Thus, the Tokyo Metropolitan Government's screening system which excludes foreign nationals from managerial positions is a rational one and therefore it does not violate either Article 14 of the Constitution or Article 3 of the LSA.

§3. Regulations Concerning the Conclusion of Individual Contracts

145. Like other contracts, the principle of autonomy of the parties applies to contracts of employment. Thus, the people basically have: the freedom to conclude contracts of employment; freedom to choose the partner; freedom to decide the terms of a contract of employment; and freedom to decide the form of the contract. Therefore, an individual contract can only be concluded with the consent of both parties. It follows that involuntary servitude is prohibited, except as a punishment for crime. Moreover, since Japanese workers before World War II had the experience of being forced to work by various means, the LSA enacted the following prohibition to eliminate such causes of forced labour. First, the LSA prohibits employers from forcing workers to work against their will by means of violence, intimidation, imprisonment, or any other unfair restraint on their mental or physical freedom. Second, it prohibits conclusion of labour contracts for a period longer than one year, although there are some exceptions. Third, it prohibits employers from making a contract which fixes in advance either a sum payable to the employer for breach of contract or an amount of indemnity for damages. Fourth, it prohibits employers from offsetting wages against advances of money or other credits the payment of which is made a condition for work. Fifth, it prohibits employers from requiring a contract for savings or making a contract to take charge of savings incidental to the labour contract.[39]

39. LSA, Arts 5, 13–14 and 16–18.

146. As far as contracts of employment are concerned, the above-mentioned general principle of autonomy of the parties is restricted to some extent. In particular, the parties' freedom to decide the terms of the employment contract is severely restricted. Article 2(1) of the LSA provides that working standards should be determined by the workers and employers on an equal basis. This provision takes it for granted that the inequality of bargaining power between them generally exists. Accordingly, Article 13 of the LSA provides for the minimum standards of working conditions along with penal sanction, and the contracts which provide for working conditions which do not meet these minimum standards shall be null and void with respect to such portions. The invalid proportions shall be governed by these minimum standards. The parties' freedom to decide the form of the contract is also somewhat restricted. Article 15 of the LSA requires the employer to specify the wages, hours of work and other working conditions for the worker when he or she concludes the contract. It also provides that certain matters shall be stated in the manner prescribed by ordinance. The Enforcement Ordinance of LSA requires the employer to notify in writing wages, scheduled working time and other matters. The employer's failure to comply with this obligation may result in penal sanctions. If the real working conditions are different from those stated, the worker is entitled to cancel the contract and the employer must pay the travelling expenses incurred by the worker who has changed residence to take up the work if he returns home within fourteen days of the cancellation. Moreover, it is generally agreed that the parties' freedom to choose the partner should also be restricted by public policy consideration. Therefore, some judicial and academic opinions argue that it is illegal for an employer to refuse to hire an employee in violation of the constitutional guarantees of freedom of thought and equality of treatment; the employee is entitled to sue the employer for damages. However, the Supreme Court has stated 'it cannot of course be unlawful even when an employer refuses to hire someone because of that person's beliefs or creed'.[40]

147. In general, the nullity and cancellation of the contract because of threats, coercion, deceit, error or the incapacity of the parties is to be judged according to civil law principles. A contract which is contrary to imperative legal norms, public order or morality is also null and void. However, according to LSA, Article 13, when a contract provides for working conditions inferior to the standards set by the law only these conditions are invalid, and they are replaced by the conditions stipulated in the Act. The TUA, Article 16, concerning contracts contrary to collective agreements and the LCA, Article 12, concerning contracts contrary to work rules have the same effect. Thus, the fact that the individual contract contradicts the provisions of the LSA, collective agreements and work rules does not make the contract as a whole null and void, but only the provisions concerned; and the conditions otherwise stipulated take their place.

148. If a contract is null and void, it is a principle of civil law that the invalidity or cancellation acts retroactively. However, quite often a labour relationship has in

40. The *Mitsubishi Jushi* case, the Supreme Court in 1973, *Saikosaibansho Minjisaibanreishu* (SMS), Vol. 27, No. 11.

fact developed and progressed when the contract's nullity is declared or when it is cancelled. So, legal precedents, taking notice of the actual relationship between employer and employee, have often recognized the existence of the contract in the past. For instance, in spite of the nullity of the contract, the employee's wage claim is admitted without trying to find the unnecessary legal detour of indemnity. Another typical case which shows respect for the facts rather than for the existence of a legal contractual relationship is the recognition of the employer's obligation to pay extra overtime rates for overtime work carried out illegally.[41] Furthermore, generally speaking, the contents of individual employment contracts are formulated by either collective agreements or work rules – with the contract itself becoming more and more a mere formality or a legal fiction, and the fact of actually providing labour becoming more important.

§4. Conclusion of the Employment Contract and the Probation Period

I. Tentative Decision of Employment (*Naitei*)

149. Under the lifetime employment practices, about one year before their supposed graduation, high school, college and university students usually start to contact or visit companies which they want to join and companies also initiate contact with students whom they want to recruit. Accordingly, during the period of April to July, the employment process is extraordinarily intense. This frenzy of job-hunting begins to subside around August when companies complete recruitment and start to send the students letters promising employment from April of the following year. Such a letter is called *naitei tsuchi* in Japanese. *Naitei tsuchi* means a notice of tentative decision of employment. However, an entry ceremony usually takes place and a written appointment to the job is given to the students receiving *naitei tsuchi* some day in April, therefore, it has been questioned whether *naitei tsuchi* constitutes the conclusion of an employment contract.

150. According to the Supreme Court's decision in the *Dainihon Insatsu* case, the student's application for a place with the company is regarded as the offer of an employment contract, and the *naitei tsuchi* constitutes an acceptance of the offer. Therefore, an employment contract is formed when the employer notifies the worker of their *natiei* (tentative decision of employment). This contract is accompanied by a starting date of work and preserves the employer's cancellation right. However, causes for cancellation are limited to those which the employer could not or was not expected to know at the time of the tentative decision of employment and which, viewed in light of the aims and objectives in reserving a cancellation right, can justify dismissal on objectively reasonable grounds and is permissible with regard to the common sense of society.[42] This *naitei* doctrine was originally established to protect students who were given *naitei tsuchi* but later dismissed without a socially

41. The *Kojima Nenshi* case, the Supreme Court in 1960, *Saikosaibansho Keijisaibanreishu* (SKS), Vol. 14, No. 9, p. 1139.
42. The *Dainihon Insatsu* case, the Supreme Court in 1979, SMS, Vol. 33, No. 5, p. 582.

admissible reason before the starting date of work, but it has sometimes been applied to mid-career employees. For example, in the *Informix Company* case,[43] an engineer who had been working for IBM was headhunted by the defendant company in December 1997 on the condition that he would be a manager of the consulting group section on 6 May 1998. But the company proposed to offer a different non-managerial post to him on the grounds of its abolishment of that section before that date. The plaintiff refused it so the company gave notice to cancel the original Job offer. The Tokyo District Court treated this as a *naitei* case and the cancellation was held void without a socially admissible reason for it. However, it might be treated as an ordinary dismissal case if both parties might be seen to have concluded a formal and not tentative contract of employment.

II. Probationary Period (*Shiyo kikan*)

151. Most regular employees are placed on probation for a fixed term after they are hired (or after the starting day of work if they are hired by *naitei tsuchi*). During this period, the employee's performance and ability are monitored and evaluated to determine whether the employee is to be employed further or not. LSA stipulates that after the first fourteen days of the probation period, the employer must give thirty days' notice to terminate the contract. Except for this legal requirement about the period of notice, the law says nothing about the probationary period. The major issue is really whether the employer can dismiss the employee more easily for unusual reasons. According to the Supreme Court decision in the *Mitsubishi Jushi* case, the probationary contract is an employment contract with a right of cancellation reserved by the employer. The reservation of the cancellation right during the probationary period is intended to reserve a later determination based on investigation and observation. The scope of the freedom to dismiss based on such a reserved cancellation right should be recognized as broader than an ordinary dismissal. However, the exercise of a reserved cancellation right should be permitted only when viewed in light of the aims and objectives in reserving a cancellation right, there is an objective reason and the exercise is permissible with regard to the common sense of society.[44]

152. There has sometimes been a question of whether a fixed term was agreed as a probationary period or the duration of employment. In *Kobe Koryo Gakuen* case,[45] the Supreme Court has held as follows:

> When an employer proposed a fixed term to an employee at hiring, if his purpose is to see and evaluate the employee's ability and aptitude, then the term is not for the duration for which the contract will continue but for the

43. The *Informix Company* case in 1997, RH, No. 726, p. 37.
44. The *Mitsubishi Jushi* case, the Supreme Court in 1973, SMS, Vol. 27, No. 11, p. 1536.
45. The *Kobe Koryo Gakuen* case, the Supreme Court in 1990, SMS, Vol. 44, No. 4, p. 668.

probationary period unless there are special circumstances which indicate that both parties clearly agree that the contract will automatically terminate at the expiry of that term.

153. However, this judgment was criticized on the grounds that there is no law that restricts the purpose of using fixed-term employment contracts. Therefore, an influential view is that the period should be understood to mean the probational period only if there is no clear agreement that the contract will be terminated at the expiry of that period. In a later case, where a lecturer was hired on a fixed-term contract with a one-year renewal limit of three years, with the condition that the contract would be converted to an indefinite contract if the College deems it necessary in consideration of work performance, the Supreme Court overruled the appeal court's decision that interpreted the three years period as the probation period and confirmed that the lecturer's employment had been terminated at the expiration of the three years period.[46]

§5. Variation of Contractual Terms

154. Where the terms of an employment contract are no longer tenable due to circumstances, the parties have to amend those terms. In such cases, the parties will, in principle, need to obtain the consent of the other party to amend those contract terms although the employer can change the content of employees' jobs and duties within the scope of their personnel rights given by the original contract. If an employee's consent to the employer's request for a lowering in working conditions is obtained through fraud, duress, mistaken motives, etc., its validity may be denied. In addition, courts often decide whether an employee's consent was based on his free will, citing the imbalance in bargaining and information-gathering power between employees and employers. For example, in the *Yamanashikenmin-Shinnyokumiai* case where the effectiveness of disadvantageous changes in retirement allowances pursuant to new shugyo-kisoku was contested, the Supreme Court held as follows:

> Regarding whether or not a worker consents to changes in working conditions regarding wages and retirement allowances stipulated in the shugyo-kisoku, it is determined not only whether the employee has acted to accept the change, but also from the perspective of whether there are objectively reasonable grounds for recognizing that the act was made based on whether the act was carried out by the employee's free will based on factors such as the nature and extent of disadvantage which the change will cause to the worker, the circumstances and manner in which the employee committed the act, and the content of information provided or explanations given to the worker prior to the act.

155. Where an employer may change working conditions by collectively bargaining with a union and entering into a collective bargaining agreement. The

---

46. The *Fukuhara-Gakuen* case, the Supreme Court in 2016, RH, No.1156, p. 5.

employer may also change contract terms by the variation of shugyo-kisoku (i.e., work rules), as long as the requirements of public knowledge and reasonableness of it are met. However, there are individual special working conditions that cannot be changed by changing the *shugyo-kisoku* (Article 10 proviso, the Labour Contracts Act). For this or some other reasons, based on case law and theory, there has been discussion about *henko-kaiyaku-kokuchi* (notices to demand either a change of working conditions or dismissal), with reference to Germany's *Änderungskündigung*.

156. Henko-kaiyaku-kokuchi may be defined as a notice for dismissal with the condition of termination being that the employee refuses to change working conditions. There are conflicting precedents regarding its treatment. In the Scandinavian Airline case,[47] one court decided as follows: 'Where the change in working conditions is essential for the operation of the company's business, the necessity outweighs the disadvantage to the worker due to the change in working conditions, and the application for concluding a new contract involving the change in working conditions is not accepted, a company may dismiss an employee who does not respond to an offer to conclude a new contract if it is deemed unavoidable enough to justify the dismissal and if sufficient efforts have been made to avoid the dismissal.' However, another court in the Osaka Health Center case,[48] held that 'Unless the employee agrees to the new working conditions, he or she will be forced to make a tough choice and be fired. Unlike German law, in Japan, where there is no explicit statutory text, it is not appropriate to establish an independent category of henko-kaiyaku-kokuchi in order to change the working conditions.'

157. Article 529 of the Civil Code provides that if the offeree has accepted the offer by adding a condition or making other modifications, it is deemed that the offeree has refused the offer and made a new offer and accordingly it is generally understood that the employee accepts the employer's application to change the working conditions with reservations and cannot legally dispute the propriety of the change.

---

47. The Tokyo District Court in 1995, RH, No. 675, p. 13.
48. The Osaka District Court in 1998, RH, No. 751, p. 38.

Chapter 2. Rights and Duties of the Parties During Employment

§1. Overview and Structure of Employment Contract

I. Overview

158. The Labour Contract Law provides that an 'employment contract is established by agreement between a worker and an employer on the basis that the worker will work by being employed by the employer and the employer will pay wages for such work' (Article 2 (1)). Thus, under an employment contract, the employee has the duty to work and the employer has the duty to pay compensation therefor. In other words, the employer has the right to order his employee to work and the employee has the right to demand his employer to pay wages as compensation. In business organizations, employers are considered to have the personnel rights necessary to make employees work efficiently in an organized manner based on employment contracts. In Japan, employers have widely recognized authority to manage human resources, including the placement of workers within companies, education and training, performance evaluations, positions and ratings.

II. Personnel System

159. The personnel system that most Japanese companies have used to determine employee positions and wages is called the '*shokuno-shikaku* system' (i.e., ability-based grading).[49] Under the system, the position and wages of each employee are graded by his categorized job ability. However, the shortcomings of the *shokuno-shikaku* system have been recognized; for example, the difficulty of objective evaluation of job ability, the imbalance between employees' contribution to the company and wages, or the inability to attract talented external personnel. Therefore, many companies are beginning to introduce systems such as job-based or function-based grading systems in addition to the *shokuno-shikaku* system, nevertheless, it is considered that the *shokuno-shikaku* system is maintained as the basic personnel system.

III. Personnel Evaluation, Promotion, Demotion Etc.

160. Companies regularly conduct personnel evaluations of each employee's job ability and performance in order to determine the need for his or her promotion or demotion. Under the *shokuno-shikaku* system, there are two different types of promotion or demotion: one is to raise or lower the grade of employees, and the other is to raise or lower the managerial position of employees. The former is accompanied by up-down fluctuation in basic wages, and the latter is accompanied by up-down fluctuation in position allowances. Personnel evaluation usually consists

---

49. T. Araki, Labor & Employment Law in Japan (Japan Institute of Labor, 2002), p. 72.

of ability evaluation (including knowledge, skills, judgment, planning ability, technical ability, leadership ability, etc.), emotional evaluation (including level of challenge, sense of responsibility, cooperation, discipline, customer orientation, etc.) and performance evaluation. In many large companies, when performing a personnel evaluation, the employee evaluated first submits his or her self-evaluation to his section manager who then evaluates him, and sometimes, the department manager makes re-evaluation and finally the human resource department makes a final evaluation. Basically, the employer has the discretionary power to evaluate personnel, but if the exercise of this discretion amounts to an abuse of the right, he will be liable for torts. Thus, the Osaka High Court[50] held that the employer could be liable for torts, where he misunderstood the facts on which the evaluation was based, where he had an improper motive, or where he disregarded important matters or emphasized unimportant matters.

161. It is considered that under a typical *shokuno-shikaku* system, even if an employee's sales performance or work performance deteriorates, it is not planned that the ability will be evaluated as lacking. Therefore, employers have to include a clear regulation that they can lower an employee's grade if his work performance deteriorates.[51] Even if there is such regulation, the employer should not abuse his right power to lower the grade. Therefore, to determine the abuse of such power, courts generally take into account various circumstances such as the existence and extent of business and organizational necessity on the employer's side; the existence of extent and degree of attribution such as lack of ability and aptitude on the employee's side; and the nature of the disadvantage suffered by the employee.[52] If the court finds that the employer abused his power, the reduction in grade will be void. As opposed to downgrading, it is understood that an employer is permitted to lower a managerial position even if there is no clear stipulation for it, as long as it does not constitute an abuse of rights.[53]

§2. Employees' Duties

I. The Duty to Work under Employer's Orders

162. In the notion of 'subordinate labour', distinguished from 'independent work' as the fundamental factor in the employment relationship, there is an implicit acceptance of the fact that the employee has an obligation to do work under the command, authority and control of the employer and to obey his orders. However, the way in which an employee should work is determined in accordance with his employment contract. The duty to work is not limited to mere mechanical performance of one's duties but encompasses the duty to perform the work in good faith. The employer has not only the power to order the employee to work in a particular

50. The *Koyouseiko* case, the Osaka High Court in 1997, RH, No. 729, p. 39.
51. The *Ark-Shoken* case, Tokyo District Court in 2000, RH, No. 785, p. 45.
52. The *Joshuya* case, Tokyo District Court in 1999, RH, No. 774, p. 12.
53. The *Equitable-Seimei* case, Hiroshima High Court in 1990, RH, No. 565, p. 79.

way but also the power to order him or her to do something necessary for the general good of the business. The latter power to order is called the 'business-related order'. According to the Supreme Court, the authority to issue a business-related order is based on the employment contract. Therefore, what the employer is entitled to order as a business-related order is determined according to a particular employment contract.[54]

163. In order to make a decision as to whether the employee is obliged to obey the employer's order, the court determines whether or not the order is valid. The employer's order is invalid where it violates statutory provisions or public policy. Thus, for instance, the inspection of an employee's belongings might infringe on the employee's civil liberty. The dismissal of a taxi driver for his refusal to have his belongings inspected according to the provision of work rules (*shugyo-kisoku*) was held to be valid, but the court indicated the following four conditions necessary to validate the regular inspection of the employees' belongings: the necessity of the inspection, the reasonability of the way of inspection, the uniform operation of the inspection, and the legal authorization by stipulation in the *shugyo-kisoku* or the like.[55] Where an order is not within an employer's authority given by his employment contract, the employee is entitled to refuse to obey that order. Thus, dismissal of a taxi driver for his refusal to shave his moustache was held to be invalid on the grounds that the provision of the *shugyo-kisoku* should be construed to require the employee only to shave an untidy or odd-looking moustache.[56] The employee is not obliged to obey an order requiring him to perform unexpectedly dangerous work.[57]

164. Many of the cases in which dismissal of an employee for disobedience has been disputed in the courts are concerned with the employees' refusal to accept the employer's decision to change the employee's job content and work. Where the type of work which an employee is required to do is specified in his employment contract, the employer may not unilaterally change it. Therefore, for example, an employee who is specified as an announcer, cabin attendant, professor or nurse may refuse the employer's order to work as a clerical worker. For example, it was held that two workers employed as assistant nurses were not obliged to obey the employer's order to do cleaning, washing and laundry.[58] Similarly, where an employee's place of work is fixed under his employment contract, the employer may not unilaterally change the employee's place of work. However, in reality, the transfer of the employee between different working places and kinds of work within the company is the prevalent practice in the Japanese industry. This is closely connected to a lifetime employment policy which means that employers need to mobilize their employees within the company in order to make use of their ability efficiently and keep their morale. Therefore, companies generally stipulate in their *shugyo-kisoku* that the employee shall be transferred to different working places and kinds of work

---

54. The *Denden-kosha Obihiro* case, the Supreme Court in 1986, RH, No. 470, p. 6.
55. The *Nishi Nihon Tetsudo* case, the Supreme Court in 1968, MSM, Vol. 22, No. 13, p. 3050.
56. The *Eastern Airport Motors* case, the Tokyo District Court in 1980, *Rodokankei Minjisaibanreishu* (RMS), Vol. 31, No. 6, p. 1202.
57. The *Denden Chiyodamaru* case, the Supreme Court in 1968, SMS, Vol. 22, No. 13, p. 3050.
58. The *Kamoshima Chuobyoin* case, the District Court in 1984, RH, No. 431, p. 117.

within the company. For example, it was held that an employer had the authority to order an employee, working as an announcer, to work as an office worker. The employee in this case was not trained as an announcer before entering employment with the company, and she signed a written pledge stating that she would accept the company's *shugyo-kisoku*. The *shugyo-kisoku* provided that the company was entitled to change the employee's place and contents of work.[59]

165. Even if the employer is found to have the right to transfer or re-assign, there is still room for the court to hold that his order of transfer or re-assignment is not valid because of his abuse of the right to make such an order in certain circumstances. The Supreme Court made it clear in the *Toa Paint Company* case how the principle of abuse of rights should be applied to the employer's order of transfer. In this case, an employee working in the Kobe branch refused to obey an order of transfer to the Nagoya branch because of his family circumstances. Both the district and appellate courts rejected the effectiveness of the order of transfer of employees. The appellate court gave the following reason: it was not necessary for the company to transfer the employee to the Nagoya branch since it was not impracticable for the company to transfer another employee there instead of him. Furthermore, if the employee had moved to the Nagoya branch, he would have been compelled to leave his family. In fact, his daughter was then only two years old, his wife was working in a nursery school as an unqualified nurse in order to obtain a nursing qualification, and his wife's mother, who was seventy-one years old, and who had always lived in Kobe, also lived with him. However, the Supreme Court allowed the company's appeal against the appellate court decision and remitted the case to the appellate court. The Supreme Court stated as follows:

> An order of transfer is not regarded as an abuse of right by an employer unless it is made without any business necessity or with an illegal motive or intention even though there is some business necessity. This is the rule unless there is a particular disadvantage to business necessity. This is the rule unless the disadvantage to the employee is such that he cannot be reasonably expected to endure it or unless there are any other special circumstances. The meaning of the aforesaid 'business necessity' should not be limited to the narrow one that the employer has had difficulty in finding someone else suitable for the position to which he wants the employee to move. The court should find that the aforesaid 'business necessity' exists if it recognizes certain facts which contribute to the reasonable operation of the company, such as proper allocation of manpower, promotion of business efficiency, development of employees' capacities, enhancement of employees' incentive to work, facilitation of business operation and so forth.[60]

166. The employer sometimes transfers the employee to another company. In many cases of transfer between companies, the employee's contractual status

---

59. The *Miyazaki Hoso* case, the Miyazaki District Court in 1976, *Rodo Hanrei Sokuho* (RHS), No. 924, p. 4.
60. The *Toa Paint* case, the Supreme Court in 1986, RH, No. 477, p. 6.

remains with the company which has transferred him although he works in and for the company to which he has been transferred. This type of transfer between companies is called *shukko* or *zaiseki-shukko* (farming-out). In cases of *shukko*, a transferred employee is usually expected to be returned to the former company within a certain period of time, and his wage differences between the former company and the latter company are usually compensated by the former company.

167. Nevertheless, compared with the law concerning transfer within the company as described above, the law concerning transfer between different companies is more restrictive. The Civil Code, Article 625, provides that an employer cannot assign his rights to a third person without the consent of the employee. LSA, Article 15, also requires the employer to state the working conditions for the worker when he concludes an employment contract. Therefore, it is generally considered that the employer's right of *shukko* should be clearly stipulated in the work rules (*shugyo-kisoku*) or the collective agreement. The employer's order of *shukko* may be legally binding on the basis of the employee's general consent at the time of hiring. It is considered that the *Shin-Nihon-Seitetsu (Nittetsu-Unyu No. 2)* case is a leading case in this regard.[61] In this case, the employees (the appellees) were firmed out by their company (the appellant) to another company (the child company of the appellant). The appellees have been worked in the transport section of the appellant. When the appellant company decided to entrust the child company with the whole business of the transport section, it ordered the appellees to farm out to the child company. The legal effect of such order was disputed by the appellees. The Supreme Court decided that the order was effective. They held that the appellant had a right to order firming-out because the appellant's works rule (*shugyo-kisoku*) provided that the employer had a right to order faming-out both when the appellees were hired and when they were ordered to faming-out and that the collective agreement with the union also provided so with precise terms and conditions of employment after their farming-out.

168. However, even if the employer has the right of *shukko*, the exercise of his right is rather limited by the rule of abuse of right.[62] The LCA now provides that the order of *shukko* (farming-out) is void if it comes under the purview of abuse of right in the light of its necessity, selection of employees for farming-out, and other relevant circumstances (Article 14). There is a different type of transfer between companies known as *tenseki* (moving out or *iseki-shukko*). *Tenseki* means that the employee will lose contractual status as an employee of the employer who transfers him to another company and will gain contractual status as an employee of the company which accepts the transfer. Therefore, the employee's agreement is required both for termination of the existing contract of employment and for conclusion of a new contract of employment. Furthermore, some courts have held that it requires the employee's individual consent at the time of the event. However, there are also some cases in which the courts have held that the employer's order of *tenseki* is

---

61. The *Shin-Nihon-Seitetsu (Nittetsu-Unnyu No.)* case, the Supreme Court in 2003, RH, No. 847, p. 14.
62. The *Gold Maritime* case, the Osaka High Court in 1980, RH, No. 572, p. 114 (affirmed by the Supreme Court in 1991, RH, No. 609, p. 14).

legally binding on the basis of the employee's general consent at the time of hiring where the company has a long-standing practice of *tenseki* to a particular company.[63]

169. If the employer abusively exercises his right to order the employee to do something, that constitutes an abuse of right. Then, his order is not only void but also illegal and therefore may constitute a tort. For example, it was held that a transfer of an employee from a managerial position to a receptionist position constituted a tort because it was intended to infringe on his personal right, isolate him, discourage him from working and eventually retire him from the company.[64]

II. The Duty of Good Faith and Observation of Workplace Discipline

170. An employment contract establishes an ongoing personal relationship and therefore mutual trust between the employer and employee is essential to maintain the contract. Thus, the employee has the duty of good faith which includes the duty not to misappropriate or damage the employer's property, the duty not to damage the employer's credit and reputation, the duty to respect company secrets, the duty not to do competitive work or business, and the like. The courts hold that the employee also has the duty to observe reasonable workplace discipline.[65] However, the employer does not have disciplinary action without any legal authorization. There is some disagreement among academics about why the employer has the power to take disciplinary action against his employees. Some consider that such power derives from his rights to business or the nature of employment relations. However, some consider that disciplinary power is given to the employer by the employee's consent to the disciplinary provisions of the *shugyo-kisoku*. Others consider that the employer is given disciplinary power by the disciplinary provisions of the *shugyo-kisoku* which is given normative effect by LSA. The Supreme Court has recently held in the *Fuji Kosan* case that in order to take a disciplinary action against his employee he should stipulate the kinds of disciplinary action and the causes of such action in the *shugyo-kisoku* in advance.[66] This requirement for employer to inform the employee of the rule of disciplinary action stipulated in the shugyo-kisoku in advance is now specified under the LCA, Article 7.

171. LSA, Article 89, requires the employer employing ten or more employees to provide stipulations concerning sanctions and other such matters in the *shugyo-kisoku*. The *shugyo-kisoku* usually stipulates causes for disciplinary action in order to establish workplace discipline. It usually stipulates disciplinary measures such as a reprimand, a reduction in wages, suspension, demotion and 'disciplinary dismissals' (*chokai-kaiko*). The employer's disciplinary action may be illegal and void in

---

63. The *Hitachi Seiki* case, the Chiba District Court in 1981, RH, No. 372, p. 49 (affirmed by the Tokyo High Court in 1988, *Rodo Horitsu Junpo* (RHJ), No. 1195, p. 55).
64. The *Bank of America Illinois* case, the Tokyo District Court in 1995, RH, No. 685, p. 17.
65. The *Kansai-denryoku* case, the Supreme Court in 1983, RH, No. 415, p. 29.
66. The *Fuji Kosan* case, the Supreme Court in 2003, RH, No. 861, p. 5. Also *see* the *Kokutetsu Sapporo Untenku* case, the Supreme Court in 1979, SMS, Vol. 33, No. 6, p. 647.

some circumstances. The Supreme Court held in 1974 that 'the employer's disciplinary action is void because of abuse of the employer's right, where it is found to be without any rational basis and not to be permissible with regard to social norms, having regard to the circumstances in the case'.[67] This rule is now basically confirmed under LCA, Article 15. Moreover, a disciplinary action that is not based on the causes stipulated by the *shugyo-kisoku* or the collective agreement or which deviates from past practices in similar cases or is not proportionate to the degree of the violation of discipline will be illegal and void. Disciplinary action which does not comply with procedural requirements stipulated by the *shugyo-kisoku* or collective agreement is also illegal and void.

172. 'Disciplinary dismissal' is a special sort of dismissal that is punishment for an employee's wrongdoing that is used to maintain discipline in the workplace. An important characteristic of 'disciplinary dismissal' is not only that it bears the name of 'discipline' which creates a serious stigma towards re-employment but also that the employee usually loses part or all of his retirement allowance along with his employment. Many *shugyo-kisokus* provide lists of causes for such a 'disciplinary dismissal'. However, the causes for a 'disciplinary dismissal' sometimes are not stipulated independently of those for other disciplinary actions. Even if the reasons for a 'disciplinary dismissal' are independently stipulated, there is often a stipulation such as 'the action may be reduced to ordinary dismissal or suspension in certain circumstances'. In many cases, causes for 'disciplinary dismissal' listed in the *shugyo-kisoku* are as follows: continuous absence from work without the employer's permission, violence or intimidation against other employees, refusal to obey the legitimate orders of the employer, misrepresentation of personal history, being employed by the employer's competitor or establishing competitive business, stealing money or articles belonging to the employer, deliberate destruction of the employer's property, receiving a rebate by using the position of employment and the like. It should be pointed out that the employer usually can dismiss the employee for incapacity, violation of his duty and economic reasons. Dismissal of this sort is called 'ordinary dismissal'.

A. The Duty Not to Misappropriate or Damage the Employer's Property

173. An employee is obliged not to appropriate his or her employer's money and to defraud the employer of his or her money. An employee also must not receive a rebate by using his position of employment. The employee, of course, must not steal or destroy the employer's property. Theft of a small sum of money by an employee who has easy access to the company's money may justify disciplinary dismissal. It was held that a taxi driver's pocketing only JPY 510 was a grave menace to the discipline of the company irrespective of how much he wrongfully took from the taxi fare and therefore it justified dismissal.[68]

---

67. The *Daihatsu Kogyo* case, the Supreme Court in 1974, RH, No. 415, p. 16.
68. The *Daiei Taxi* case, the Matsuyama District Court in 1974, RH, No. 200, p. 20.

B. The Duty Not to Damage the Employer's Credit and Reputation

174. In principle, what an employee does outside his workplace and hours of duty is free from the employer's intervention. However, when an employee has committed a crime, such as violating the local regulations on outdoor assembly, indecency or obscenity, outside his workplace and hours of duty, the employer may take disciplinary action against him on the grounds that his conduct damages the company's credit or reputation. The courts have held that the employer is entitled to take disciplinary action against the employee if his conduct may have a serious influence on the reputation and image of the company, having regard to all the circumstances of the case including: the nature of the employee's conduct; what the circumstances of that conduct were; what industry the company belongs to; the type of company; the size of the company; the position which the company occupies in the economic community; what policy the company has; what work the employee is engaged in the company; what position the employee occupies.[69] Recently, employees' 'whistleblowing' has become an important topic in labour law because malpractices in public bodies and private companies were discovered by it. However, it is a difficult question to what degree 'whistleblowing' has to be protected since it involves an employee's, an employer's and public interests. The problem usually arises when an employer takes disciplinary action against an employee on the grounds that his conduct damages the company's credit or reputation where the latter disclosed to a public office or mass media an employer's conduct that he believes to constitute malpractice. The courts have developed case law which is rather generous to whistleblowers, taking the following factors into consideration: what, how and whom the whistleblower informed of, whether he did so in public interest, whether the information was true or not, whether it was appropriate for him to believe that the information was true, whether he should have first given the information to someone within his organization, whether anonymity should be allowed and how he acquired the information.

175. Because case law is neither well-known nor comprehensible to the public, the Whistleblower Protection Act (WPA) was enacted in 2004. However, besides WPA, the existing case law still kept its significance for employees' protection. This is because WPA provides for a narrower protection than case law does since it specifies undisputable minimum standards to protect whistle-blower who does so in public interests. The coverage of WPA includes despatched workers and contract workers as well as employees (Article 2(1) and Article 4). The reportable facts of the degree and way in which WPA protects workers' whistle-blowing are 'criminal acts' provided for by or violation of disposition pursuant to those laws that are listed in WPA or a cabinet order as statutes concerning the protection of interests such as the protection of individuals' lives and bodies, the protection of interest of the consumers, the conservation of the environment, protection of fair competition, and the protection of citizen's lives, bodies, property and other interests (Article 2(3) and Annexed list). The main rules of WPA are specified by Article 3 as follows:

---

69. The *Nihon Kokan* case, the Supreme Court in 1974, SMS, Vol. 28, No. 2, p. 265.

Where a whistleblower is dismissed by the business operator .... on the basis of whistle-blowing provided for in each of the following Items in the respective case, the dismissal shall be void:

(i) To make a whistle-blowing to the business operator, etc. where a reportable fact is considered to have occurred, or be about to occur:
(ii) To make a whistle-blowing to an administrative organization with the authority to impose disposition or recommendation, etc. where there are reasonable grounds to believe that the reportable fact has occurred, or
(iii) To make a whistle-blowing to any person to whom such whistle-blowing is considered necessary to prevent the occurrence of the reportable fact or the spread of damage caused by the reportable fact, (a) where the whistleblower has reasonable grounds to believe that he will receive dismissal or other disadvantageous treatment if he does whistle-blowing as provided for in the preceding two items; (b) where the whistleblower has reasonable grounds to believe that the evidence pertaining to the reportable fact might be concealed, counterfeited, or altered if he makes a whistle-blowing as provided for in item (i); (c) where the whistleblower was requested by the business operator, without any justifiable reason, not to make a whistle-blowing provided for in the preceding two items; (d) where the whistleblower does not received notice from the business operator, etc., about the commencement an investigation on reportable fact within twenty days from the day of the whistle-blowing provided for in item (i)made in writing ... or the business operator, etc., does not investigate without any justifiable reason; or (e) where the whistleblower has a justifiable reason to believe that some damage to the life or body of an individual is caused or about to be caused.

C. The Duty to Respect Professional Secrets

176. Given the traditional broad notion of employees' loyalty to the enterprise, ethically speaking the employee's obligation not to disclose his employer's trade secrets or confidential information is much emphasized. However, legally speaking, the nature and extent of this obligation is not so clear. Generally, it is believed that an employee is free to use the skill and experience (or know-how) acquired through his employment to find another job after his contract has terminated. On the other hand, it is also generally accepted that he should not disclose the employer's secret documents and correspondence or abuse his connections with customers. Anyhow, such obligations rarely become legal issues, except in connection with the obligation to avoid competition after the termination of the contract, and in connection with the disclosure of company secrets or confidential information in order to protect the public.

D. The Duty Not to Engage in Competitive Work or Business

177. Since an employment relationship is a continuous human relationship, in order to maintain that relationship, both parties are required not to unfairly infringe on the interests of the other party. In other words, both parties have a contractual duty of good faith under their employment contract. Therefore, employees have a duty of confidentiality to their employers and employees' use or disclosure of business secrets during the period of employment is in breach of this duty. Since this duty is attached to every employment contract, it arises even without a special agreement or shugyo-kisoku. The company usually stipulates in its *shugyo-kisoku* that disciplinary action will be taken against an employee who discloses or has disclosed company secrets. Thus, on the basis of such a *shugyo-kisoku* provision, the employer may take disciplinary dismissal action against an employee for disclosure of the knowledge and techniques peculiar to the company. There are conflicting views as to whether this duty will remain after the termination of an employment contract. The prevailing view is that the duty disappears upon the termination of the contract. Therefore, a special agreement is required to prohibit an ex-employee from using or disclosing business secrets after the termination of employment contract.

178. Even if there is no special agreement as such, serious secret leak may constitute a tort and the former employee who leaked the information may be liable for damages. In addition, under the Unfair Competition Prevention Act (UCPA) of 1934 as amended in 1993, when a worker uses or discloses a trade secret (i.e., a method of production, a way of selling or other technological or business information which is controlled as a secret and is not publicly known), which the worker was shown by his employer, for the purpose of illicit gain by engagement in unfair competitive business or other misconduct, or to damage a person holding the secret, the employer may bring an action in the courts for an injunction of such use and disclosure and compensation for damages or other remedies.

179. Employees also have a duty not to compete with their employers during the period of employment. Like a duty of confidentiality, this duty arises even without a special agreement or shugyo-kisoku. If the shugyo-kisoku provides for disciplinary action against an employee for engagement in his or her own competing business or in any completing business of other company, the employer may take disciplinary action against him or her. However, an employee often engaged in a competing business after his retirement from the previous company. It is generally considered that employers need a special agreement with their employees in order to impose a duty of non-competition after the termination of employment. This is not only because the non-compete duty under the employment contract loses effectiveness but also because the employee has the freedom to choose his or her occupation (Constitution, Article 22).

180. Therefore, if the restrictions on non-competition after the termination of employment exceed reasonable limits, unreasonably restrict the employee's freedom to choose his or her occupation, and threaten the employee's survival, the agreement will be invalid as being contrary to public order and morals (Civil Code,

Article 90). The reasonableness of such restriction should be determined by the duration and area of restriction, the scope of restricted jobs and compensation for such restriction from the viewpoint of the employee's interests, the employer's interests and the public interest.[70] Looking more precisely, courts make decisions by comprehensively taking into consideration factors such as: (i) the employer's interests worthy of protection (e.g., customer lists, the company's proprietary technology and know-how, special technology acquired abroad for a large sum, etc.), (ii) the employee's status and job content (handling confidential technology or have access to management strategies, etc.), (iii) the duration and location of non-competition (depending on the type of information), (iv) the scope of occupations subject to restrictions, (v) compensation measures for employees (i.e., payment of compensatory wages or allowances), and (vi) societal interests. After all, if an employer proves that an express and valid non-compete agreement exists with an employee and that the employee has violated that agreement, the employer can seek judicial relief such as damages and injunctive relief. In addition, even if an employment contract does not provide for such covenants not to compete, the employer can resort to tort remedies when its employees engage in a competing business after retirement. However, under tort law, damages are available only when employees' conduct deviates from the permissible range of free competition by, for example, utilizing the employer's trade secrets or defaming the employer's business.[71]

181. In many companies, a reduction in the amount of retirement allowance is prescribed for those who retire in order to work for another company in the same trade. In the *Sankosha* case, where an advertising company (the plaintiff) claimed the restoration of half the amount of a paid retirement allowance from an employee (the defendant) who had been employed by another advertising company just after his retirement, the Supreme Court upheld the Nagoya High Court decision which repealed the Nagoya District Court ruling that reducing retirement allowance is illegal. The Supreme Court stated as follows:

> Restricting a sales employee's freedom to be employed by another company in the same trade for a certain period of time after his or her retirement does not constitute an unjust restraint on his or her freedom to choose his or her occupation. Accordingly, taking into consideration that the retirement allowance is a reward for an employee's meritorious service as well as remuneration for his or her continuous service, it is not an unreasonable measure to draw up retirement allowance rules (a part of the shugyo-kisoku) which provide that the amount of allowance will be half as much in the case of violating the rule of such employment restriction as that of non-violation.[72]

182. However, in a more recent case in which an advertising company paid no retirement allowance to an ex-employee on the grounds of the *shugyo-kisoku* which provided that retirement allowance would not be paid if the employee was

70. The *Foseco Japan* case, the Nara District Court in 1970, HJ, No. 624, p. 78.
71. *Sakusesu* et al., case, the Supreme Court, RH, No. 1005, p. 5.
72. The *Sankosha* case, the Supreme Court in 1977, RHS, No. 958, p. 25.

employed by another advertising company within six months after his or her retirement, the Nagoya High Court held that taking into consideration that the retirement allowance is remuneration for his or her continuous service and that non-payment of it is so severe that an employer seriously restricts the employee's freedom to choose his or her employment, non-payment of retirement allowance should be limited to the case in which the employee's work for a competitor company is considered to be especially perfidious.[73] Accordingly, it can be said that the reduction in retirement allowance on the grounds of employment by a competitor company must be also justifiable from the viewpoint of the employee's interests, the employee's interests and the public interest.

III. Employee's Invention

183. On the premise that the right to obtain a patent belongs to an employee who made an invention, the Patent Act (Act) before the 2015 amendment provided as follows:

> where an employee obtained a patent on an invention which he or she made in the line of his or her duty and within the employer's business purpose, that employer can exercise that patent though not exclusively (Art. 35(1)). In any other case, any contract, work rule or other provision which gives an employer the right to have a patent or to exclusively exercise a patent when an employee made an invention is void (Art. 35(2)). Where an employee agrees to a contract, work rule or other provision which gives an employer the right to have a patent or to exclusively exercise a patent, he or she is entitled to reasonable compensation for it (Art. 35(3)). Where a contract work rule or other provision stipulates the amount of such compensation, that amount must not be unreasonable having regard to consultation between the employees and the employers concerning laying down the standard to make compensation, the disclosure of those standards, the reflection of the employees' opinion on compensation, etc. Where there is no stipulation or an unreasonable stipulation on the amount of compensation, the amount of compensation is determined on the basis of the amount of profits which the employer may obtain from that invention and the degree to which the employer has contributed to that invention (Art. 35(4)).

184. Recently, the number of disputes concerning 'reasonable compensation' which an employee as an inventor may receive in return for giving his employer a patent or exclusively exercising a patent is increasing perhaps partly because employees' consciousness regarding the monetary value of invention is increasing and partly because their expectation for lifetime employment is decreasing. Courts generally held that, where compensation paid to an employee for his invention is

73. The *Chubu Nihon Kokokusha* case, the Nagoya High Court in 1990, RH, No. 569, p. 37.

less than a reasonable one, the employee is entitled to the difference between the paid compensation and a reasonable one which the court decides according to PL, Article 35(4).[74]

185. The 2015 amendment of the Patent Act made considerable modifications to the above legal principles. The amendment made it possible for employers to *originally* acquire the right to receive patents regarding employees' inventions through employment contracts or work rules. On the other hand, the amendment provided that the employee whose invention is acquired by or succeeded to the employer is entitled to fair compensation. The amount of the compensation can be prescribed under the employment contract or work rules unless the amount is unreasonable.

§3. EMPLOYER'S DUTIES

I. The Duty to Provide Work

186. It is not entirely self-evident that an employer has an obligation to provide work or to actually use his or her worker in addition to paying his or her wages. This question was first raised when an employer refused an employee access to the workplace after dismissal was declared null and void by the court and while the employer was still paying his wages. A similar situation occurred when the employer prevented the employee from working when an employee was unlawfully suspended or placed on leave. However, the judicial opinion generally indicates that there is no right to engage in work except where there is a special contractual agreement on such a right or where the employee has reasonable interest in actually working.[75] Where a cook employed at a restaurant was dismissed, the court held that it was such an exceptional case in which an employee's right to engage in work should be recognized because it is crucial for the cook to learn cooking skills under the instruction of a head cook and to maintain his acquired skill through everyday cooking.[76] It should be noted that if an unfair labour practice by the employer is involved, the employee's interest in having access to the workplace is vital, especially in a country such as Japan where union activity at the enterprise is indispensable under the conditions of enterprise unionism. Under the TUA, Article 27, the Labour Relation Commission may order and compel the restoration of the worker to his original work.

II. The Duty to Care for Employees' Safety and Health

187. It is held that an employer has the duty of good faith to his or her employee just as the employee has it to the employer. However, the employer's duty of good faith to the employee has been understood as rather limited in its content. One major

74. The *Olympus Kogaku Kogyo* case, the Tokyo High Court in 2001, RH, No. 812, p. 21.
75. The *Yomiuri Shinbun* case, the Tokyo High Court in 1958, RMS, Vol. 9, No. 5, p. 831.
76. The *Restaurant Swiss* case, the Nagoya District Court in 1970, RHS, No. 731, p. 7.

duty imposed on an employer as the duty of good faith towards his or her employee is the duty to care for employee safety and health. However, it is relatively recent that it was established by the courts as the employer's contractual duty. In Japan, where an employee can claim that he or she has suffered an injury or illness resulting from duty, he can claim insurance benefits under the WACIA of 1947. Separately, he or she can claim damages from the employer if such an injury or illness was caused by the employer's negligence or breach of duty to create a safe work environment. In this case, of course, the employer will be exempt, up to the amount of insurance benefits, from responsibility for civil damages. Claims for civil damages have often been upheld on the grounds of negligence until 1971. However, after the enactment of the Industrial Safety and Health Act of 1972, the courts held that an employer had a duty to ensure safety in the workplace under his employment contract.[77] Eventually, the Supreme Court held that when the parties have entered into relations involving special social contact, the duty to care for safety would be generally recognized as imposed on one or both parties towards the other, based on the good-faith principle.[78]

188. As stated above, there are two channels to compensate for a labour accident (worker's accident). The LSA provides that, in the event that 'an employee suffers an injury or illness resulting from his employment', the employer is required to furnish medical treatment (Article 75), compensation for lost time (Article 76), compensation for discontinuance (Article 81), compensation for disabilities (Article 77), survivors' compensation (Article 79), payment compensation in instalments (in place of the disabilities compensation and survivors' compensation) (Article 79) and funeral expenses (Article 80). However, since the WACIA has extended its coverage of the workplace, been improved in its content of insurance payments, it is the principal law governing labour accidents. This Act also covers employees' accidents occurring on the way to and from work. According to administrative interpretation, 'resulting from employment' means 'caused by employment' and the initial test determining whether it is caused by employment is whether it occurs 'in the course of employment'. Therefore, an employee's injury does not result from employment if it does not occur 'in the course of employment'. However, even if it does, it does not necessarily mean that such an injury was caused by employment. The main question is whether one can say that the employee's injury had a proper causal relationship with the employee's engaging in his duties. The scope of 'illness resulting from his employment' is established in the Ordinances of LSA that list various kinds of illnesses. New kinds of illnesses may be added on the basis of the latest medical knowledge on illnesses resulting from employment. However, even though an employee's illness does not fall under the listed illnesses, it will be treated as illness resulting from employment if the employee or his survivor proves that his illness is attributable to the employee's duties. It is highly controversial whether an employee's brain, heart disease or suicide is regarded as having been caused by duties. In Japan, a death due to brain or heart disease caused by employment is called *karoshi*; if the employee commits suicide, it is called *karojisatsu*.

77. The *Moji Koun* case, the Fukuoka District Court in 1972, HJ, No. 694, p. 235.
78. The *Jieitai Sharyo Seibi Koji* case, the Supreme Court in 1975, SMS, Vol. 38, No. 6, p. 557.

189. The Ministry of Health, Labour and Welfare has issued administrative guidelines to deal with this problem. Especially, how to deal with employment-related suicide has attracted public attention. Therefore, in 1999, the Ministry issued new guidelines, which were revised in 2001, with respect to mental disorders and suicides due to work-related fatigue which are covered by workers' accident compensation insurance. These guidelines set up new standards. As for suicides due to overwork, the new standards will allow for compensation when suicides are committed in a state of mind where the employee's normal judgment has been impaired as a result of his or her duties at work.

190. Another channel to compensate for a labour accident is provided by civil law litigation against an employer. The employee or his survivor may pursue his employer's responsibility for damages. Civil litigation based on tort or breach of contract is still important since the WACIA provides for fixed-rate compensation and does not provide for compensation for injured feelings. After the Supreme Court held that 'on the basis of certain legal relations, the aforesaid duty to care for safety when the parties have entered into relations involving special social contacts will also be generally recognized as devolving on one or both parties toward the other based on the good-faith principle',[79] the civil litigation based on breach of contract became the main vehicle for claiming damages against employers. Based on this case law, Article 5 of the LCA provides that an employer shall, in association with a labour contract, give the necessary consideration to allow a worker to work while securing the safety of his/her life, body and the like.

191. There are some significant differences between civil litigation based on tort and one based on breach of duty to care for safety: limitation periods (three years for contractual breach and three years for tort), damages for survivors' injured feelings (not granted for contractual breach), and the starting point for reckoning a delayed loss (from the day after the accident in tort and from the day after the claim in contractual breach). However, regarding factors constituting tort or breach of duty in caring for safety, the following comments made by an influential scholar are worth noting:

> It should be noted that, if a worker must allege and prove in concrete terms the employer's violation of its duty to care for safety, then even where non-performance of that duty is established, it cannot be said to be more advantageous than establishing a tortuous act based on the same type of care under the law governing tortuous acts, the view that, in order to prevent workers from suffering injuries and diseases in the course of their duties, the employer must exercise a high degree of foresight and avoidance, may become generalized.'[80]

192. It is worth noting here that there are an increasing number of cases in which an employee's survivors claimed damages against his employer on the grounds that

79. *Ibid.*
80. Sugeno & Yamakawa, *Rodoho* 618 (Kobun-do 13 ed. 2024).

the employee's death from heart or brain disease or suicide was caused by overwork. There are cases in which courts have upheld survivors' claims of *karoshi* and *karojisatsu*. Moreover, the Supreme Court has recently upheld claim of *karojisatsu*.[81] In that case, the Supreme Court stated that employers in general have a duty under tort law to organize the work of their employees so that mental and physical illness would not result from the accumulation of excessive fatigue or stress.

III. The Duty to Care for Employees' Interests Other Than Safety and Health

193. The employer's duty of good faith to the employee is extended beyond the duty to care for the employee's safety and health. For example, he has to make a due effort to let the employee take annual leave. Another example is that the employer is required to mitigate the expenses of the employee when he transfers him to another area. However, what is the most prominent is that the employer is required to make the best effort to avoid dismissing the employees even when the workforce reduction is unavoidable due to a bad financial situation.

IV. The Duty Not to Infringe upon Employees' Personal Rights

194. Besides the responsibility for safety care, it is often held that the employer has the duty not to infringe upon the employee's personal rights. For example, it has been held to be illegal for an employer to watch upon or 'put a tail on' an employee in order to survey his political ideology.[82] It has been also held to be illegal for an employer to have made a medical check on the HIV antibody of an employee without his consent during a regular health examination.[83] An employer transfers or assigns an employee to an unnecessary and intolerable job with an illegal or wrongful motive, it has been held that such transfer or assignment constitutes infringement of the employee's personal rights.[84] In cases of sexual harassment, several courts have held that the employer has a contractual duty to provide satisfying working environments in order that the employees can pleasantly work there.[85] Several courts have held that an employer has a contractual duty to provide working environments in which the employees cannot be forced to resign or that an employer has a contractual duty to refrain from exercising his right of personnel management wrongfully.[86]

195. Several enacted statutes obligate employers to take necessary measures for employment management to ensure that employees are not disadvantaged in terms

81. The *Dentsu* case, the Supreme Court in 2000, RH, No. 779, p. 13.
82. The *Kansai Denryoku* case, the Supreme Court in 1995, RH, No. 512, p. 12.
83. The *T Koyogyo* case, the Chiba District Court in 2000, RH, No. 785, p. 10.
84. For example, The *Air France* case, the Chiba District Court in 1994, RH, No. 647, p. 11.
85. For example, The *Mie Sexual Harassment* case, the Tsu District Court in 1997, RH, No. 729, p. 54.
86. For example, The *Efupiko* case, the Shimozuma Branch, the Mito District Court in 1999, RH, No. 763, p. 7.

of working conditions or the working environment is harmed due to various types of harassment in the workplace. The Employment Opportunity Act of 1985 imposes an obligation on employers to take necessary precautions in employment management to prevent sexual harassment between men and women (EEOA, Article 11). In addition, the same law, the Childcare and Family Care Leave Act, and the Worker Dispatch Act require necessary employment management measures to prevent acts that are unacceptable to the working environment by co-workers due to pregnancy, childbirth, childcare, or nursing care. (EEOA, Article 11.2; CFLA, Article 25: WDA, Articles 47.2 and 47.3). Furthermore, the Act on Comprehensively Advancing Labour Measures, etc. (ACALM), Article 30.2 (1) provides as follows: In order for an employer to preclude any behaviour (so-called power harassment) that is based on behaviour that constitutes bullying in the workplace which exceeds the scope necessary and reasonable in the course of business from damaging the work environment of the employer's workers, the employer must provide consultation to those workers and take measures necessary in terms of employment management, such as developing a necessary system for appropriately handling such behaviour.

196. These statutes provide that the directors of Prefectural Offices may give any necessary advice, guidance or recommendation to the parties to resolve any harassment disputes prescribed above (EEOA, Article 17; CFLA, Article 52.4; WDA, Article 47.7; ACALM, Article 30.5) and that he may also refer the competent Disputes Adjustment Commission for conciliation of disputes (EEOA, Articles 30.6 and 30.7; CFLA, Articles 52.5 and 55.6; WDA, Articles 47.8 and 47.9; ACALM, Articles 30.6 and 30.7). In addition, when an employer is in violation of the above statutory provisions, the Minister of Health, Labor and Welfare may give employers advice, guidance, and recommendations (EEOA, Article 29; CFLA, Article 56) and, if the employer has not complied with recommendations, may make a public announcement of such violation. (EEOA, Article 30; CFLA, Article 56.2; Article 33).

197. Apart from these statutory measures, if the perpetrator of harassment is the victim's boss or co-worker, he will be liable for damages for tort under Civil Code, Article 709. The employer of the perpetrator will also be held liable for tort if the damages are inflicted on the victim with respect to execution of his business. Besides, Employers are understood to have an obligation to create and maintain a good working environment for workers as a subsidiary obligation under the employment contract, and therefore harassment in the workplace is considered a breach of that obligation. Thus, the employee harassed by his or her boss or co-worker may directly pursue liability for damages in the contract against his employer (CC, Article 415).

V. The Duty to Provide Decent Working Conditions

198. Article 1, section 1 of LSA provides that working conditions must be such as will meet the needs of the worker who lives a life worthy of a human being. From this and other provisions which aim to secure the decent and humane treatment of workers, one can conclude that there is an obligation on the part of employer to have proper concern for the welfare of his or her employees. This obligation requires the employer not only to observe the various protective labour law provisions governing safety, hygiene and other working conditions but also to endeavour to raise standards above the minimum laid down by the legislation (Article 1(2)). The extensive nature of this obligation is exemplified by the provisions in LSA which require the employer to pay transport costs to employees less than 18 years old who have been dismissed and who are going back home within fourteen days (Article 64), but also to those who have terminated their contracts because they have found the actual conditions to be different from what was stated before the contracts were concluded (Article 15(3)). The employer also has an obligation to allow his employees the necessary time off to exercise their right to vote and other civil rights, and to carry out their public duties (Article 7).

VI. The Duty to Draw up Work Rules (*Shugyo-kisoku*)

199. As described in the earlier section, the employer who employs more than ten employees continuously must draw up his *shugyo-kisoku* (for a more precise description of the employer's obligation and the effects of the *shugyo-kisoku*, *see* General Introduction, Chapter 6, section 6), which should contain the following working conditions, and submit its copy to the Labour Inspection Office (LSA, Article 89):

1. hours of work, rest hours, holidays, vacations and shifts;
2. wages – methods of decision, computation and date of payment, promotion and so on;
3. matters concerning retirement and dismissal.

If there are any of the following benefits, systems or measures the employer must also stipulate them in the *shugyo-kisoku*:

1. retirement allowances, bonuses, minimum wage and so on;
2. the cost charged to the employees for food, equipment and other expenses;
3. regulations covering safety, sanitation and related matters;
4. regulations about vocational training;
5. regulations governing accident compensation and relief for injury and illness sustained outside work;
6. official commendations or sanctions (disciplinary measures);
7. other stipulations applicable to all employees.

VII. Employer's Obligations at the End of the Employment Contract

200. The employer must provide the retiring or dismissed worker, on his request, with a certificate giving details of the period of employment, the type of his occupation, his position in the enterprise, his wages and reason for the termination. He may not insert in the certificate anything which the employee does not ask for. Also, he must not conspire to send or circulate information about the nationality, creed, social status or union activities of the employee, nor make any secret mark on the certificate. In addition, the employer must provide the reason for dismissal in writing without delay when the employee has requested it in the period between being given the advance notice of dismissal and the day of leaving employment (LSA, Article 22). Furthermore, again on request, he must pay all wages and return any reserves, bonds, savings or other funds and valuables belonging to the employee within seven days of his retirement, death or dismissal (Article 23).

Chapter 3. Hours of Work, Overtime and Holidays

§1. Hours of Work

201. 'Working hours' as regulated by the LSA are the actual working time excluding rest periods, and the total hours regardless of change of workplace (Articles 32 and 38(1)). However, for pit work, working hours are regarded to be the time from entry into the mouth of the mine to exit from the mouth of the mine, including rest periods (Article 30(2)). There is no legal provision about what the actual working hours are. According to a widely held view, working hours are the hours during which an employee is under his or her employer's direction and supervision. However, the most influential academic view defines working hours as 'the time spent under the employer's work supervision and direction or in performing the employer's business on the basis of the employer's express or implied instructions'.[87] This is because work engaged in for an employer does not necessarily occur under the employer's supervision.

202. The employer is required to stipulate the starting and ending times for working hours in the work rule, i.e., *shugyo-kisoku* (LSA, Article 89(1)). The hours between the starting time and the ending time less the scheduled rest periods are called 'scheduled working hours'. Therefore, when work is carried out according to a schedule, working hours normally correspond to scheduled working hours. However, the question is still likely to arise as to whether the time needed to get ready for work and to finish work should be included in the working time or not. Generally, the following points are significant:

1. Even if preparation for work such as checking the machines and tools is carried out before the beginning of scheduled working hours, they will be regarded as a part of working hours. If morning meetings and exercises are carried out under the control of management, they will also be regarded as a part of working hours. Changing clothes and putting on safety helmets and other equipment before scheduled working hours are normally regarded as a part of working hours if such conduct is at least effectively obligated.[88]
2. Finishing activities after the end of scheduled working hours, such as checking machines, cleaning, handing over to the next shift and changing clothes are regarded as a part of working hours. However, cleaning hands, taking a bath and the like are excluded from working hours.[89]
3. Although rest periods are in principle excluded from working hours, waiting time is included in working time. For instance, when an employee in a sushi shop takes a recess at the workplace but must stay there and be ready to work if customers come in and need to be served, recess time is regarded as waiting

87. K. Sugeno & R. Yamakawa, *Rodo Ho (Labour Law)* 421 (Koubundo 13th ed. 2024).
88. The *Mitsubishi Nagasaki Zosen* case (No. 1), the Supreme Court in 2000, RH, No. 778, p. 8; the *Mitsubishi Nagasaki Zosen* case (No. 2), the Supreme Court in 2000, RH, No. 778, p. 11.
89. The *Mitsubishi Nagasaki Zosen* case (No. 1) and (No. 2), *supra*.

time and included in the working time.[90] Similarly, recess hours in which a security guard may take a nap but, when alarms are sounded, should perform a necessary task are regarded as a part of working hours.[91]

4. Participation in training, education, QC circle (Quality Circle) or recreational activities is regarded as a part of working hours if they are compulsory and further the company's business.

203. When employees work outside the premises during a part of or the entire working time, control and calculation of the total working hours become difficult and sometimes even impossible for the employers. In such cases, it is presumed in principle that they have worked for the scheduled working hours in the relevant premises. However, where it would normally be necessary to work in excess of the scheduled working hours in order to accomplish the duties in question, the number of hours worked will be deemed to be the number of hours normally necessary to accomplish such duties. In such cases, if there is a so-called worker-management agreement, which is a written agreement between an employer and a majority union (or a person representing a majority of the employees if there is no majority union) in the workplace, the number of hours specified in the agreement will be regarded as the number of hours normally necessary to accomplish the duties in question. An employer must submit the agreement to the LSIO (LSA, Article 38.2(1) (3)).

204. After April 1997, the maximum working hours for adult workers employed in all enterprises are in principle eight hours per day and forty hours per week. Although LSA was amended in 1987 to reduce the maximum working hours per week from forty-eight hours to forty hours, the maximum has been reduced step by step by Cabinet Orders, i.e., forty-six hours (in 1988), forty-four hours (in 1991) and eventually forty hours (in 1994). Even since 1994, the forty-hour system has not applied to all enterprises because the Cabinet Order has excluded certain enterprises from it according to their trade and size. However, after April 1997, the exemption of the forty-hour system is limited to enterprises with nine or less employees which engage in certain trades such as selling, distributing, hairdressing, entertaining, health and hygiene services, hotel, restaurant, or snack bar work (Enforcement Ordinance of LSA, Article 25.2(1)). Such enterprises are subject to the forty-four-hour maximum for the time being.

205. The employer should provide rest periods totalling at least forty-five minutes for more than six hours' work and at least one hour for more than eight hours' work. Rest periods should be given to all employees at the same time, except if the employer has a worker-management agreement which permits him or her to do otherwise. The employer must not interfere with the use made by his employees during their rest periods (LSA, Article 34).

---

90. The *Sushidokoro Sugi* case, the Osaka District Court in 1981, RHS, No. 1091, p. 3.
91. The *Oboshi Biru Kanri* case, the Tokyo High Court in 1996, RH, No. 706, p. 26.

§2. Flexible Arrangements of Working Hours

206. When the LSA was amended in 1987 to reduce the maximum number of working hours, several statutory flexibility arrangements were added to the LSA at the same time. Since the 1994 amendment, the LSA has permitted five arrangements to make working hours flexible: (1) uneven distribution of working hours (average working time system) over a period not exceeding one month (Article 32-2), (2) flex-time (Article 32-3), (3) uneven distribution of working hours over a period not exceeding one year (Article 32-4), (4) uneven distribution of working hours over a one-week period (Article 32-5), and (5) unrebuttable presumed working hours for discretionary work for professional jobs (Article 38-3). The 1998 amendment also created (6) another discretionary work arrangement for unrebuttable presumed working hours regarding workers who are engaged in managerial planning jobs (Article 38-4). Arrangements (2)–(5) require the employer to have a worker-management agreement on the relevant points and to submit it to the LSIO. Arrangement (6) requires the employer to have a worker-management agreement.

207. The first of the above-listed flexible arrangements allows an employer to distribute work hours unevenly over a period not exceeding one month on the condition that the employer stipulates the working hours to be distributed each day and week in the worker-management agreement or the *shugyo-kisoku* and the average scheduled working hours per week do not exceed the weekly maximum working hours.

208. The second of the flexible arrangements allows the employer to engage employees beyond the daily maximum working hours so long as the average working hours over the specific unit period not exceeding one month do not exceed the weekly maximum. In order to implement this arrangement, the employer must stipulate the framework of the arrangement (the scope of workers to be covered by this arrangement, the period of the arrangement, the number of total hours to be worked within the period, the periods of core-time and flexible-time, etc.) have a worker-management agreement or work rules.

209. The third of the flexible arrangements allows an employer to distribute work hours unevenly over a period not exceeding one year (Article 32-4). In order to implement this arrangement, the employer must stipulate the following items in a worker-management agreement: (1) the scope of workers whom the employer may have working under this arrangement; (2) the period to which this arrangement applies (a period exceeding one month but not exceeding one year during which the average working hours per week do not exceed forty hours); (3) the specified period (e.g., an especially busy period), (4) working days in the applicable period and working hours for each of the said working days (in cases where the applicable period is divided into periods of one month or more, working hours for each working day in the initial period division and working days and total working hours of each period division); (5) other items as stipulated by order. In the case where the applicable period is divided into periods of one month or more and the working days and the total working hours for each period division excluding the initial period division are stipulated, the employer must, with the worker-management agreement, set the working hours for each working day in each period division no later than thirty days before the first day of the period division. Where the period to which this arrangement applies is under three months, daily and weekly working hours should not exceed ten and fifty-two hours respectively. In both cases, the employer must ensure one rest day per week (Enforcement Ordinance of LSA, Article 12-4(3)).

210. The fourth of the flexible arrangements allows small businesses in the service sector to adjust their daily working hours to cope with unforeseeable shifts between active and slack days. On the condition that the employer has a worker-management agreement, he is allowed not to fix the working hours for each day of the work week. Instead, the employer may notify the employees of them by the end of the preceding week. He may also have employees work for up to ten hours per day.

211. The fifth of the flexible arrangements relates to calculation of the number of hours of discretionary work. According to Article 38-3 of LSA, if the employer, pursuant to a worker-management agreement, assigns a worker to duties for which it is difficult for the employer to give concrete directives regarding such decisions as the means of accomplishment and allocation of time because of its discretionary nature and stipulates that calculation of the working hours will be in accordance with the said agreement, the working hours will be regarded as the number of hours set forth in the agreement regardless actual working hours. Working hours of employees engaged in research and development activities or other duties shall be in accordance with such an agreement and the working hours of employees shall be regarded as the number of hours set forth in the agreement. The duties for which this system is permissible are specified under the Enforcement Ordinance and notice issued by the Minister of Health, Labour, and Welfare. The worker-management agreement must stipulate measures to promote those employees' health and welfare and to process their grievances regarding the implementation of this arrangement.

212. The 1998 amendment added Article 38-4 to LSA in order to introduce another kind of discretionary work arrangement for workers who are engaged in managerial planning jobs. This discretionary work arrangement is available for employees if their duty is planning, investigation, and analysis of matters regarding management of the enterprise and if they have knowledge and experience related to performing such duties. Under this discretionary work arrangement, how to accomplish such duties must be left mostly to the discretion of such employees and no concrete direction will be given to them regarding the means of performance or the allocation of time. Those covered by this arrangement are high-level white-collar employees while those covered by the discretionary work arrangement under Article 38-3 are mainly professional employees. The implementation of a discretionary work arrangement under Article 38-4 requires a worker-management committee to be established. Half of its members must be appointed within a specific period of appointment by a majority union (or a person representing a majority of the employees), in the workplace and be approved by a majority of employees. The committee must, by a majority of four-fifths or more, determine the duties and scope of employees covered by the arrangement as well as the number of hours which will be regarded as their working hours. The committee must resolve that the employer shall take measures to promote those employees' health and welfare, to process their grievances and shall obtain the individual employee's consent regarding the implementation of this arrangement. This resolution must be filed with the LSIO.

§3. HOLIDAYS

213. The employer must in principle provide his employees with at least one rest day per week. However, this principle of 'one rest day per week' is not applied to an employer who provides at least four rest days during a four-week period if the first day of the period is specified (LSA, Article 35 and Enforcement Ordinance of LSA). The legal maximum is a six-day working week, but a five-day week is more popular in practice (59.8% of all regular employees employed by private enterprises with thirty or more employees in 2022). National holidays, which amount to fourteen days per year, are not legally binding in the private sector, but today most offices and factories including private ones are closed on such holidays.

§4. OVERTIME

214. Where an employer has employees work either beyond the maximum working hours (eight hours per day or forty hours per week) or the maximum hours under the flexible working hour arrangements, the employer may be punished. This is also the case where an employer does not give required rest days to employees. However, overtime or rest day work is permitted under the following conditions. If an employer has concluded a worker-management agreement, and submitted it to the Labour Inspection Office, overtime or rest day work is permissible to the extent that the agreement stipulates (LSA, Article 36). The payment of overtime or rest day wage is necessary even where overtime or rest day work is permissible. Before the 2018 amendment of the LSA, the Minister of Health, Labour and Welfare merely set a standard with respect to the limit of overtime work to be stipulated by the worker-management agreement. This standard was not mandatory, although it makes the ground for administrative guidance. The 2018 amendment of the LSA created a provision that directly establishes a limitation on overtime work as stipulated under the worker-management agreement. In principle, a provision regarding overtime work that is made permissible under the worker-management agreement must not exceed forty-five hours per month and 360 hours per year (Article 36, item 4). A stricter limitation is provided regarding the average working time arrangement (Article 32-4) over the period of one year at the longest. In a special situation where this limitation cannot be applied due to extraordinary circumstances such as an unforeseeable increase in workload, the overtime work that can be permissible under the worker-management agreement can be 100 hours per month (at most six months in a year and working hour on rest day work is included here) and 720 hours per year (item 5). A provision under the worker-management agreement that stipulates this special exception is called ‘special provision’. Furthermore, another restriction on overtime is imposed regardless of the existence of the worker-management agreement. The employer may not have employees work beyond 100 hours per month and the average overtime hours during 2, 3, 4, 5 and 6 months must not exceed eighty hours (hours of rest day work included (item 6)). With respect to hazardous work, the maximum overtime hour is 2 hours. This limitation has existed before the 2018 amendment. There are certain jobs such as medical doctors where these strict limitations do not apply and different standards are established. LSA

215. However, it does not necessarily impose a duty upon individual employees to work overtime hours or on the rest days prescribed by the agreement. There must be a contract with that effect to create a legal obligation for individual employees to do overtime work. According to the Supreme Court decision in the *Hitachi Musashi Factory* case, only where, in addition to a written agreement between the employer and the majority union in the factory, there is a provision in the *shugyo-kisoku* that the employer may request the employee to work overtime, the employee has a duty to comply with the request to work overtime, provided that it is considered to be reasonable.[92]

216. The employer is required to pay an increased rate of wages: at least 25% over the normal wages for overtime work and at least 35% extra for rest-day work. Similarly, if the employer has the employee work between 10 pm and 5 am, he is required to pay night-work pay, at least 25% over the normal wages (Article 37). However, if the employer has the employee work between 10 pm and 5 am beyond forty hours (or on a rest day), he is required to pay an increased rate of wages at least 50% (or 60%) over the normal wages (Enforcement Ordinance of LSA, Article 20). In addition, where overtime working hours are over sixty hours per month, the rate must be at least 50% over the normal wages for each hour beyond sixty hours. However, the employee can take a paid hour leave instead of being paid such an increased rate of wage for each overtime working hour over sixty hours if a worker-management agreement so stipulates. There are many judgments on the question of whether the employer has fulfilled its obligation to pay overtime wages by paying a certain sum of remuneration to the employee who was engaged in overtime work. The Supreme Court has announced that the employer must meet two requirements. First, the remuneration must be clearly distinguished from the normal wages that should be paid to the employee regardless of overtime work.[93] For example, the agreement stipulating that the employer should pay a monthly salary of a certain fixed amount including overtime wages does not satisfy this requirement as long as the amount of normal wages cannot be specified under this agreement. Second, the money that is paid to the employee must have the nature of consideration or

92. The *Hitachi Musashi Factory* case, the Supreme Court in 1991, SMS, Vol. 48, No. 7, p. 127.
93. The *Koshin Kai* case, the Supreme Court in 2017, RH, No. 1168, p. 49.

remuneration for the overtime work, since the remuneration for the performance of special duty such as dangerous work rather than overtime does not qualify as overtime wages.[94]

§5. Employees Exempted from Regulations on Working Hours, Etc.

217. In the following cases, not only the legal principle of maximum working hours but also all the regulations concerning rest periods and weekly rest days are not applied (Article 41 of the LSA):

1. In agriculture, animal husbandry and fishing.
2. Employees in a supervisory or management post or employed in a confidential capacity.
3. Employees engaged in security guard duties and intermittent labour with the approval of the LSIO (LSA, Article 41).

218. There are numerous cases where it is disputed whether employees who are called 'managers' by their employers are legally exempted from the regulation of working time under Article 41 of the LSA. According to lower court decisions, the exemption status is determined not by the titles given by the employer but by the factual situations in each case. The relevant factors may include the job contents and responsibilities, discretion in working time, and economic status such as the amount of salaries.

219. Regarding these exempted workers, the employers need not pay overtime and holiday premiums, although they must pay premiums for night work.[95]

220. The 2018 amendment of the LSA introduced a new type of exempt employees who are not qualified as employees in a supervisory or management post under Article 41. This exemption is applied to employees who have an advanced level of expertise, are engaged in professional work specified under the Enforcement Ordinance of the Ministry of Health, Labour and Welfare such as research and development and are paid more salary as prescribed under the Ordinance. This new exemption scheme is called the 'highly professional' arrangement. LSA Article 41-2 provides, where: (1) a worker-management council adopts a resolution by a majority of four-fifths or more of its members regarding highly professional employees as specified above (the employer must notify the Labour Inspection Office of that resolution), (2) the resolution stipulates certain required matters such as the entitlement of rest days that are more favourable than the requirement under the LSA as well as measures to secure their health and welfare, and (3) the employer has such employees work with their consent and in accordance with the worker-management resolution, provisions under the LSA concerning the working hours, breaks, days off and premium wages for work at night time do not apply.

94. The *Nihon Chemical* case, the Supreme Court in 2018, RH, No. 1186, p. 5.
95. The *Kotobuki* case, the Supreme Court in 2009, RH, No. 1000, p. 5.

§6. Night Work

221. Night work is defined by LSA as work done between 10 pm and 5 am, and it can be changed to that done between 11 pm and 6 am by the Ministry of Health, Labour and Welfare if it proves necessary in a particular area or season. Payment for night work must be at the increased rate of at least 25% above normal wages (Article 37, item 4). Where employees responsible for the care of children under the age of admission to elementary school and/or other family members who are in need of case specified in the Child and Family Care Leave Law have so requested, the employer shall not employ them for night work. For minors, there are special regulations concerning hours of work in general which will be described in Part I, Chapter 6.

§7. Annual Paid Leave

222. LSA, Article 39 provides that the minimum length of annual paid holidays is ten days for those who have been employed for six months and were present for over 80% of the total working days in that year. The number of holidays is increased up to twenty days according to the length of service as follows: eleven days after 1.5 years, twelve days after 2.5 years, fourteen days after 3.5 years, sixteen days after 4.5 and eighteen days after 5.5 years and twenty days after 6.5 years. For part-time employees, the number of annual paid holidays is fixed by ordinance with due consideration for the ratio of the number of days specified by ordinance as the prescribed working days in a week for ordinary workers. During holidays the employer should pay the employee his average or normal wages. The employee may take his holidays 'consecutively or separately' whenever he likes during the year, but the employer may change the date of his employee's holiday if it disturbs the normal operation of the enterprise (Article 39(5)). The word 'separately' in Article 39 was added to the original draft during the enactment of LSA. The reason for this amendment was the absence of the custom of annual holidays in Japan. As a result of this legislative wording, and also because of the absence of the custom of annual holidays in pre-war Japan (except the end of the year, New Year and early summer for a few days), the way of using the annual vacation has taken a rather peculiar form from the Western point of view. The main reasons that employees do not take all their holidays or long continuous holidays are that they feel it is difficult to use them because of inconvenience to other employees in the same workplace or that they want to use them in case of illness or another emergency. They are mostly taken one or two days at a time. Holidays for a long period like a week or two are quite a recent phenomenon and are still exceptional. Often some of the vacation days to which employees are entitled are left unused at the end of the year (37.9% of total holiday entitlements were not used in 2023). Unused paid holidays may be carried over only to the next year. The 2008 amendment to LSA made it possible for employees to take annual paid holidays by an hour unit instead of a day unit if a worker-management agreement so stipulates. This amendment is purported to make it easier to take paid holidays (Article 39(4)).

223. The low rate of taking holidays may be caused by Japanese group working practices, the high costs of travel, reduced bonuses and sometimes a negative performance evaluation as a result of increased absence due to taking vacations. However, it may also be caused by the way of determining the date and period of holidays. According to the LSA, an employee has a right to determine the date and period of holidays subject to the employer's right to change in order to avoid the disturbance of the normal operation of the enterprise (Article 39(5)). This makes it rather difficult to coordinate all employees' holiday seasons. In order to increase the rate of holidays taken, the 1987 amendment introduced the possibility of planned vacations by an agreement between an employer and a majority union or a representative of the majority of workers when there is no majority union. In accordance with such an agreement, employees are requested to take their vacations on planned days. However, a minimum of five days per year is reserved for personal choice in order to meet the individual convenience for the sake of the Japanese style of annual holidays (Article 39(6)). Also, in order to decrease unused paid holidays, the 2018 amendment of the LSA requires the employer to designate its employee's holidays up to five days if the employee has ten or more holidays unless the employee has taken the holidays before the designation by the employer (Article 39(7)).

§8. Child and Family Care Leave

224. Balancing work and family life has been one of the most important policy goals in the last couple of decades in Japan. The CFLA was enacted in 1991 against the background of declining birth rate and population ageing. At that time there was no general legal requirement for child and family care leave except for maternity leave, the purpose of which is the protection of the health of female workers from the viewpoint of childbearing. Since this enactment, the Act has been amended a number of times. Recently, the labour policy has been focused on the promotion of male workers to take childcare leave. Where an employee, male or female, applies to the employer for leave to take care of his or her child who is less than a year old, the employer must give him or her leave for childcare subject to certain exceptions such as a fixed-term employee whose employment is clearly expected to terminate within one year and six months (Articles 2 and 5). Although the childcare leave may continue until the child becomes one year old, the employee may require the extension to the maximum of two years if there are special circumstances such as the difficulty in finding childcare facilities. Although female employees may take maternity leave under the LSA (Article 65) for eight months after childbirth in addition to six months before childbirth, the employees who need to take care of their child may also take so-called post-childbirth childcare leave (Article 9-2 of the CFLA) within the eight months after the childbirth. Since female employees usually take maternity leave mandated under the under the LSA, This 'post-childbirth' childcare leave is mainly supposed to be taken by male employees. As such, the employee can work during the 'post-childbirth' childcare leave under the conditions prescribed by the worker-management agreement (Article 9-5). The employee is paid a benefit under the Employment Insurance Law which is equivalent to 67% of his or her former wages until the end of the 180th day and 50% after that (the EIA, Articles 61-7, etc.). The 2024 amendment increased the amount of this benefit up to 80% for a certain period.

225. In addition to childcare leave, the CFLA requires the employer to make several arrangements so that the employee can continue to work without difficulty in balancing work and childcare, such as part-time work arrangement, exemption from and limitation on overtime work and night work, short period leave when the child is ill or needs care for certain matters. The 2024 amendment expanded the scope of such arrangements, including the requirement for the inclusion of 'tele-work' or 'work from home' as one of the measures available when the part-time arrangement is difficult.

226. The employer is also obliged to give family-care leave to take care of a 'subject family member' in conditions requiring constant care for a period where an employee applies to the employer for it (CFLA, Article 11). The 'subject family member' may be the spouse (including a person in de facto marital relations with the worker), parents and children or parents of the spouse who live with the employee applying for family-care leave. The conditions requiring constant care are provided by the Ministry of Labour Ordinance (Article 2). The employee can divide the period into three periods. The maximum period of family-care leave given to an employee is ninety days in total for each subject family member. As with the child-care leave, the Act also requires the employer to make certain arrangements such as part-time work so that the employee can continue to work without difficulty in balancing work and family care.

Chapter 4. Remuneration and Benefits

§1. Pay Systems

227. Generally speaking, the Japanese wage system can be described as a person-based and organization-based wage system. The scale of wages is determined by an employee's expected personal ability to perform his duty but not by his job duty. It is determined by the company's factors and not directly affected by the market's factors. It is also determined according to an employee's functional grades reflecting past points of performance evaluation but not according to an employee's present contribution to the company. Therefore, in Japan, it is more difficult to reflect the employee's present performance on the job in determining his wages. It is generally accepted that the Japanese wage system, including retirement allowances, is highly dependent on age and length of service rather than on skill or job evaluation. Although recently the trend has been to emphasize evaluation more than in the past, and although some research done by economists suggests that the correlation between the amount of wages, the length of service and age is not as different from that in Western countries as was generally presumed, the difference still exists both in statistical fact and, more especially, in attitudes and ideas. Statistics from the Ministry of Health, Labour and Welfare show that age has an increasing effect on wage differentials except for the older groups (Table 13). Employees' starting wages are usually decided according to the employee's level of education rather than his ability, and then basic wages are typically increased according to his length of service in many enterprises. In many enterprises, differences caused by promotion which are more based on the individual's merit gradually appear after several years of service.

Table 13 Wage Differences by Age of Male Workers (100 = Wages for 20–24)

Year	*1980*	*1990*	*2000*	*2010*	*2023*
Age 20–24	100.0	100.0	100	100	100
25–29	127.4	123.3	117	119	116.8
30–34	155.9	149.7	152	139	131.7
35–39	180.5	174.2	186	164	147.4
40–44	193.6	195.4	213	185	162.1
45–49	197.6	210.8	237	205	173.1
50–54	194.0	209.7	266	209	182.2
55–59	169.3	183.4	260	196	186.4
60–64	138.3	142.3	202	142	145.7

Source: Ministry of Labour (currently Ministry of Health, Labour and Welfare), *Chingin Kozo Kihontokei Chosa* (Basic Surveys of Wage Structure).

228. However, many enterprises have gradually been introducing performance-based or merit-based wage systems to revise their traditional wage systems in recent years. Moreover, many companies have recently applied the annual salary system to their white-collar employees, especially managerial employees. The annual salary system started to be introduced by some enterprises in the second half of the 1970s and became popular in the 1990s. Several surveys have recently found that a majority of enterprises have already introduced or plan to introduce such systems. However, most Japanese annual salary systems are rather different from those in Western countries. Their term of one year only means the duration in which the employee's performance is evaluated to determine his wages, and it does not mean the duration of his employment contract itself. Nevertheless, such annual salary systems enable the employer, in determining an individual employee's wages, to exclude certain factors such as the length of his service and his working hours. The implication of annual salary systems is rather significant in that determination of wages is individualized by being done through negotiation between an employer and an individual employee. Recent official surveys on wages have been witnessing the fact that factors on which companies take account in deciding the basic wages have recently been shifting from factors of the employee's age, length of service and educational background to his ability, function and results. This is the case not only for managerial employees but also for non-managerial employees. In this sense, the Japanese wage systems are in the process of changing into more merit- or performance-based systems.

229. Japanese wages usually consist of Contractual monthly earnings and annual special earnings (bonuses and other special payments). Monthly earnings are composed of scheduled earnings and non-scheduled earnings. Scheduled earnings consist of basic wages and various types of allowances such as family, commuting, housing and regional allowances, allowances for foremen, supervisors and other positions, for special jobs, special work, technical work, high attendance rates and subsidized living expenses. Non-scheduled earnings include payments for overtime work, work on rest days and night work (*see* Figure 1). In many companies, basic wages are linked to some extent with age, to some extent with seniority and to some extent with ability and job duties. Bonuses, which in most cases are paid twice a year at the end of the year and in the summer, are a very important part of wages, being equivalent to a few or several months' wages in total for a year on average. Besides these wages, retirement allowances paid in lump sums and often accompanied by pensions are also regarded as a part of wages. In 2023, 74.9% of enterprises employing more than thirty workers had retirement allowance schemes. The allowance is paid to employees as a lump sum in 69.0% of cases, as an annuity in 9.6% of cases, and partly as lump sum and partly as annuity in 21.4% of cases. Senior high school leavers who have worked as production workers until mandatory retirement age get, on average, 34.3 months' pay as a retirement allowance. University graduates who have worked as administrative, clerical or technical workers until mandatory retirement age received, on average, 36.0 months' pay in 2023.[96]

---

96. Ministry of Health, Labour and Welfare, Shuro Joken*Sogo Chosa* (Comprehensive Survey on Working Conditions), 2023.

§2. The Notion of Wages

230. Wages are defined by Article 11 of the LSA as every payment to the employee from the employer as remuneration for work, whether called wages, salaries, allowances, bonuses or anything else. Although the Act prohibits the employer from paying wages other than in cash in principle, it is in fact allowed if otherwise provided for by law, order or agreement (Article 24, paragraph 1). Payment must be to the employee from the employer. Thus, the tips earned by waiters or waitresses are not wages unless there is an arrangement by which the employer takes all the tips received from customers and divides them between the employees. Payment must be made as remuneration for work. Thus, payments which the employer gratuitously made to the employee are not wages. Accordingly, some payments in cash, such as the money given by the enterprise to celebrate a wedding or express sympathy upon the death of a close relative, are not regarded as a part of wages as long as the precise, detailed conditions of the payments are not laid down in work rules (*shugyo-kisoku*), collective agreement, or individual contract. Similarly, goods and other benefits are not regarded as a part of wages if they form a part of the welfare facilities of the enterprise. However, housing provided by the employer is regarded as a part of wages when the employer pays a housing allowance of equal value to those not living in company accommodation.

§3. The Notion of Average Wage

231. Although in principle wages are remuneration for the work done by the employee, in some cases, LSA requires the employer to make payments for periods during which no work is done at all. Such payments include payment in lieu of notice in a case of dismissal (Article 20), payment during the period of business suspension (Article 26), payment during the annual vacation (Article 39), payment during time off caused by an accident at work (Article 76) and so on. In these cases, the amount of payment is calculated on the basis of the employee's 'average wage'. LSA provides a rather detailed definition of the average wage in Article 12. According to this provision, the 'average wage' means the quotient obtained by dividing the total amount of wages for a period of three months (or the period of employment if this is less than three months) preceding the day on which the calculation of the average wage became necessary (or the final day of the wage calculation period if it exists) by the number of days in this period; however, the amount shall not be less than the amount computed by one of the following methods:

1. If the wages are calculated by the working day or the working hour, or paid at piece rates or by result, 60% of the quotient is obtained by dividing the total sum of the wages by the number of working days during that period.
2. If a part of the wage is defined by the month, week or any other fixed period, an aggregate of the quotient is obtained by dividing the total sum of these parts by the number of days during that period and the sum calculated by the foregoing method.

232. The amount of wages on which the 'average wage' is calculated does not include extraordinary wages and those paid periodically at more than three-month intervals (such as bonuses, allowances for non-absence service, etc.).

233. The 'average wage' differs from the 'normal wage' which is used for the purpose of determining the amount of increased wages for overtime work, rest-day work and night work. If wages are paid monthly, the amount of the 'normal wage' is calculated by dividing the prescribed amount of monthly wages by the prescribed number of working hours within a month. However, certain types of wages are excluded from the calculation of increased wages. Those are family allowances, commutation allowances, children's education allowances, and specially paid wages and wages paid for periods of more than one month (Article 37 and the Ordinance for Enforcement of LSA, Articles 19 and 21).

§4. Civil Code Provisions Concerning Wages

234. An employee cannot demand wages before he has completed his/her work (Civil Code, Article 624(1)). This indicates that the employee's right to demand wages becomes concrete after the employee has carried out his/her work. This is called the principle of 'no work, no pay'. Where wages are fixed by periods, the employee can demand wages only after the expiration of each period (Article 624(2)). However, these rules are not mandatory and therefore the parties can make a contract of employment in contradiction of these rules. An employee's performance of duty must be done actually and in strict accordance with the tenor of the obligation (Article 493). However, where his/her performance of duty becomes impossible because, for example, his/her employer does not allow him/her to perform it, the employee has a right to be paid if such impossibility is caused by the employer (Article 536(2)), for example, in a case where the employer discharges the employee without good cause. In the *Katayamagumi* case, an employee who was suffering from Bosedow's disease was suspended without payment although he requested his employer to assign him to desk work instead of supervision of work on construction sites. The Supreme Court held that, where an employee has not agreed to engage only in a specific job under his/her contract of employment, the employee may perform an appropriate alternative work in strict accordance with the tenor of his obligation if there is a possibility that he may be assigned to it having regard to his ability, experience, position and the company's size, trade, etc.[97] In other words, the employer's refusal to assign the employee who cannot perform the duty of the present position because of his/her physical condition to the position he/she can perform is regarded as the employer's responsibility, and the employee has the right to demand his/her wages if the employee's contract is not restricted to the present position.

97. The *Katayamagumi* case, the Supreme Court in 1998, RH, No. 736, p. 15.

§5. REGULATIONS CONCERNING THE PAYMENT OF WAGES

235. The LSA provides that wages must be paid in cash and in full directly to the workers themselves (Article 24 (1)). This provision contains three important principles for payment of wages; payment-in-cash, direct payment and full payment. Wages must also be paid at least once a month on a definite date, except for extraordinary wages, bonuses and the like specified by the Enforcement Ordinance of LSA (Article 24 (2)). This is known as the principle of periodical payment. Payment other than in cash may be permitted if otherwise provided for by law, order or collective agreement. Deductions from wages may also be permitted if otherwise provided for by law, order or a written worker-management agreement with the majority union or, if there is no majority union, with the representative of the majority of employees. However, even if such agreement exists, deductions to offset the employer's claim against an employee are only permissible within the limit of one-fourth of the total amount of wages in a payment period (Article 510 of the Civil Code and Article 152 (2) of the Civil Enforcement Act).

236. Exceptions to the above-mentioned standards which are in common use are the deduction of tax, social security fees; the repayment of debts to the employer; the payment of fees and payment for benefits and goods provided by the employer under the worker-management agreement written above. The deduction of union dues and fees under the check-off system is also permissible if the employer and the union conclude a worker-management agreement. However, the employer may not make a contract fixing in advance either the sum payable for breach of contract or the amount of indemnity for damage caused by the employee's negligence (Article 16); neither may the employer deduct the money advanced or make any other such claim as a condition of work (Article 17). Concerning the principle of payment in cash, payment by check and payment into the employee's bank account once became controversial issues, but this was legitimized by the Enforcement Ordinance. Also, payment in the form of virtual currency has recently become permissible under certain limited conditions prescribed by the Enforcement Ordinance (Article 7.2).

237. There was some controversy on the possibility of the deduction of overpaid wages from wages in a later pay period and that of the employee's voluntary agreement to deduction of a debt owed to the employer from his wages. The Supreme Court affirmed the effectiveness of those deductions. The Court has held that an employer's wage offset conducted pursuant to the consent of an employee does not contravene the principle of full payment so long as the consent is based completely on his free will.[98] Similarly, the Supreme Court has upheld the legality of an employer's failure to pay wages when the employee has abandoned wage claims of his own free will.[99] The Court has also held that the deduction of previously overpaid wages from wages in a later pay period is permissible where an employer acts to correct and adjust an overpayment reasonably close to the time it

98. The *Nisshin Seiko* case, the Supreme Court in 1990, SMS, Vol. 44, No. 8, p. 1085.
99. The *Singer Sewing Machine Company* case, the Supreme Court in 1973, SMS, Vol. 27, No. 1, p. 27.

was overpaid, gives the employee advance notice, and the sum is not so large as to risk the stability of his or her economic well-being.[100]

238. When an employee requires money for an emergency use such as childbirth, disease, accident or something else specified by an ordinance of the Ministry of Health, Labour and Welfare, the employer shall pay the accrued wages before payday (Article 25). This is generally known as the principle of emergency payment.

§6. Retirement Allowance

239. There are some cases where retirement allowance rests at the employer's discretion and therefore is not regarded as a wage. However, since most retirement allowances are paid on the basis of the provisions of work rules (*shugyo-kisoku*), collective agreements or individual contracts, they are usually regarded as a wage. The amount of retirement allowance generally depends on the employee's basic wage, length of employment and reason for employment termination. In general, the longer the employee's duration of employment, the higher the amount of retirement allowance he/she is entitled to obtain. The *shugyo-kisoku* often provides that, for example, a retirement allowance will be paid to an employee in the following cases: (i) when he/she retired at the mandatory retirement age; (ii) when he/she retires or is dismissed because he/she becomes unfit for work due to mental disability, injury or illness; (iii) when he/she died; (iv) when he retires for his/her own personal reasons; (v) when he/she retires or is dismissed due to unavoidable circumstances, e.g., for business reasons. Most *shugyo-kisoku* provisions stipulate a smaller amount of allowance in the case of (iv) than in other cases and stipulate that an employee who is subject to a 'disciplinary dismissal' action is entitled to no allowance or a reduced amount of allowance. These provisions have generally been authorized by the courts. According to the courts, the right to retirement allowance does not accrue 'bit by bit' throughout the period of employment, in which case the reduction of retirement allowance is regarded as non-payment of wages, but accrues at the time of employment termination. The amount is determined by the standard stipulated in the *shugyo-kisoku* or other regulations, according to the degree of the employee's contribution to the company which is squarely calculated at the time of the termination by the employee's duration of service, the manner of termination, and the cause of termination. The courts do not approve reduced payment where the consequences are so harsh that they constitute violation of 'public policy and good morals'.[101] However, the amount of retirement allowance is usually larger if the retirement or termination is caused by the employer as in the case of (v).

100. The *Fukushima Kenkyoso* case, the Supreme Court in 1969, SMS, Vol. 23, No. 12, p. 2495; the *Gunma Kenkyoso* case, the Supreme Court in 1970, SMS, Vol. 24, No. 11, p. 1639; the *Shizuoka Kenkyoso* case, the Supreme Court in 1975, HJ, No. 778, p. 100.
101. The *Sankosha* case, the Supreme Court in 1977, RHS, No. 958, p. 25.

§7. Bonuses

240. As with retirement allowances, the payment of and the criteria for bonuses are usually stipulated by the *shugyo-kisoku* or collective agreement. In such cases, bonuses constitute a part of wages. It has often been a topic of dispute whether the employer may require that an employee must be in employment status on the date of payment of the bonus in order to be entitled to the payment even though the employer was in employment status during the period for which his/her contribution is evaluated. The Supreme Court has held that the *shugyo-kisoku* provision requiring such a condition is reasonable and therefore is binding even without the individual employee's specific consent.[102]

§8. Minimum Wages

241. Article 27 of LSA provides that the employer must guarantee a fixed wage proportionate to the working hours of those workers who are paid piece rates or by results. This minimum fixed wage is interpreted as guaranteeing a certain amount of income to the employee, but the minimum amount is not specified in the law. The Ministry of Health, Labour and Welfare says that the size of the fixed wage should be defined so as to guarantee an amount which is not drastically lower than normal income. However, a court has held that, where an employer has not stipulated any guaranteed wage, his employee cannot claim any guaranteed wage on the basis of Article 27.[103]

242. So far in Japan there is no fixed flat-rate minimum wage applied to all industries at a national level. Statutory minimum wages were first introduced under the Minimum Wages Act of 1959 (MWA), and the present system was established under that law amended in 1968. Since then, Minimum wages have been determined either on the basis of collective agreements in a certain district (Article 11) or on the research and deliberations of the Minimum Wages Councils (MWC) (Article 16). MWC has been set up both at the national level (Central MWC) and at the local level (Local MWC) and is composed of three delegations: workers, employers and the public. The collective agreement-based minimum wage has been decided by the Ministry of Health, Labour and Welfare or the Director of the PLB upon the unanimous request (based on agreement) of the employers and unions covered by collective bargaining agreements with substantially the same provisions regarding minimum wages, and applied to the majority of workers of the same kind and their employers in a certain district. In deciding minimum wages in this way, the Minister or the Director of PLB should ask the opinion of MWC (Article 13). However, since a collective bargaining agreement has been usually concluded between an individual enterprise and an enterprise union, there have been very few examples of regional minimum wages based on collective bargaining agreements.

102. The *Daiwa Ginko* case, the Supreme Court in 1982, RH, No. 339, p. 11.
103. The *Daisan Kujimaru* case, the Kanazawa District Court in 1961, HJ, No. 274, p. 30.

The low level of minimum wage has recently been severely criticized especially as even being lower than the level of public assistant benefits provided under the Livelihood Protection Act.

243. However, in 2007, MWA was amended to a great extent, although MWC remains the same. The principal changes in the amended MWA are written below. In recent years, there has been a considerable increase in the amount of minimum wages throughout Japan. The gist of the minimum wage regulation is as follows:

i. In order to secure the minimum level of wage, a minimum wage shall be determined in every area of the nation (Article 9(1)).
ii. The amount of the minimum wage in each area shall be decided by taking account of the living costs, wages and ordinary enterprises' ability to pay in the area concerned (Article 9(2)). In deciding living costs, the standards of public assistant benefits under the Livelihood Protection Act shall be taken into consideration in order to enable workers to maintain a wholesome and culturally wholesome standard of living (Article 9(3)).
iii. The Minister of HLW or the Directors of the PLBs shall seek the central or the local MWC to investigate and deliberate in each area, seek the necessary opinions and thereafter decide the amount of minimum wage for each area (Article 10(1)).
iv. A person representing all or part of a portion of employee groups and employers who belong to specific trade or profession may request the Minister or Director to decide or repeal the amount of 'specific minimum wage' which applies specially to their trade or profession (Article 15(1)).
v. The minimum wage (or a specific minimum wage) that applies to a dispatched worker shall be one of the areas in which his/her workplace is located (Articles 13 and 18).
vi. The minimum wage shall apply to all employees but the employer may pay a minimum wage at a certain reduced rate to specific kinds of employees, with the permission of the Director. The specific kinds of employees include those having a considerably small capacity for work due to a mental or physical disability, those in a probationary period, those receiving vocational training for the basic skills and knowledge and those engaging in light and easy work (Article 7).

§9. Guarantee of Payment on the Employer's Insolvency

244. The wage claims of employees are protected by the already-described regulations on the payment of wages: in cash, in full and by direct and periodical payment. Thus, the delayed payment of wages can be punished by a fine. Also, the Labour Inspection Office requires the employer to pay unpaid wages through administrative guidance. But, of course, it is possible that the enterprise may go bankrupt and leave delayed wages unpaid. The Civil Code gives persons possessing wage claims a general preference over all the assets of the enterprise.[104] In addition, the Civil Code gives agricultural employees a special preference in the products of their labour for one year's wages and factory employees for the last three months' wages.[105] However, a general preference is inferior to a special preference or to a security right over specific property (especially, mortgages), and both preferences cannot be carried out against moveable property which has been transferred to a purchaser. The Bankruptcy Act, the Civil Rehabilitation Act and the Corporate Reorganization Act provide some protection for payment of wages.

245. First, the Bankruptcy Act under which a claim for salary by an employee of the bankrupt entity for the three-month period preceding the commencement of bankruptcy proceedings, or for retirement allowance for a like period, or for part of the salary and/or retirement allowance will be considered a claim on the bankrupt's estate, and will be paid at any time before other claims (Articles 141, 151 and 98). Other wage claims that are, as stated above, given preferences under the Civil Code have status of preferential claims among bankruptcy dividends. Likewise, under the Civil Rehabilitation Act, a claim for salary or retirement allowance preceding the commencement of rehabilitation proceedings will be a claim with general priority and may be paid at any time without going through civil rehabilitation proceedings (Article 122). Also, under the Corporate Reorganization Act, a claim by an employee for salary and employee for the six-month period will be common benefit claim and may be paid at any time without going through corporate reorganization proceeding. A claim for retirement allowance, the higher amount of either the total amount of the employee's salary for the six-month period or one-third of the total amount of retirement allowance will be a common benefits claim.

246. Furthermore, in practice, as most enterprise bankruptcies are carried out through private settlement procedures to avoid complex and lengthy legal measures, it is very difficult to protect payment of wages. Accordingly, the SWPA of 1976 introduced special measures under which the government must pay unpaid wages in the place of the employer who has become unable to pay owing to serious financial difficulties or even bankruptcy.

247. Under SWPA, an employee who has been covered by the Workers' Accident Compensation Insurance and engaged in the given undertaking for more than one year will be entitled to government payment of unpaid wages in the place of his employer in one of the following circumstances: where the employer has been adjudged to be bankrupt or has received a preliminary order for special liquidation; where the employer has received a preliminary decision in a rehabilitation procedure, a preliminary order in a composition or a preliminary order in a reorganization; or where, if the undertaking concerned is a medium and small enterprise, the suspension of the employer's business activities is confirmed by the LSIO as being without hope of resumption (SWPA, Article 7, Enforcement Order, Article 2; Enforcement Ordinance, Article 8). The government payment covers 80% of the

104. Articles 306 and 308.
105. The Civil Code, Arts 311 and 324.

total amount of the employee's unpaid periodic pay running from the day after the six months preceding the termination to the day before his claim is made and is subject to the upper and lower limits. The upper limit varies according to the employee's age. It is JPY 3,700,000 for those 45 years old and older, JPY 2,20,000 for 30 years old but under 45, and JPY 1,10,000 for those under 30 (Enforcement Order, Article 4).

§10. Remuneration During Time-Off

I. Suspension Allowances

248. If the employer is responsible for causing a suspension of business, he/she shall pay an allowance equivalent to at least 60% of the average wage to the employees who cannot work because of such suspension (LSA, Article 16). Theoretically, the employer is liable to pay the full wage under the Civil Code, Article 536, paragraph 2, if work becomes impossible because of his negligence or intention. Thus, the purpose of the suspension allowance is to guarantee 60% of the average wage as a minimum with sanction of fine and allow employees to claim the rest of their wages using ordinary civil law procedure. At the same time, the legal precedents have tended to interpret the employer's liability to pay suspension allowances more broadly than under the Civil Code. For instance, closure of a factory because of financial difficulties, a lack of materials caused by a strike held by another union and a strike in the supplying company are a few examples of cases in which it was held that the employer should pay a suspension allowance. In all these cases, if the employer has paid a suspension allowance and then been found liable in the Civil Code to pay the full wages, he is obliged to pay the difference between the full wages and the amount already paid in a suspension allowance.

II. Accidents at Work and Occupational Diseases

249. During a period of incapacity for work caused by an industrial accident or occupational disease, the employer must pay the employee 60% of the average wage as 'non-work compensation'. The employer who fails to pay this allowance is liable to punishment by imprisonment or fine, although the amount will be actually paid as a benefit under the WACIA of 1947 which covers all employees. If the employer is found to be liable for the accident under civil law, the employee is entitled to claim the difference between his full wages and the amount of compensation paid for the damage caused by the accident.

III. Leave of Absence

250. Besides the annual paid holidays already mentioned, there are five different sorts of leave of absence to which the employee is legally entitled. These are leave for childbirth, menstruation, childcare, family care and time off work to carry out official duties. The leave for childbirth and menstruation will be described in Part II, Chapter 6. Leaves for childcare and family care are provided for by the CFLA of 1995. The contents of the CFLA are explained in Part II, Chapter 6, section 8.

251. The employer must give the employee leave of absence during working hours to exercise his franchise and other civil rights and to execute his public duties, at the request of the employee (LSA, Article 7). Whether this time off is with or without pay depends completely on each company's *shugyo-kisoku* or collective agreement, depending on the length of the absence. For instance, a short absence from work in order to vote is permitted without a wage cut, while a longer leave of absence (necessitated by election to public office or even to the legislature) will be without pay. In most enterprises, the latter situation will be treated as a reason for suspension (*see* the next section).

252. Most companies provide various kinds of leave of absence: sick leave, leave for marriage, for the funeral of a family member, for union activities and for other reasons with the permission of the management. Sick leave of a few days is allowed without a doctor's certificate. The right to short periods of leave to undertake union activities may be provided for by collective agreement. Longer leave for full-time union officials is treated as a reason for suspension (*see* section 11 *below*). Such leave is only given without pay, as otherwise it would be regarded as giving financial assistance to the union fund and this is prohibited as an unfair labour practice (*see* Part II, Chapter 7). Other leaves of absence – including those guaranteed by law can be given with or without pay depending on the agreement, or often on provisions of the *shugyo-kisoku*. In many companies, wages are not deducted for a short period of illness, especially in the case of a monthly paid employee. During sick leave and maternity leave, employees receive approximately 60% of their average wages for the Health Insurance scheme which covers all employees (the Health Insurance Act, Articles 45 and 50).

§11. Suspension Period

253. The notion of suspending the employment contract is not very widespread in Japanese industrial relations. Instead, most enterprises have a system called the suspension period, during which the contract continues to be in force except for work and wage payment. The suspension period is a period during which the employee is released from the obligation to work and wages are not paid or only partly paid. Thus, the difference between this period and the leave of absence is not very clear, except that they are stipulated in a different way and suspension is usually for a longer period.

254. There are two kinds of suspension periods. One is a period of incapacity for work which the employer tolerates without dismissing the employee. Such a period may be when the employee is ill or injured and unable to work when he becomes a union official when he undertakes full-time training or study (even abroad), or in other special circumstances. Except in cases of suspension due to illness and to training or study, the suspended employee is not paid. In cases of suspension due to illness, wages are often not paid at all and rarely paid in full but sometimes paid in part, depending on the reason and the length of the period. For instance, if the employee is ill, he gets 80% of his wages for the first six months, 60% for the next six months and so on. The maximum period tolerated is also different – depending on the reason – but it can be as much as two or three years. Where the employee who suffered injury or contracted a disease resulting from employment is entitled to temporary disability benefit equivalent to 60% of his wages and special suspension benefit equivalent to 20% of his wages during a period of disability under the WACIA, Articles 22-2 and 23. During the period when the employee cannot work and thirty days after this period, the employer is prohibited from discharging the employee (LSA, Article 19), unless there are certain special circumstances under the Act. If the employee suffered injury or contracted a disease resulting from other than employment, then he is entitled to sickness benefit equivalent to 60% of his daily standard wages under the Health Insurance Act, Article 99. An employer can suspend his employee for his illness only where his illness is too serious to perform his duty. However, in Japanese companies, where an employee's duty is usually not narrowly specified because of prevailing hiring practices, suspension is often not allowed if the employer has some alternative work available to the employee. Legal problems may arise as to whether the employment contract then ends altogether or revives fully. In cases of suspension for ill health, many *shugyo-kisokus* or collective agreements provide for the expiration of the suspension period as a cause for dismissal or automatic termination. If it is a cause of dismissal, the law of dismissal will apply to it. Therefore, the employer must give notice of dismissal and have a substantial burden of proof to justify dismissal (*see* the next chapter). On the other hand, where the expiration of the suspension period is a cause of automatic termination of employment, the employee cannot use protective provisions and the doctrine of abusive dismissal to dispute the effect of employment termination. However, even though the expiration of suspension period is a cause of automatic termination of employment, some courts have held that the employer who insists upon the effect of automatic termination must prove the reason for his refusal of reinstatement at the end of the suspension period. One court held that 'the employer has to prove that the degree of ill-health can justify dismissal having regards to all circumstances including prospect of recovery of ill-health, availability of places for reinstatement, etc.'[106]

255. Another kind of suspension period is imposed as a disciplinary action or to decide on a punishment. Suspension as a disciplinary action should be laid down in the *shugyo-kisoku* with precise reasons and degrees (*see* Part I, Chapter 2). Suspension while deciding on disciplinary action is used when the employee is being prosecuted for a crime which would justify a disciplinary action – such as disciplinary dismissal – and the employer waits to hear the decision of the Court. The legal effect of a suspension while deciding on disciplinary action is highly debatable because it is usually accompanied by a wage decrease or wage cut. Such a suspension is not a

106. The *Air France* case, the Tokyo District Court in 1984, RH, No. 423, p. 23.

disciplinary action in itself but is still as disadvantageous as a severe disciplinary action. This is true especially where criminal proceedings before the court are prolonged. Therefore, the court will examine the appropriateness of suspension while deciding on disciplinary action, from the viewpoint of probability that the employee's continuation to work may damage workplace discipline or customers' confidence in the employer or that court proceedings may considerably disrupt the employee's work. This probability has been evaluated according to causes of prosecution, the employee's job and position in his workplace, and all other circumstances.[107]

107. The *Nihon Yakin* case, the Fukuoka District Court in 1975, RH, No. 219, p. 49.

Chapter 5. The Termination of Employment

§1. Job Security in General

256. Article 27, section 1 of the Constitution provides for the right to work as a fundamental human right of the Japanese people. This is interpreted as meaning that the Government has a political obligation to try and provide jobs for all those who are able and willing to work. The obligation to work imposed by the same provision is interpreted as meaning that, with regard to those who are able to work but who do not want to, the Government has no obligation to assure them of the 'wholesome and cultured life' which is guaranteed by Article 25 of the Constitution. Under Article 27, the government should take the necessary measures to guarantee jobs, such as public employment agencies, public works to provide work for the unemployed, a training scheme to improve the workers' chances of getting better jobs and finally an unemployment insurance scheme. All these measures are put into effect by a number of laws including the Employment Measures Act of 1966, the ESA of 1947, the Vocational Ability Development and Promotion Act of 1969, the EIA of 1974 and the Local Employment Promotion Act of 1987 and other special laws to promote the employment of the old and the handicapped and to give job security to workers in certain industries such as ports and coal-mining.

257. Apart from the above-mentioned governmental obligation, Article 27 of the Constitution is also interpreted so as to make the promotion of job security a matter of public order. Thus, the decisions of the courts often proclaim that the employer must respect this public order and not abuse his right of dismissal. Reflecting the extraordinary nature of the dismissal of regular employees under the lifetime employment practice (although this practice is losing its significance as a dominant practice), the courts have developed a rather strict attitude towards dismissal, requiring 'just cause' even for dismissal with notice. Another important characteristic of the law on dismissal in Japan is that the courts always declare the dismissal null and void and affirm the applicant worker's status as an employee in the defendant company whenever they find it to be unreasonable in the circumstances of the case (*see* Doctrine of Abusive Dismissal, *infra*). The result is that the dismissed employee is always reinstated unless he prefers to claim damages instead. This is mainly due to the lifetime employment practice. Under this practice, it is difficult for the dismissed employee to find another employment equivalent to his previous employment since many companies generally recruit few people other than new school leavers. Even if the dismissed employee finds alternative employment, he often has to start over in a less favourable job.

§2. Ending the Contract Other Than by Dismissal

I. Extinction of a Party

258. The contract of employment is regarded as a personal contract and the death of the employee or, in the case of an individual employer, of the employer, brings the contract automatically to an end. In the case of a corporate employer, the death of the representative does not affect the contractual relationship. Only the extinction of a company as a legal entity will terminate the contract of employment. Therefore, the bankruptcy or insolvency of a company does not automatically terminate the contract. Until the final dissolution of a company, a contract of employment can be terminated by dismissal. It is generally considered that the merger of companies does not terminate the contracts of employment between the extinguished company and its employees because the successor company inherits all the rights and obligations of the extinguished company. By contrast, when a business is transferred from one company to another, it is usually considered that the contracts of employment are not transferred to the latter company unless the transfer of those contracts is agreed to by the agreement to transfer business and consented to by the employees in question. Therefore, this raises the problem of how to protect the employees' employment. Many courts have held that the parties to the transfer of business are usually deemed to have agreed to succeed in employment contracts of all the employees.[108] Details of this and related problems will be discussed below (*see* Merger and Split of Company and Transfer of Business, *infra*).

II. The Expiry of a Fixed-Term Contract

259. There are a number of temporary employees who are employed under fixed-term contracts (*see* Part I, Chapter 1). As a general principle, a contract for a fixed term automatically terminates at the expiry of such a term. The significance of a fixed-term contract is dual. On the one hand, the employer cannot lawfully dismiss the employee during the term unless any unavoidable causes exist (Civil Code, Article 627). Thus, a fixed-term contract has the function of employment security. On the other hand, the employee cannot unilaterally terminate the employment (*see below*). Thus, a fixed-term contract also has the function of inducing the employee to stay in the company. It was considered that the latter function might lead to forced labour. Therefore, Article 14 of the LSA provides that a contract of employment shall not be made for a period longer than three years, except for the completion of a specific task. However, the maximum period may be five years for newly employed workers with highly specialized knowledge, technology etc. or for workers aged 60 or older. Except in these cases, even if the parties made a contract stated to be for five years, the contract is only effective for three years (Article 13) and will terminate at the end of that period. The maximum period prescribed by Article 14 was one year without any exception until 1998. However, according to deregulation policy, the 1998 Amendment introduced the exceptional maximum period of three years for workers with highly specialized knowledge, technology etc. or for workers aged 60 or older and the 2003 Amendment extended one year as the principle and three years as the exception to respectively three years and five years.

260. LSA, Article 14 excludes not only the newly employed workers with highly specialized knowledge, technology, etc. and 60 or older workers but also the

108. The *Harima Tekko* case, the Osaka High Court in 1963, RMS, Vol. 14, No. 2, p. 439.

completion of a specific task from the application of the rule of 'a fixed term – no more than three years'. Therefore, it is legal to conclude a contract of a certain duration over three years if that is the period necessary, for instance, to construct a bridge. However, it is not clear whether Article 14 allows the employer to conclude a contract with an uncertain duration of over one year. An administrative interpretation affirms it on condition that such a contract with an uncertain duration must not last so long that it limits the employee's freedom.[109]

261. On the other hand, it is considered that the employment of a certain employee is firmly secured for the employee during the term of a fixed-term employment contract. The Civil Code, Article 628 provides that, even where the parties fix the term of the contract, either party may instantly discharge the contract if there are unavoidable circumstances. Accordingly, this has been interpreted in such a way that the employer cannot dismiss the employee during the term without unavoidable circumstances. However, a few courts have held that Article 628 does not prohibit the parties from agreeing to widen the meaning of 'unavoidable circumstances'. Such a change purposes to secure the right to discharge if there are 'unavoidable circumstances'. As a result, in order to clarify previous judicial interpretations, the LCA of 2007, Article 17 (1) provides that an employer may not dismiss a worker during the term of the contract unless there are 'unavoidable circumstances'. Accordingly, an individual agreement that allows for dismissal during the term in the absence of 'unavoidable circumstances' is not valid.

262. Where the employee continued to render service after the expiration of a fixed term and the employer did not raise any objection to it, it should be considered that the parties entered into a new contract on the same terms as before (Civil Code, Article 629). In this case, leading theories and judicial opinions have held that it is converted to a contract of indefinite duration. However, there is an influential view that it should not be construed as converted to a contract of indefinite duration, mainly because it is very difficult to dismiss the employee under contracts of indefinite duration because of the law of abusive dismissal.[110]

263. Contracts for a fixed term are often renewed several times or even many times for economic reasons. Fixed-term contracts provide employers with a very convenient means to adjust the quantity of the workforce in response to fluctuation of business demands. On the other hand, they put workers on an unsecured position of employment. This might be regarded as the employer's evasion of the law of dismissal. To strike a balance between the interests of employers and fixed-term employees, the courts have developed a flexible rule to deal with the termination of fixed-term contracts on the expiry of their terms. The court imposes the legal analogy of the law of abusive dismissal on the refusal to renew the employee's contract on the grounds of the expiration of its term (*see infra*). One of the leading cases concerning repeated renewal of a fixed-term contract is the Supreme Court's *Hitachi*

109. Ministry of Labour, *Zentei Shinpan Rodokijunho Jo* (Labour Standards Law, New Edition Vol. 1), *Romugyoseikenkyujo*, 1994, p. 196.
110. Sugeno & Yamakawa, *supra*, p. 819.

Medico case where the appellant was employed as a 'temporary employee' under a written contract for a term of two months. The contract was renewed five times; the 'temporary employees' scheme' was made for the purpose of adjusting the workforce in response to the state of the demand for their products. The standards used to recruit 'temporary employees' were not very demanding, compared to those for regular employees. The company's policy was to engage 'temporary employees' in simple work. The Supreme Court addressed this question in the following way: the 'temporary employees' in the factory in question were not employed for temporary work such as seasonal work or work for particular products. Thus, their employment was expected to continue to some extent. The appellant's contract was renewed five times. According to these facts, legal regulation on the analogy of the law of dismissal should be applied to the refusal to renew his contract on the grounds of the expiration of its term.[111] It may be said that by using the analogy of the law of dismissal, the courts have imposed certain legal restrictions on the employer's refusal to renew a fixed-term contract based on the inference of a tacit agreement with his employee or the employee's reasonable expectation of continuous employment.[112] More recently, a lower court extended this logic to a taxi driver who had reasonably expected to be continuously employed at the beginning. In this case, the defendant taxi company has never refused to renew fixed-term contracts of so-called temporary drivers and had converted them to contracts of indefinite duration. The court held that it was in contravention of the contractual duty of good faith and therefore impermissible for the defendant to refuse to renew the plaintiff driver on the grounds of the expiration of the term of his contract.[113]

264. The above-described application of the analogy of law of dismissal, more precisely the law of abusive dismissal to fixed-term employment contracted was accommodated by the LCA in 2012. Thus, Article 19 of the LCA provides:

> Where (i) the status of a fixed term employment contract should not be regarded in general societal terms as substantively different from an employment contract without a definite term as a result of repeated renewals of the contract; or (ii) the continuation of employment even after the expiration of the term of a fixed-term employment contract should be reasonably expected. The fixed-term employment contract is deemed as renewed if there is no justifiable reason for the non-renewal or it is deemed to be socially acceptable.

265. However, recently there have been an increasing number of cases where employers have set a renewal limit for fixed-term contracts in advance, or, after several renewals, have inserted non-renewal clauses into renewal contracts stating that the contract will not be renewed the next time. In such cases, courts take into account all the relevant circumstances of the case and make a judgment on whether the employees' expectation of renewal is still reasonable. For instance, even if an

---

111. The *Hitachi Medico* case, the Supreme Court in 1986, RH, No. 486, p. 6.
112. The *Toshiba Yanagimachi* case, the Supreme Court in 1974, SMS, Vol. 28, No. 5, p. 927.
113. The *Ryujin Taxi* case, the Osaka High Court in 1991, RH, No. 581, p. 36.

employment limit was specified at the time of concluding the contract if the employer's words or actions lead to an expectation of continued employment beyond that limit, the employee's reasonable expectation of continued employment may arise. Similarly, even if an employer unilaterally specifies a renewal limit or non-renewal clause in the contract at the time of renewal, if a reasonable expectation of continued employment has already arisen, this will not automatically be lost unless the employee agrees. On the other hand, if an employee agrees to such clauses, it will be rather difficult to deny that the employee will lose his or her reasonable expectation of continued employment. However, even in such a case, careful examination is required to determine whether the agreement was based on the employee's free will.

266. In addition, the LCA introduced a provision (Article 18) which is influenced by EU law regarding the conversion of a fixed-term employment contract to a contract without a definite term. That is to allow an employee employed over five years in total under a fixed-term employment contract to convert his contract to one without a definite term by addressing such a request to his employer. This five-year period may be extended to ten years for certain researchers and university lecturers. Also, this period may be extended under certain requirements regarding persons reemployed after mandatory retirement as well as employees who have expertise and earn wages more than a certain amount under the Special Measures Act on Workers with Expert Knowledge Employed by Fixed-term Contract, which was enacted in 2014. Further, where there is a period of inactivity exceeding six months during which no employment contract was in effect, any duration of fixed-term employment contracts before such a blank period will not be counted into the total period of employment. This blank period may become a contract term shorter than one year. The working conditions of those employees shall remain the same as those under their employment contract before the conversion unless otherwise stipulated.

III. The Occurrence of Events Agreed to as Causes of Termination

267. Whether or not an agreement to terminate the contract can be concluded beforehand is a controversial question. Such provisions are often stipulated in the *shugyo-kisoku* or collective agreement. Most typically, the expiration of a suspension period of ill-health and the attainment of compulsory retirement age are very often stipulated as causes of automatic termination of employment. The former has been discussed in Part I, Chapter 4. Like the expiration of a suspension period, compulsory retirement age is stipulated either as a cause of dismissal (so-called *teinen-kaiko*, i.e., dismissal at retirement age) or as a cause of automatic termination of employment (so-called *teinen-taishoku*, i.e., resignation at retirement age). The law of dismissal will apply to *teinen-kaiko* but not to *teinen-taishoku*. One of the problem issues has been whether it is lawful to provide for the attainment of compulsory retirement age as a cause of dismissal or of automatic termination of employment. Thus, some academics argue that the compulsory retirement age should be unlawful since it ignores differences in expertise and aptitude of individual workers and therefore violates the constitutional provisions of people's right to live (Constitution,

Article 25) and right to work (Article 27).[114] The Supreme Court, however, stated that while older workers' ability generally decreases, their wages conversely increase; the provision for compulsory retirement is intended to keep the structure and operation of an enterprise proper and therefore it cannot be unreasonable.[115] Another problem is whether a system requiring retirement at a certain young age is valid. However, Article 8 of the OPESA of 1971 (as amended in 1994) provides that a compulsory retirement age must not be younger than 60 except for those occupations which the Ministry of Labour Ordinance lists as difficult jobs for older persons. Moreover, Article 9 (as amended in 2004) requires the employer who has a compulsory retirement scheme providing for a compulsory retirement age of 60 or more but less than 65 to take measures either to raise that retirement age, to continue employing workers who want to continue working or to remove the retirement age.

IV. Termination by Agreement

268. A termination to which both parties agree is not a dismissal and is not subject to the law of dismissal. Similar to the conclusion of a contract, there is freedom to terminate a contract of employment by agreement. In theory, the agreement of termination is formed when one party accepts an offer which the other party has made involving the termination of a contract. In practice, an employer often invites an employee to make an offer of termination agreement. After having made such an offer, the employee sometimes contests its effectiveness in a lawsuit. In such cases, the courts often hold that an agreement of termination is void because of mistake, duress or mental reservation or that an employee's offer to terminate has been effectively revoked before the employer accepts it. The reason why an employer often tries to get his or her employee's agreement to terminate employment is to avoid any future dispute about the effectiveness of termination based on the law of dismissal.

V. Resignation

269. A resignation is a termination of the contract of employment by the employee. The employee may lawfully terminate a contract of employment at any time without any reason by giving two-week notice if the contract is one without a fixed term. However, this notice period does not apply to employees who are employed under an agreement that wages are fixed by periods, for example, a month. In such a case, the notice of termination may be given only for the ensuing month and such notice shall be given during the first half of the current period

114. G. Kimura, 'Taishokusei wo Meguru Hotekimondai', 56 *Rodoho Gakkaishi*, 1984, p. 29.
115. The *Shuhoku Bus* case, the Supreme Court in 1968, SMS, Vol. 22, No. 13, p. 3459.

(Civil Code, Article 627). In contrast, a contract of a fixed term may be immediately terminated by the employee during the term only if any unavoidable cause exists. However, if such cause has arisen due to the fault of one of the parties, such party is liable for compensation for damages to the other party (Article 628).

270. There are two delicate questions concerning the resignation. One is whether the employee's submission of resignation is, in a legal sense, a notice of resignation or an offer to make an agreement to terminate an employment contract. This distinction is practically rather important. If the submission of a letter of resignation is an indication of agreement to terminate employment, many courts have held that the employee may revoke it before the employer accepts it. The courts have not treated submission of resignation as a notice of resignation unless it is evident that the employee has made a firm decision to terminate employment in any event.[116] The other important question is whether the employee has resigned or been dismissed in cases where the employee's resignation is de facto caused by the employer's conduct, such as humiliating an employee before his subordinates, imposing intolerable working conditions, giving him or her only non-substantial work, and the like. Until recently, most courts have neither established any special concept such as 'constructive dismissal' nor positively regarded the termination induced by an employer's conduct as dismissal. This seems due to the fact that dismissal is usually considered in the context of whether or not a dismissal is effective in law.

271. However, because of the structural changes in employment, there are an increasing number of cases in which the employee does not claim a judgment affirming his status as an employee but a judgment ordering damage payment. Indeed, it is clear that the employer's harassment or imposition of intolerable working conditions itself constitutes a tort (Civil Code Article 709). Thus, it is rather easy for courts to make a judgment ordering damage payment for the employee's injured feelings caused by forced resignation. The question is whether the employee may also make a claim for the loss of his wages accrued but for resignation.[117] Recent courts' decisions have affirmed this question. Indeed, several courts have accepted an employee's damages claims for wages accrued but for resignation enforced by the employee's harassment on the basis of the employer's contractual duty to provide a satisfying working environment.[118] Apart from these cases, many courts have held with regard to unfair labour practice that an employee's resignation or agreement to terminate employment is void if it is motivated by the employer's anti-union intent.[119]

116. The *Tanabe Tekkojo* case, the Osaka District Court in 1973, *Rodokeizai Hanrei Sokuho*, No. 819, p. 22.
117. F. Komiya, *Hogaku Seminar*, 1996, No. 493, p. 94.
118. The *Kyoto Sexual Harassment* case, the Kyoto District Court in 1997, RH, No. 716, p. 49; the *Efupiko* case, the Shimozuma Branch, the Mito District Court in 1999, RH, No. 763, p. 7.
119. The *Iizima Sangyo* case, the Tokyo High Court in 1976, RMS, Vol. 27, No. 3/4, p. 243.

§3. STATUTORY REGULATION

I. Notice of Dismissal

272. The Civil Code provides the following rules of notice. Where a contract of employment is for a fixed term, the employer may not dismiss the employee during that period but is permitted to dismiss the employee immediately only if any unavoidable cause exists (Civil Code, Article 628). Where that cause is due to the employer's fault, the employer will be liable to the employee in terms of damages. In contrast, where a contract of employment is without a fixed term, the employer may dismiss the employee at any time without any reason by giving either two weeks' notice or wages in lieu of notice. However, where the employee is employed under an agreement of monthly pay, the notice may be given only for the ensuing month and such notice must be given during the first half of the current period (Article 627).

273. In contrast with this civil law principle, Article 20 of LSA provides that the employer must give at least thirty days' advance notice before dismissal. Exceptions to this notice requirement are where the continuance of the enterprise is made impossible by reason of some natural calamity or other unavoidable cause, and where the employer dismisses the employee for reasons for which the employee is responsible. Such exceptions are interpreted as much narrower than 'unavoidable cause' under the Civil Code (Article 628). The employer who does not give thirty days' notice shall pay money equivalent to thirty days' average wages or more. The employer may be punished by imprisonment or by a fine in violation of Article 20. The court may also order the employer to pay, in addition to the unpaid wages, an additional payment of an identical amount (Article 114). There is some conflict between judicial decisions on the effectiveness of dismissal where the employer had not given thirty days' notice. The Supreme Court however held that, unless the employer insisted on the summary effectiveness of the dismissal, the dismissal became effective either when the thirty days passed or when the employer paid money equivalent to thirty days' average wages or more.[120]

274. Article 21 of LSA excludes the application of the minimum notice requirement from the following employees: (i) those employed on a daily basis; (ii) those employed for a fixed term of no longer than two months (four months in the case of seasonal workers); (iii) those in a probationary period. However, the application does not exclude where workers coming under (i) have been employed for more than one month, where workers coming under (ii) have been employed for longer than two months (four months in the case of seasonal workers) or where those under (iii) have been employed for more than fourteen days. There are two conceivable cases in which workers coming under (ii) would have been employed for longer than the original contract period: (a) where the worker continues to work after the expiration of the contract period without the employer's objection; (b) where the worker and the employer agree to renew the contract. In the case of (a), Article 20

120. The *Hosoya Fukuso* case, the Supreme Court in 1960, SMS, Vol. 29, No. 4, p. 403.

rather than 21 applies (*see* section 1, II). There is some disagreement among academics as to whether the minimum notice requirement applies to the expiration of the contract period after the renewal in the case of (b). However, most academics agree with the view that the minimum notice requirement should apply to the expiration of a fixed-term contract where such a contract has been maintained on the premise that it is to be automatically renewed unless either party gives notice of non-renewal.

II. Other Statutory Regulation

275. In addition to all the above-described basic regulations on dismissals, there are several statutory provisions which regulate dismissals as follows. First, Article 19 of LSA prohibits an employer from dismissing an employee during a period of incapacity for work caused by an accident at work or occupational disease and within thirty days thereafter, and from dismissing a female employee during statutory leave for childbirth (i.e., six weeks before childbirth, or in cases of multiple births, fourteen weeks, and eight weeks following childbirth) and within thirty days thereafter. An employer who dismisses an employee in violation of Article 19 is subject to punitive sanctions and such dismissal is void. Article 7 of the TUA of 1949 prohibits dismissal on the grounds of trade union membership or activities. Not only does violation of Article 7 constitute an unfair labour practice and result in a remedial order by the LRC, but also the dismissal in contravention thereof is void (*see* Part II, Chapter 7). Article 3 of LSA prohibits discriminatory dismissal on the grounds of the nationality, race, creed or social status of an employee. Article 9 of the EEOA of 1985 prohibits an employer from dismissing female employees on the grounds of marriage, pregnancy, childbirth or taking childbirth leave. Citing marriage, pregnancy or childbirth as a reason for the retirement of female employees is also illegal. Such discriminatory dismissal will be void. Furthermore, Article 14 of the Constitution prohibits discrimination on the grounds of race, creed, sex, social status or family origin and dismissal on any of these grounds is void without justification because it is in contravention of public policy and good morals (Civil Code, Article 90). Clearly, discriminatory dismissals are rather widely regulated by statutory provisions. LSA (Article 104), the Industrial Safety & Health Act (Article 97) and the SWPA (Article 14) prohibit an employer from dismissing an employee on the ground that he or she has reported the employer's violation of these Acts to the administrative offices. Such dismissal is also void.

§4. Regulation Through Work Rules (Shugyo-kisoku) and Collective Agreements

276. The *shugyo-kisoku* usually provides for a disciplinary dismissal as well as an ordinary dismissal. A disciplinary dismissal (*chokai-kaiko*) is a punishment for the employee's wrongdoing for the purpose of maintaining discipline in the workplace (*see* Part I, Chapter 2, section 1). Article 89 of LSA requires the employer to include, together with terms and conditions of employment, matters pertaining to termination of employment and, if disciplinary measures are set up, matters pertaining to their nature and limits. It is generally considered that an employer may take disciplinary action against his employee only if so stipulated by the *shugyo-kisoku*, and therefore the causes of disciplinary action are limited to those specified in the *shugyo-kisoku*.[121] This means that a disciplinary dismissal without any specified cause is void. The *shugyo-kisoku* often requires detailed procedures before a disciplinary committee prior to the disciplinary dismissal. There is disagreement among the courts as to the question of whether the disciplinary dismissal contravening such procedures is void. As far as an ordinary dismissal is concerned, opinions are divided as to whether the causes of it are limited to those specified in the *shugyo-kisoku*. However, even if they are not so limited, a dismissal which is not based on the *shugyo-kisoku* is inevitably presumed to be abusive under the doctrine of abusive dismissal as mentioned below. Another important measure to regulate dismissal is a collective agreement. Many collective agreements stipulate the causes and procedures for an ordinary dismissal as well as a disciplinary dismissal. The courts have held that a dismissal which is not based on the reasons specified in the collective agreement is void.[122] Most courts have also held that a dismissal which has not gone through consultation procedures provided under collective bargaining agreements is void.

§5. Doctrine of Abusive Dismissal

I. Regulation

A. *Basic Rules*

277. Japan did not enact special statutory provisions requiring just cause for dismissal until 2003 although there have been demands for, and discussions concerning, the enactment of such provisions. The regulation of dismissal has, however, been developed by courts applying the principle of the abuse of rights as provided for by Article 1(3) of the Civil Code. According to the Supreme Court's decision in the *Nihon Shokuen Company* case, 'if dismissal is found to be without any rational reason and not to be permissible with regard to the common sense of society, such dismissal is void because of abuse of the employer's right of dismissal'.[123] The courts have also been very reluctant to find dismissal valid unless the reason for it is very serious with regard to all the circumstances. A leading case is the Supreme Court's decision in the *Kochi Hoso* case.[124] In this case, the company dismissed the plaintiff, an announcer, who overslept and missed his ten-minute news program on two occasions within two weeks. As a result, the news broadcast was cancelled on one occasion and shortened on the other. The Supreme Court stated as follows:

121. The *Kokutetsu Sapporo* case, the Supreme Court in 1979, SMS, Vol. 33, No. 6, p. 647.
122. For the effect of collective agreement in general, refer to Part II, Ch. 5, §3.
123. The *Nihon Shokuen* case, the Supreme Court in 1975, SMS, Vol. 29, No. 4, p. 456.
124. The *Kochi Hoso* case, the Supreme Court in 1977, RH, No. 268, p. 17.

(The announcer's failure in his duty comes into the category of an 'ordinary dismissal' prescribed in the shugyo-kisoku of the company). But even where there is the reason of an 'ordinary dismissal', the employer is not necessarily entitled to dismiss the employee for that reason. Even in such a case, the dismissal is void because of the abuse of the employer's right to dismiss where it is regarded to be considerably unreasonable in the circumstances of the case and therefore is not permissible with regard to the common sense of society. In this case, it may well be considered that the dismissal is not permissible with regard to social justice.

278. This case is important not only in order to understand the Japanese standard for determining the abusiveness of dismissal but also to understand the position of the burden of proof in abusive dismissal litigation. It is generally considered that unless the employer proves a permissible reason for dismissal, the dismissal will be held to be abusive and therefore void. Furthermore, the employer is required to prove the facts to substantiate his reasons for dismissal. Once the employer discharges his burden, the employee will take on the burden of proving that the dismissal is still impermissible with regard to the common sense of society according to the circumstances of the case.

279. Around 1993 when companies' restructuring began on a large scale after the collapse of the Japanese 'bubble economy', the fierce discussion on enactment of general regulation of dismissal started between both sides of industry. The employers' side mainly argued that the test of abusiveness applied by courts under the law of abusive dismissal was too severe for employers to comply with in order to effectuate their business under competitive circumstances. On the other hand, the workers' side mainly argued that the law of abusive dismissal was too fragile to maintain because it was not provided for by a statutory provision. Their disagreement also concerned the standards of abusiveness, the coverage of the law, the burden of proof, the remedy for the dismissed and the court procedure. However, that long discussion only resulted in inserting a new provision of abusive dismissal into the LSA in 2003. Thus, the LSA, Article 18-2 provided 'if dismissal is found to be without any rational reason and not to be permissible with regard to the common sense of society, such dismissal is void because of abuse of the employer's right of dismissal'. This provision was transplanted in the LCA in 2007 (Article 16). It is generally considered that the court practices concerning the law of abusive dismissal might not be substantially affected by enactment of Article 18-2 although the existence of the law of abusive dismissal became more visible to the people.

280. Many courts have stated that it was not essential for the employer to give the employee a reason for dismissal, and therefore that the employer was entitled to allege a reason other than that indicated to the employee at the time of dismissal. However, there is some conflict among judicial views as to whether the employer was entitled to rely on a reason of which he was not aware at the time of the dismissal. However, as far as disciplinary dismissals are concerned, the Supreme Court has decided that the employer is not entitled to rely on a reason for which he was unaware at dismissal.[125] It is still not clear whether this ruling can be applied to ordinary dismissal cases.

281. The rules which the courts have applied to a disciplinary dismissal are almost the same as those applied to an ordinary dismissal. Even if there is a type of conduct which constitutes one of those stipulated by the *shugyo-kisoku* as a cause for a disciplinary dismissal, the courts have further determined whether the disciplinary dismissal is abusive in certain circumstances. Thus, the Supreme Court held in the *Daihatsu Kogyo* case that the employer's disciplinary action was void because of abuse of the employer's rights, 'where it is found to be without any rational basis and not to be permissible with regard to the common sense of society, having regard to the circumstances of the case'.[126] This ruling is reflected in the current Article 25 of the LCA as follows: If an employer may take disciplinary action against an employee, and such disciplinary action lacks objectively reasonable grounds and is not found appropriate in general societal terms in light of the characteristics and mode of the act committed by the employee pertaining to such disciplinary action and any other circumstances, such disciplinary order is being treated as an abusive of rights and is invalid. It is generally considered that even in a case of a disciplinary dismissal, non-disclosure of the reason for it does not automatically make the disciplinary dismissal void. However, the Supreme Court held that, in order to determine the abusiveness of a disciplinary dismissal, the court could take into consideration only matters which the employer knew of at the time of dismissal.[127]

282. Even if an employee's conduct constitutes grounds for disciplinary dismissal, if it also justifies grounds for ordinary dismissal, the employer may choose ordinary dismissal rather than disciplinary dismissal. However, when an employer expresses its intention to issue a disciplinary dismissal, there is a question as to whether this can be recognized as valid to the extent that it is an ordinary dismissal. Many court decisions deny its effectiveness as an ordinary dismissal. This is because of disciplinary dismissal and ordinary dismissal, so it cannot be interpreted that an intention to disciplinary dismissal includes an intention to ordinary dismissal.

B. Just Cause

283. Rational reasons which may justify an ordinary dismissal under the doctrine of abusive dismissal can be roughly divided into four types: (i) misconduct, (ii) incompetence, (iii) economic reasons, and (iv) requirement of union shop agreement. Among these causes, (iii) will be discussed in the next paragraph and (iv) in Part II, Chapter 2. (i) may also be a reason for a disciplinary dismissal. This means

125. The *Yamaguchi Kanko* case, the Supreme Court in 1996, RH, No. 708, p. 31.
126. The *Daihatsu Kogyo* case, the Supreme Court in 1983, RH, No. 415, p. 16.
127. The *Yamaguchi Kanko* case, *supra*, the Supreme Court in 1997, RH, No. 708, p. 31.

that an ordinary dismissal will sometimes perform one of the functions of disciplinary action. However, a higher degree of culpability on the employee's part is generally required in disciplinary dismissal cases than in ordinary dismissal cases, on the grounds that a disciplinary dismissal often deprives the employee of all or part of the retirement allowance which would otherwise be paid.

284. Causes which may justify a disciplinary dismissal include falsification of one's past employment record at hiring, neglecting contractual duties, violation of job-related orders or workplace discipline, criminal activities, working for a competing company, etc. (*see* Part I, Chapter 1, section 2, II). When the courts determine if it was abusive for the employer to have dismissed (or taken a disciplinary dismissal against) the employee, they have generally taken into consideration the following factors: the size and type of the company, the position which the company occupies in the business community, the nature and extent of damages, the nature of the employee's misconduct, the extent of the employee's repentance after committing misconduct, the employee's history of misconduct or work-performance, the employee's occupation and position in the company and a comparison with disciplinary measures taken against other employees for the same and similar misconduct. As to (ii), 'incompetence' includes incapacity, lack or loss of skills or qualifications, etc. As far as dismissals for incompetence are concerned, judicial decisions indicate that, before dismissing an employee, the employer has to ascertain whether or not the employee shows a total lack of ability to work or an incorrigibly bad attitude towards his or her work. In order to do so, the employer is usually required to transfer the employee to a workplace which is more suitable to him and which may give him cause for reflection.

C. *Dismissal for Economic Reasons*

285. The employer's economic situation may constitute a rational reason for dismissal. However, dismissal for such a reason is also subject to the question of whether it is permissible with regard to the common sense of society. Since there is no fault on the part of the employees in cases of dismissal for economic reasons, the courts have intervened actively in disputes concerning these dismissals. The courts have developed four criteria for determining whether dismissal for economic reasons is valid. Those criteria are (i) whether there was a genuine financial need to reduce the workforce, (ii)whether the employer made a reasonable effort to avoid dismissal, (iii) whether the employer bargained or consulted with the unions, and (iv) whether the standards by which he selected the employees for dismissal were reasonable and whether the employees were in fact selected in accordance with that standard.[128] Regarding criterion (i), the courts decided whether it was probable that the company would have fallen into severe financial difficulties unless it reduced the workforce. Under criterion (ii), the courts look into whether the employer implemented measures such as voluntary retirement, transfer, or reductions in the number of temporary or part-time employees. With regard to criterion (iii), no matter

128. The *Toyo Sanso* case, the Tokyo High Court in 1979, RMS, Vol. 30, No. 5, p. 1002.

whether or not there is a collective agreement requiring the employer to consult with the union prior to dismissal, the courts hold that dismissal is void if the employer has failed to consult with the union. As to criterion (iv), if the employer uses an unreasonable standard or unreasonably departs from the standard used in selecting employees for dismissal, the dismissal is held to be void. However, since there is no rigid rule such as the American seniority rule, the courts have had difficulty in deciding whether a particular standard is unreasonable or not.

II. Remedial Rules

286. When the courts find that the employee's case is abusive under the doctrine of abusive dismissal, they usually deliver a judgment affirming his status as an employee in the defendant's company, and order the defendant to pay the unpaid wages, plus interest, between the date of dismissal and the date of final oral argument before the court, and order continuation of monthly payment accruing each month after the date of final oral argument until the issuance of the judgment. Provisional execution for payment is also usually admitted because without such an order the court's judgment ordering the employer to pay wages is not enforceable on appeal to the higher court. The sum of unpaid wages is subject to reduction for earnings from other employment in the period between the plaintiff's dismissal and the date ending oral argument (Civil Code, Article 536, paragraph 2). However, any reduction for interim earnings from other employment is limited to 40% of the unpaid wages (LSA, Article 26).

287. Provisional dispositions have been widely used in disputes arising from labour and employment relations. The provisional disposition procedure is subordinate to the formal litigation procedure for the purpose of preserving the enforceability of the alleged right. In order to obtain a provisional disposition order, the applicant must show that his case is likely to have merits and that his rights are likely to be damaged without such an order. The standard of proof required in the provisional disposition procedure is lower than that in formal litigation. It is enough for the applicant to convince the judge of his allegation that his claim is likely to be real; it is not necessary to convince the judge that it is real. A case may be conducted on the basis of an inquisitorial hearing (Civil Preservation Act, Article 23).

288. In addition to a judgment affirming an employee's status and ordering unpaid wages, the courts may order on the basis of the employee's injured feelings. However, there are cases in which the courts held that the employee's injured feelings will be consoled by the decision to affirm his status as an employee and the payment of wages which are due. There have been an increasing number of cases in which courts have held that dismissal without rational reasons may constitute a tort and therefore that the employee may seek damages for injured feelings. It may be inferred in such cases that the employer failed to prove the existence of rational reasons. However, because abusive dismissal is void, the dismissed employee may not lose his right to wages accruing from his employment after dismissal if he is ready to work for the employer. Since a wage is remuneration for work, if an employee is not ready to work for his employer, the tortious dismissal does not constitute the cause of the non-payment of wages. Accordingly, a court held that the employee was not entitled to claim damages for wages which would have accrued but for dismissal.[129] Another court stated that, if the employee does not claim the status of employee on the grounds of voidance of dismissal, this should not be regarded as dismissal by his employer but as voluntary resignation and therefore damages should not be awarded.[130] However, it is the employer that breaks the relationship of mutual trust with his employee through abusive dismissal, and once the relationship has lost its binding trust, it is extremely difficult to reconstruct. This view is not seen as persuasive at all. Moreover, the question here is not the effectiveness of dismissal as a judicial act, but whether dismissal as factual conduct satisfies the conditions required to constitute a tort. Many courts have recently begun to admit damage claims for accrued wages.[131] However, the assessment of such accrued wages is necessarily speculative.

§6. Notice Requirement for Workforce Reduction

289. It should be noted that, besides the judicially developed rules of dismissal for economic reasons, there is a statutory notice requirement concerning collective termination of employment. Namely, where an employer reduces the workforce by more than thirty employees through dismissal or retirement in one establishment in any one month because of reduction of scale of operations or some other reason, he must give notice to the PESO one month prior to the date of that workforce reduction. However, where the entire reduction does not occur at the same time, notice may be given prior to the date of the last dismissal or retirement. If the employer fails to do this, he can be fined. The purpose of this requirement is to make it easy for the Government to take action, to promote the employment of redundant workers through employment security agencies and public vocational training agencies.[132]

§7. Measures for Employment Stabilization

290. In the 1970s, the government introduced a number of pieces of legislation to protect workers from dismissal for economic reasons and to promote re-training and re-employment of those hit by the recession which followed the oil crisis. In 1974 the government replaced the 30-year-old Unemployment Insurance System with the Employment Insurance System which introduced the Employment Adjustment Grant Scheme. This scheme was integrated into the Employment Stabilization

129. The *Yoshimura* case, the Tokyo District Court in 1992, RH, No. 617, p. 31.
130. The *Waiwai Land* case, the Osaka District Court in 2000, RH, No. 793, p. 49.
131. The *Informateck Company* case, the Tokyo High Court in 2008, RH. No. 978, p. 93.
132. The Employment Measures Act of 1966, Art. 21; the Enforcement Ordinance of EMA. Art. 4.

Fund System which was established in 1977 and aims to assist redundant workers by providing grants to employers who introduce various measures to prevent dismissals for economic reasons.

291. The Employment Stabilization Fund System consists of the Employment Stabilization Service and the Employment Stabilization Fund. The former aims to prevent unemployment and to correct the employment situation, to increase employment opportunities and to otherwise stabilize employment. The Employment Stabilization Fund provides the funds for the effective operation of the above services. Considering that the Employment Stabilization Service will be greatly affected by business fluctuations and that large sums will therefore be paid out during recessions while little will be spent during boom times, an Employment Stabilization Fund was set up in the Labour Insurance Special Account (Employment Accounts). The amount of money needed for the Service is accumulated in this Fund, to be effectively appropriated for the Service when necessary.

292. The Employment Stabilization Services include the following:[133]

1. Where employers have been compelled to reduce business activities due to changes in business or in the industrial structure and other economic reasons, providing assistance to employers who have put employees on temporary suspension from work or who have had workers undergo vocational training or employers who take other measures necessary for stabilizing the employment of employees. The Employment Adjustment Grant is typical of the grants based on this service and will be given to employers in the industries designated by the Minister of Health, Labour and Welfare if they are compelled to minimize business operations due to business fluctuations or a change in the industrial structure or for other economic reasons, but conduct temporary suspension from work with wages paid and provide education and/or training and transfer their employee.
2. Providing assistance to employers who take measures such as providing for leaves of absence for their employees who are compelled to terminate their employment relations so that they can prepare for obtaining other employment opportunities.
3. Providing assistance to employers who extend the employment of older workers by raising the retirement age, re-employing those who have reached the retirement age, and the like, assist older retirees in their re-employment or hire older people, and to employers who take other measures necessary for stabilizing the employment of older workers. Under this service, the following grants may be given to certain employers: grants for promoting continuous employment of older workers, grants for arranging an appropriate working environment for older workers, grants for giving workers of age 45–65 paid holidays to prepare for their future working life, and other grants.
4. Providing assistance to employers who newly employ workers by moving undertakings to areas where an increase in employment opportunities is

133. The EIA, Art. 62; the Enforcement Ordinance of EIA, Arts 102.2 and 120.

needed, to employers who employ, throughout the year, workers in areas where many seasonally unemployed workers live, and to employers who take other measures necessary for stabilizing the employment of workers in areas where improvement of the employment condition is necessary. Under this service, the following grants are available for certain employers: grants for employment creation in the designated areas, grants for promotion of mass employment creation in the designated areas, and other grants.

5. Other services, as prescribed by Ministry of Labour Ordinance, which are necessary for promoting the employment of physically disabled persons and others having difficulty in finding employment, and for stabilizing the employment of insured persons, etc. A typical example of the grants available for certain employers under this service is the grant for employment stabilization of employees responsible for family care or childcare.

§8. Regulations Regarding the End of the Contract

293. At the end of the employment contract the rights and obligations of both parties are terminated – except for those which have already been realized; that is, the worker's (this means the former employee's) right to wages for the work done and to such things as workers' accident compensation, and the worker's obligation to return any property belonging to the employer (this means the former employer) which he used in his work, such as tools, a uniform or a key for a locker. Workers also have a certain obligation after the contract has ended to respect the secrets of the employer and to avoid competing against him, which will be described in Part I, Chapter 7. Also, LSA imposes a certain obligation on the employer to protect the worker's interests after the contract has ended.

294. The employer must provide a certificate giving details of the worker's period of employment, his occupation, the type of his position in the enterprise, his wages and a reason for the termination of employment (including a reason for dismissal, when the employee is dismissed) upon the request of the worker at the end of the contract. He shall not insert in the certificate anything which the worker does not require. Furthermore, the employer shall not send any communication or put any secret mark on the certificate in conspiracy with a third party indicating the nationality, creed, social status or union activities of the worker with the intention of impending his future employment (LSA, Article 22). This is the prohibition of the blacklist. However, the employer may provide certain information about former employees if asked to do so by their new or prospective employers.

295. At the end of the contract the employer shall complete the payment of wages and return whatever reserves, bonds, savings or other funds and valuables he has which belong to the worker within seven days of the claimant asking for them (the claimant may be the bereaved family of a dead employee) (LSA, Article 23). Wages here are taken to include retirement allowances.

296. The employer must pay the necessary travelling expenses of the worker who returns home within fourteen days of the cancellation of the contract if the worker has cancelled it because the real working conditions were different from those which were specified before the contract was concluded (LSA, Article 15, paragraph 3). The employer must also pay the necessary fare in the case of minors under 18 years of age who wish to return home within fourteen days of dismissal except if they were responsible for their own dismissal and the employer has obtained authorization from the LSIO to this effect (LSA, Article 64).

§9. Merger and Split of Company and Transfer of Business

297. Where companies A and B are amalgamated into company C, company C will take over the rights and duties of companies A and B which cease to exist in consequence of such amalgamation (Companies Act, Articles 750 and 754). Therefore, company C will take over the rights and duties which the two companies have towards their employees. This means that the employees of companies A and B automatically become the employees of company C in consequence of amalgamation. Those employees, however, may terminate the contract of employment with company C if they do not want to remain as employees of company C.

298. On the other hand, there is no statutory provision for cases of transfer of business. Some courts have held that even in cases of transfer of business, the transferee company automatically takes over the status of an employer from the transferor.[134] However, this interpretation of law is not sustainable not only because there exists no statutory provisions prohibiting the transferee from refusing the employees of the transferor but also because Article 625 of the Civil Code provides that the employer cannot assign his rights to a third person without the consent of the employee. Therefore, many courts have found the existence of an implied agreement between the transferor and the transferee that the transferor takes over the transferee's status of an employer.[135] However, this also means that, if the transferee clearly rejected such succession at concluding a contract of business transfer, the employees of the transferee cannot claim for their status of an employee of the transferee.

299. What happens if the transferor dismisses all of his employees just before the business transfer and then the transferee re-employs those employees, except certain employees? The courts sometimes apply the doctrine of piercing the corporate veil to cases where the transferor company is the transferee's subsidiary and is liquidated by the transferee either if the transferor company can be regarded as a so-called empty shell case or if the transferee company has real power to control the transferor company and has an illegal purpose such as getting rid of trade union members (a so-called abuse of corporate status case). In order for the courts to treat

134. For example, the *Harima Tekko* case, the Osaka High Court in 1963, RMS, Vol. 14, No. 2, p. 439.
135. For example, the *Matsuyama Shimin Byoin* case, the Matsuyama District Court in 1965, RMS, Vol. 16, No. 3, p. 394.

a subsidiary as an empty shell, they have to find such particular factors as commingling business activities with those of the parent company, absence of separately held corporate assets, commingling of funds and other assets with those of the father corporation, failure to maintain corporate formalities and corporate minutes or adequate corporate records. Therefore, cases where courts have found 'empty shell cases' are few. A typical one of such cases is the *Kurokawa Construction Company* case. In this case, Company *A* was a member of S group of companies. All stock of Company *A* was owned by the Kurokawa Construction Company (Company *K*), Company *B*, Company *C* and the president of Company *K*. Plus most stock of Company *K* was owned by Company *C*, 99% of whose stock was owned by the eldest son of the president of Company *K*. Each of these companies of S group was regarded as a section of Company *K* and each companies personnel and financial affairs were controlled by the administration department and financial department of Company *K*. All decisions on selection of directors, personnel affairs and wages of employees were substantially made by the president of Company *K*. The bankbooks of Company *A* are held by a financial division of either Company *K* or other companies of S group. The president of Company *K* substantially controlled all the assets and properties of Company *A*. Operating profits of Company *A* had been absorbed by Company *K* through the pretence of settling accounts. Based on these facts, the Tokyo District Court held Company *A* had been an empty shell and should not be recognized as a legal personality. Accordingly, the court ordered Company *K* to pay retirement benefits to two retired employees of Company *A*.[136]

300. Therefore, the doctrine of 'abuse of corporate status' is much more practical for the courts. The *Daiich Kotsu Sangyo* case is a good example where company A established taxi company B (a subsidiary of company A) and liquidated taxi company C (another subsidiary of company A) to replace Company B in order to get rid of trade union members employed by company B. The Osaka High Court found that company A had real power to control both subsidiaries and had an illegal purpose to getting rid of trade union members and therefore that company A should bear the employment responsibility for those employees who were trade union members.[137] However, in this case, there was some question as to whether the company bearing the employment responsibility is company A or company C.

301. In addition, even where one cannot apply the doctrine of piercing the corporate veil, some courts have affirmed that the employees of the transferor acquired

---

136. The *Kurokawa Construction Company* case, the Tokyo District Court in 2001, RH, No. 813, p. 15. Other cases where a company was recognized as an empty shell are as follows: the *Kawagishi Kogyo* case, the Sendai District Court in 1970, *RMS*, Vol. 21, No. 2, p. 330; the *Moriokashi Nokyo* case, the Morioka District Court in 1985, RH, No. 461, p. 50; the *Kitakyushu Kucho* case, the Osaka District Court in 2009, *Rodokeizai Hanrei Sokuho* (Labour Economics Law Bulletin), No. 2057, p. 27.
137. The Osaka High Court in 2007, RH, No. 975, p. 50. Other cases where a parent company was held to have the employment responsibility for the employees of its child company are as follows: the *Funai Electricity* case, the Tokushima District Court in 1975, *RMS*, Vol. 26, No. 4, p. 580; the *Nakamoto Shoji* case, the Kobe District Court in 1979, RH, No. 328, p. 52; the *Fuse Jidosha Kyoshujo* case, the Osaka District Court in 1982, RH, No. 393, p. 35. However, some courts have held that unlike the doctrine of the 'empty shell', the doctrine of 'abuse of corporate status' cannot

a status as an employee in the transferee as they have made much of the fact that the identity of business is maintained after transfer of business. Therefore, in cases where the transferee has employed all the employees of the transferor but trade union members, some courts held that the transferee should show just cause for refusing to employ those members in a similar way.[138]

302. Another question has recently arisen from the process of amending the Commercial Code in order to make a company easily split. The Commercial Code was eventually amended so that a company easily split the whole or part of business but that the split part as the whole shall be succeeded by another pre-existing or new company (a successor company) according to a written plan of company split which was approved in a general meeting of stockholders. Currently, these rules regarding company split are provided under the Companies Act (Articles 757 et seq.). Therefore, there is possibility that employees who have worked mainly in the part of business succeeded by a successor company cannot be taken over by that company if their employment contracts have not been written down in that plan as subjects of succession. On the other hand, employees having worked only partly in that part cannot remain in the previous company if their contracts have been written down in that plan as subjects of succession. In order to resolve these problems and others, the Succession of Employment Contracts Act was enacted in 2000. According to that Law, where the employment contract of an employee who has worked mainly in the part of business taken over by a successor company was not taken over by that company, the employee can make an objection to such non-succession and his contract shall then be regarded as taken over by that company. On the other hand, in principle, such an employee cannot make objection when the plan of company–split provides that his employment contract shall be taken over by the successor company. However, the employer who originally concluded the employment contract (original employer) owes a duty to consult such employee before drawing up the plan of the company split. If the employer neglects this duty, the employee who does not give consent to the succession of the employment contract can remain with the original employer and seek a court judgment declaring such contractual status.[139]

303. Next, where the contract of an employee who has worked only partly in the part taken over by a successor company was succeeded by that company, he can make an objection to such succession and his contract shall then be regarded as not succeeded by that company (Articles 4 and 5). Two weeks before the written plan of company split is approved in a general meeting of stockholders, every employee must be informed as to whether his contract will be succeeded by a successor company (Article 2). The Act also provides that, where there is a collective agreement between the previous company and the union which has applied to the succeeded

impose the employment responsibility upon a parent company for the employee of its child company. The Osaka High Court in the *Daiich Kotsu Sangyo* case, however, stated that a case of a pretended liquidation must be differentiated from one of a genuine liquidation and that the parent company should bear employment responsibility as well as monetary liabilities for such unpaid wages on the former case.

138. The *Tokyo Nisshin Gakuen* case, the *Saitama* District Court in 2004, RH, No. 888, p. 13.

139. The *Nippon IBM* case, the Supreme Court in 2008, RH, No. 1010, p. 5.

employees, it is regarded as a collective agreement containing the same contents concluded between the successor and that union (Article 7).

§10. Unemployment Benefits

304. When an employee becomes unemployed, he or she is normally entitled to unemployment benefits under the EIA of 1974, in principle, on the condition that he or she has been an insured person for at least six months within one year before becoming unemployed. The benefits consist of the employment-seeker's benefits, placement promotion benefits, educational training benefits and continuous employment benefits (EIA, Article 10(1)). The employment-seeker's benefits include basic allowance, skill acquisition allowance, lodging allowance and sickness and injury allowance (Article 10(2)). The placement promotion benefits include employment promotion allowance, removal expenses and wide area job-seeking expenses (Article 10(3)). How long the basic allowance continues to be given to the unemployed depends on his or her age, the reason for retirement, the degree of difficulty in finding employment, the hours of working, the period of employment as an insured person. The duration of basic allowance is set for 90 to 360 days although it may be extended under three kinds of special extension programme: Training extended benefits programme, wide area extended benefits programme and national extended benefits programme (Articles 24–27). The duration of basic allowance is differentiated according to the types of recipients: ordinarily qualified recipient, a specially qualified recipient and a handicapped recipient (*see* Table 14). A handicapped recipient means a person who is physically, mentally or socially handicapped to find an employment (Article 22(2)). A specially qualified recipient means a person whose separation from employment was caused by the bankruptcy, downsizing or discontinuance of the enterprise of his employer or a person whose was dismissed without serious reasons for which he should be responsible or a person who resigned for false employment conditions at employment stage, being unpaid or underpaid for more than two months, reduction in wages, employers' certain infringement of law, recommendation of resignation without monetary incentives, etc. (Article 23(2)). The daily amount of basic allowance is an amount obtained by multiplying the daily amount of wages by the percentage gradually decreasing within the range of 80% to 50% in set proportion to the increase in the daily amount of wages (Article 16).

Table 14 Duration of Basic Allowances
(a) Ordinarily Qualified Recipients

	Years as a Contributing Member of the System				
	Less Than 1	*1–Less Than 5*	*5–Less Than 10*	*10–Less Than 20*	*20 or More*
All ages	90	90	90	120	150

(b) Specially Qualified Recipients

	Years as a Contributing Member of the System				
	Less Than 1	*1–Less Than 5*	*5-Less Than 10*	*10-Less Than 20*	*20 or More*
Under	90	90	90	120	180
30–34	90	90	180	210	240
35–44	90	90	180	240	270
45–59	90	180	240	270	330
60–64	90	150	180	210	240

(c) Handicapped Recipients

	Years as a Contributing Member of the System				
	Less Than 1	*1–Less Than 5*	*5–Less Than 10*	*10–Less Than 20*	*20 or More*
Under	150	300	300	300	300
45–64	150	360	360	360	360

305. The 1994 amendment to EIA introduced a new type of benefit for continuous employment (or re-employment) of the elderly and childcare leave allowance. The benefits for continuous employment of the elderly will be paid to an employee who continues employment and whose monthly wage is reduced to less than 75% of the monthly wage received at age 60. The duration of payment is five years on the condition that the employee has been an insured person under EIA for five years or more before his or her attaining age 60. Where the new monthly wage is more than 61% of the monthly wage received at age 60, the benefits will be lowered until the total of the new monthly wage plus the benefit is 75%. The benefits for re-employment of the elderly will be paid to an employee who is re-employed after obtaining 100 or less days of unemployment benefits and whose monthly wage decreased to less than 75% of the monthly wage received at age 60. The child and family care leave allowance will be paid to the employee on child and family care leave. Each month during the childcare leave, he or she is entitled to benefits equivalent to 40% (tentatively 50%) of his or her wage.

Chapter 6. Protection of Certain Categories of Worker

§1. Minors

306. Under the Civil Code, minors (persons under 18 years of age) must obtain the consent of their legal representative if they enter a contract. If a minor makes a contract without the consent of persons with parental authority or guardians, the legal representative can rescind the contract (Civil Code, Article 5). However, to prevent exploitation by persons with parental authority or guardians, they may not enter into employment contracts on behalf of minors (LSA, Article 58), and minors may claim wages on behalf of themselves (Article 59).

307. The LSA generally prohibits the employment of children until the end of the first March 31 following their 15th birthday, to ensure the health and welfare of them (Article 56). Exceptions to this rule are allowed for non-industrial sectors (ages 13 and older) and film and theatre businesses (including those under 13 years of age) with the approval of the Director of the LSIO, if light work that does not have a detrimental effect on health and welfare is performed outside of school hours.

308. With the same purpose, minors are protected by restrictions on employment, including limitations on working hours and days off (Article 60), night work (Article 61), dangerous and harmful work specified by an ordinance of the Ministry of Health, Labour and Welfare (Article 62), and the prohibition of underground work (Article 63). The prohibitions and restrictions on the employment of workers under 18 years old have already been described in Part I, Chapter 1, section 4. For Example, the exceptions to the principle of the eight-hour working day and forty-hour working week permitted for adult workers (such as the uneven distribution of working hours, longer working hours in certain industries and overtime) are not allowed for minors under 18 years old.

§2. Expecting and Nursing Mothers

309. In June 1997, an Act to amend the existing laws concerning sexual equality in employment was passed in the Diet and brought substantial changes especially in the provisions of LSA and the EEOA of 1985. However, these amendments came into force late, in April 1999 (*see* Part I, Chapter 1, Section 5).

310. Whereas previous labour laws generally regarded women as vulnerable workers and provided for their protection, the protection which remains in LSA beyond March 1999 mainly concerns pregnancy, maternity and nursing care. An employer shall not employ women to work underground except for those who are involved for a short time in medical, nursing sector, media and natural science research work. Pregnant women and women within one year after childbirth shall not be excluded from the above prohibition (LSA, Article 64.4). Employers must not allow pregnant women or women who have given birth less than a year previously to work with heavy materials, in places where noxious gases are produced or in any other work that is harmful to pregnancy, childbirth, breastfeeding, etc. (Article 64.5). Employers are prohibited from putting women who are expected to give birth within six weeks and have applied for maternity leave to work. Similarly, employers may not require a woman to work within eight weeks of giving birth, unless she has requested to do so after six weeks of giving birth (Article 65). Where pregnant women or women within one year after childbirth have so requested, employers shall not require them to work overtime, in holiday and night (Article 66). Women who suffer badly during menstruation may request menstrual leave without pay (Article 68). A woman nursing a baby less than one year old is entitled to take at least thirty minutes' nursing time twice a day during working hours (Article 67).

§3. Elderly Workers

311. The OPESA which purports to promote the continuity of employment and so to promote the welfare of older persons was first enacted in 1971 and was amended to a great extent in 1986, 1994, 2004 and 2020. The OPESA makes any agreement on retirement age under 60 void (OPESA, Article 8). Where the compulsory retirement age in a company is older than 60 but under 65, the OPESA requires an employer to take one of three measures prescribed in order to secure the employment of older persons until the age of 65. This is because the age of eligibility for the state pension has been raised from 60 to 65, making it important to secure employment during the five-year gap. Those measures which are prescribed under the OPESA are: (1) to raise that compulsory retirement age, (2) to maintain employment beyond it by re-employing persons after retirement age, or (3) to abolish the mandatory retirement scheme (Article 9(1)). Of these three measures, re-employment is most often utilized. The employer may not refuse to re-employ qualified workers except in cases where the employer could lawfully dismiss them. The OPESA also provides for Silver Human Resource Centres which provide temporary, short-term or light working opportunities to older persons (Article 46).

312. In addition, in order to maintain the vitality of the economy and society in the midst of a rapidly ageing society with a declining birth rate and shrinking population, and to ensure that older workers who are willing to work can make full use of their abilities, the OPESA requires employers to make efforts to institutionalize one of several options for securing employment opportunities until the age of 70, including raising the retirement age and re-employment, as well as hiring the former employees under outsourcing contracts or social contribution programmes (Article 10.2).

§4. Disabled Workers

313. The DPEPA of 1960 (as amended in May 1997 and 2012) requires employers to ensure that a prescribed percentage of employees consists of physically disabled or mentally retarded persons (Article 14). The percentage is set by reference to the proportion of people with disabilities in the population and was increased in 2018 as a result of the inclusion of people with mental disabilities in the mandatory recruitment category following the 2012 amendment. In 2026, this figure will be set at 2.7% (the Enforcement Ordinance of DPEPA, Article 10.2). It imposes financial burden on the employers to encourage them to achieve the prescribed percentage. The Ministry of Health, Labour and Welfare collects a levy to encourage the employment of physically disabled or mentally retarded employees from employers normally employing more than 100 employees (Article 26). The amount of levy collected from each employer is reduced in accordance with the number of physically disabled or mentally retarded persons actually employed by him every year (Articles 27 and 28). Employers who exceed the prescribed rate for employing physically disabled or mentally retarded employees will be paid an allowance (Articles 18–19).

314. In addition, the DPEPA was amended in 2012 so that the employer owes a duty not to discriminate because of the disability of its employees as well as a duty to provide for reasonable accommodation for disabled employees. This amendment came into force in April 2016. The Ministry of Health, Labour and Welfare has issued guidelines that stipulate the matters necessary for the appropriate and effective implementation of reasonable accommodation by employers.

Chapter 7. Discrimination and Equality in Employment

§1. Overview

315. There are various laws which prohibit employment discrimination. The most important laws are the Constitution which establishes equality before the law as a fundamental human right, the LSA which embodies the provisions of the Constitution with regard to employment, and the EEOA which was enacted with the basic principle that workers should not be discriminated against on the basis of their gender. The issue of disparities in working conditions between regular and non-regular employees, which is seen as closely linked to the gender-based division of labour, has been contested as discrimination. As it is not considered discrimination but rather a policy issue that needed to be addressed, several other laws have been enacted on this issue. These are discussed below.

316. As stated above, the DPEPA now has provisions regarding employment discrimination because of disability. Also, Labour Policy Comprehensive Promotion Act (formerly Employment Measure Act) requires employers to provide for equal treatment regardless of age with respect to recruitment and hiring of workers (Article 9). However, there are a number of exceptions to this requirement. For example, it is permissible for employers to select young applicants with a view to building up their skills through long-term employment.

317. There have been an increasing number of cases which do not involve direct discrimination in working conditions but harassment related to sex, creed, etc. Although Article 3 of LSA is not applicable to such cases, employees may claim damages on the grounds that harassment constitutes a tort. Thus, in the *Kansai Denryoku* case where the employer shadowed employees belonging to a particular political party, opened their lockers without their consent and isolated them from other employees, the court held that such employer conduct infringed the employees' freedom of creed and privacy and therefore constituted a tort.[140] Similarly, in the *Fukuoka Sekuhara* case, where a chief editor compelled his female subordinate to quit the publishing company, the court held that the male chief editor's conduct harms her benefit of working in a comfortable work environment and therefore constituted a tort.[141] In these cases, the court ordered the employers to pay the employees damages for their injured feelings. Moreover, in a case where an employee resigned because of sexual harassment, a court has ordered an employer to pay her wages accrued but for resignation.[142]

140. The *Kansai Denryoku* case, the Osaka High Court in 1991, RH, No. 603, p. 5.
141. The *Fukuoka Sekuhara* case, the Fukuoka District Court in 1992, RH, No. 607, p. 6.
142. The *Kyoto Sexual Harassment* case, the Tokyo District Court in 1997, RH, No. 716, p. 49.

§2. Equal Treatment under the Labour Standards Act

318. Article 3 of the LSA prohibits discriminatory treatment with respect to wages, working hours or other working conditions by reason of the nationality, creed or social status of any employees. Article 4 separately prohibits discriminatory treatment of a woman as compared to a man with respect to wages, by reason of being a woman. These provisions intend to realize 'the principle of equality' proclaimed by the Constitution in the field of employment relations. Article 14 of the Constitution provides that all people are equal under the law and that there shall be no discrimination because of race, creed, sex, social status or family origin. If an employer violates these articles of LSA, he or she shall be punished with imprisonment or a fine. Any act or conduct having a legal effect such as a contract, notice of dismissal, etc. shall be null and void. An act or conduct violating these articles may also constitute a tort for which the discriminated employee may claim damages.[143]

319. According to the administrative interpretation, the term 'social status' means status gained by birth.[144] Thus, being a bankrupt, having been declared the person with limited capacity or having a criminal record does not constitute social status.[145] The social status also does not include the contractual status, such as being employed on a fixed-term contract, etc.[146] The term 'nationality' is generally construed to include the concept of race.[147] The term 'creed' has long been held to include both political and religious beliefs. Where, in conformity with his political creed, an employee engages in conduct which adversely affects the company's order or interests, the employer may take appropriate action to protect his or her interests.[148] It has also been held that, where an enterprise operated by an employer is inseparable from a particular ideology or creed, the employer may dismiss an employee for harbouring opposing beliefs.[149]

§3. Equal Payment of Males and Females

320. Article 4 of the LSA prohibits discrimination in terms of wages on the grounds that the employee is female. The simplest example of wage discrimination is the *Akita Sogo Ginko* case where the employer applied a wage scheme to female employees which was different from that applied to male employees. In this case, it was held that application of separate wage schemes established the presumption of illegal wage discrimination and therefore that the employer must rebut it by proving certain justifiable reason for the application of separate wage schemes. It was also

143. The *Tokyo Denryoku* case, the Maebashi District Court in 1993, RH, No. 635, p. 22.
144. *Hakki*, No. 17 (1967).
145. The *Harima Zosen* case, the Kure Branch, the Hiroshima District Court in 1959, *Rohan Shu*, No. 4, p. 189.
146. The *Juji Juko* case, the Utsunomiya District Court in 1965, RMS, Vol. 16, No. 2, p. 256.
147. The *Hitachi Seisakujo* case, the Yokohama District Court in 1974, HJ, No. 744, p. 29.
148. The *Nichibokaizuka* case, the Supreme Court in 1955, SMS, Vol. 9, No. 12, p. 1793.
149. The *Nicchu Ryokosha* case, the Osaka District Court in 1969, RMS, Vol. 20, No. 6, p. 1086.

held that the plaintiff female employees were entitled to have the difference between the amount of wages paid to them and that amount paid to male employees on the basis of Article 13 of LSA.[150]

321. There have been several cases in which the application of the so-called head of household rule to wage determination has been contested. Many companies have wage schemes which provide that employees who is positioned as the head of the household in the resident record are entitled to family allowance, housing allowance, etc. For example, in the *Iwate Ginko* case in which the wage scheme stipulated that a husband was regarded as a head of household as to family allowance where both he and his wife earned an amount of income beyond a certain level. It was held that such stipulation violated Article 4 of LSA and therefore was void.[151] There were cases where wage differentials caused by different treatment of male and female employees in hiring, job assignment or promotion were held to be unlawful discrimination. In the *Nissotosho* case, it was held that it was in violation of Article 4 for an employer not to have corrected a female employee's wage scale after she became engaged in a job which was equivalent to those of male employees.[152]

322. In most cases of wage differentials involving different treatment in job assignment, upgrading or promotion, it is difficult to apply Article 4 because that article only prohibits discrimination in terms of wages. However, the courts have held that discriminatory treatment on the grounds of sex is in contravention of Article 14 and is therefore in violation of public policy. Thus, such discriminatory treatment is void, according to Article 90 of the Civil Code and it may constitute a tort. For example, in the *Shakaihoken Shinryohoshu Shiharaikikin* case where an employer uniformly upgraded male employees but did not do so with female employees, the court held that not to upgrade female employees constituted a tort and it ordered the employer to pay the difference in wage as damages.[153] What is the most difficult for the courts is to make a judgment affirming an employee's upgraded status, partly because promotion and upgrading are considered to be based on an employer's discretion and partly because there is no statutory basis for the court to make such a judgment without the employer's decision regarding promotion. However, in the *Siba Shin-yo Kinko* case,[154] the Tokyo High Court upheld the district court's judgment affirming an employee's upgraded status. In that case, as for male employees who were hired in the same year as the plaintiffs (female employees) and were regarded as being of the same age for wage calculation as far as the plaintiffs were concerned, there was a custom in the defendant company that male employees were upgraded within a certain number of years after the time of

150. The *Akita Sogo Ginko* case, the Akita District Court in 1975, RMS, Vol. 26, No. 2, p. 388.
151. The *Iwate Ginko* case, the Sendai High Court in 1992, RMS, Vol. 34, No.1, p. 1; the *Sannyo Bussan* case, the Tokyo District Court in 1994, RH, No. 651, p. 15.
152. The *Nisso Tosho* case, the Tokyo District Court in 1992, HJ, No. 1433, p. 3; the *Shionogi Seiyaku* case, the Osaka District Court in 1999, No. 1707, RHS, No. 1707.
153. The *Shakaihoken Shinryohoshu Shiharaikikin* case, the Tokyo District Court in 1990, RH, No. 656, p. 7.
154. The *Shiba Shinkin* case, the Tokyo High Court in 2000, RH, No. 796, p. 5 and the Tokyo District Court in 1996, RH, No. 704, p. 21.

hiring. The company had a *shugyo-kisoku* which stipulated equal treatment regarding working conditions. The district court held that the custom concerning upgrade which applied to male employees should be applied to the plaintiffs according to the *shugyo-kisoku*. The Tokyo High Court upheld the district court's judgment affirming the employee's upgraded status but its reason for it was slightly different. The Court held that discrimination in upgrading is regarded as wage discrimination where the employees' grading for wage is separated from promotion in post and therefore that the appellees is entitled to upgraded status according to the essence of employment contract and the provision of LSA, Articles 4 and 13.

323. The courts have also held that any of the following agreements or stipulations in *shugyo-kisoku* were void: an employee's written pledge that she would resign upon getting married; a provision of *shugyo-kisoku* which sets different retirement ages between male and female employees; dismissal of female employees for redundancy by applying discriminatory criteria on the basis of sex.

324. However, because of the lack of a statutory basis for regulation, discriminatory treatment on the grounds of sex has been dealt with by the courts on a case-by-case basis. Therefore, female employees usually have difficulty in challenging employment discrimination. The LSIOs and Women's and Young Workers' Offices have not been able to do much in this situation. There are also no special conciliatory bodies to deal with disputes on discriminatory treatment.

§4. Equal Employment Opportunity Act

325. Six years after the adoption of the Convention Concerning the Elimination of All Forms of Discrimination Against Women by the United Nations, the EEOA of 1985 was enacted to improve the situation described above. In 1997, EEOA was substantially amended to more effectively regulate employment discrimination while LSA was amended to abolish most of the special protection for female employees (*see* Part 1, Chapter 1, section 5). A further substantial amendment to EEOA was made in 2006. The purpose of the amended EEOA was to convert protection for women against sexual discrimination into prohibition of both men and women against sexual discrimination, to introduce the concept of indirect discrimination and to extend the coverage of this prohibition.

326. The purposes of EEOA are: (1) to promote equal opportunity and treatment between men and women in employment in accordance with the principle of 'equality under the law' proclaimed in the Constitution; (2) to ensure female employees' health in work during pregnancy and after childbirth; (3) to prevent sexual harassment; (4) to secure women's health care during pregnancy and after childbirth. As far as purpose (1) is concerned, EEOA provides for the following: the employers shall provide opportunities to all persons regardless of sex, with regard to recruitment and hiring (Article 5); and the employers shall not discriminate against employees on the basis of sex, with regard to assignment (including allocation of duties and grant of authority), promotion, demotion, training, fringe benefits, change in job type, employment status, retirement recommendation, compulsory retirement age, dismissal and renewal of an employment contract (Article 6). EEOA, Article 7 now provides for the concept of indirect discrimination in a rather modest way. It prohibits an employer from taking measures which concern the recruitment and employment of workers, or any of the matters listed in Article 6 (e.g., height and weight requirement), and from applying a criterion concerning a person's condition other than the person's sex, and which is specified by ordinance of the Ministry of Health, Labour and Welfare as measures that may cause virtual discrimination by reason of a person's sex, considering the proportion of men and women who satisfy the criterion and other matters, except in a case where there is a justifiable reason relating to job and business to take such measures. On the other hand, these provisions do not prevent employers from taking measures to overcome obstacles to equal opportunity and treatment between males and females in employment (Article 8). This Article is intended to make so-called positive action permissible.

327. As regards the 'positive action', the Act on Promoting Women's Active Engagement in Professional Life was enacted in 2015. Under this Act, employers who employ 100 or more employees are required to draw up and disseminate an action plan to promote female employees' active participation in employment, based on the employer's assessment of problems regarding women's employment situations in their companies. Although the contents of the action plan are generally left to the employer's determination, some elements including numerical goals must be included. In this sense, this Act requires employers to make 'positive action' programmes based on their own assessment of problems regarding equal employment. The Act also requires employers to publicize information on situations regarding their female employees through the Internet or other measures. The contents of information to be publicized must include certain matters such as wage disparity between male and female employees.

328. As far as purpose (2) is concerned, Article 9 of EEOA provides that the employers shall not stipulate marriage, pregnancy or childbirth as a reason for retirement of female employees, shall not dismiss female employees for marriage, and shall not dismiss or give disadvantageous treatment by reason of pregnancy, childbirth or for requesting for or having taken maternity leave, or other reasons relating to pregnancy or childbirth. The Minister of Health, Labour and Welfare is empowered to issue guidelines with respect to the measures which employers shall take with regard to the matters stipulated in Articles 5, 7 and 9 (Article 10). As for purpose (3), EEOA requires employers to pay due attention in employment management to ensure that a female employee's reaction to sexual speech or conduct in the workplace does not cause any disadvantages concerning terms and conditions of employment nor cause detriment to her working environment. The Minister of Health, Labour and Welfare is empowered to issue guidelines for this purpose (Article 11). As far as purpose (4) is concerned, the employers shall secure the necessary time off to receive health guidance and medical examinations (Article 12) and take necessary measures, such as change of working hours and reduction of work, in order to enable the female employees to comply with the directions they receive based on the health guidance and medical examinations (Article 13).

329. The EEOA provides for no penal sanction to an employer for his violation of the above provisions. However, if an employer's conduct violating those provisions is a juristic act, it will be void as being a violation of an imperative. It may also constitute a tort for which the employer may be sued for damages.

330. Employers shall, when a complaint is submitted by a female employee concerning a matter stipulated in Articles 6, 7, 9, 12 and 13, endeavour to achieve a voluntary settlement, by such means as referring that complaint to a grievance body (Article 15). The Director of each PLB is empowered to give any necessary advice or guidance or make any necessary recommendation to either employee or employer – or both – if asked by them to do so (Article 17). Where either employee or employer – or both – apply for mediation, the Director shall refer their dispute, except in cases concerning recruitment and hiring, to the Equal Opportunity Mediation Commission for mediation (Article 18). The Commission, which consists of three commissioners appointed by the Minister of Health, Labour and Welfare from among persons of learning and experience, may make a settlement proposal and recommend its acceptance to the parties concerned (Articles 19, 20, 21, 22 and 23). The Commission may, when it finds no chance for resolution by conciliation, discontinue the conciliation as to the disputes pertaining to. In such a case, the Commission shall notify the parties concerning said discontinuance (Article 23). The persons who applied for the conciliation file a suit as to the claim which was the purpose of the conciliation within thirty days of the day of notification, the suit shall be deemed to be filed on the day when the conciliation was applied for in terms of interruption (Article 24).

§5. Prohibition of Discrimination and Unreasonable Treatment Against Non-regular Employees

331. In the employment management of individual enterprises, non-regular employment is classified by various terms, such as '*pa-to*', '*arubaito*' or '*shokutaku*'. Legally, 'non-regular employment' consists of three types of employment: fixed term (temporary), part-time and dispatched employment, which contradict the three characteristics of regular employee ('*Seishain*'): permanent, full-time and direct employment. Most part-time employees are also employed in fixed-term contracts, so the above characteristics often overlap.

332. In the traditional Japanese practice of long-term employment, the transfer of regular employees between jobs is a common occurrence, with no change in pay. House unions have been established to organize all regular employees within each company. Because of this practice, no clear job categories have been developed, and therefore no standard pay for each job category has been formed across industries. As a result, the level of remuneration varies greatly from company to company, depending on the size of the company and the industry or trade to which it belongs. Within each company, the remuneration of an employee is basically determined according to his or her age, length of service, educational background, performance rate, family status, mobility, etc.

333. It should be noted that such a system only applies to those who have the status of regular employees who are directly employed under an indefinite term and full-time basis in each company. It does not apply to non-regular employees employed under part-time or fixed term-based contracts. Part-time employees are ordinarily paid by hour, while full-time employees are paid by month. Their wages are determined separately from those of regular employees and in many cases, determined based on local labour market prices. In a sense, the company treats non-regular employees as outsiders. Therefore, to establish the principle of equal treatment in employment in Japan, it is necessary to reform the deep-rooted employment practices in each industry, and it would be even more difficult to make such a change all at once. However, due to intensified global competition, many enterprises are reforming their wages rather drastically, for example by introducing a more individualized performance-orientated wage system, the annual salary system, or a job-duty-based wage system. Some companies have introduced certain measures to give their part-time employees terms and conditions balancing those of full-time employees or opportunities to become full-time employees.

334. The legal problems associated with non-regular employment can be summarized in two main areas: weak employment security and poor working conditions. The issues are intertwined: weak job security gives fixed-term employees weak bargaining power, making it difficult for them to negotiate better conditions. Especially, in the case of fixed-term employment, the contract is basically terminated at the end of the term unless it is renewed by employers. Fixed-term employees cannot expect long-term employment, and they are often the target of redundancy before regular employees are dismissed at the time of company restructuring. They also tend to receive lower wages, promotions, training and benefits than regular employees.

335. Unlike EU countries,[155] Japan did not have statutory guarantee of equal treatment for part-time employees and fixed-term employees. It has not ratified ILO Convention No. 175 concerning Part-Time Work. The LCA which was enacted in 2007 only provides that the employer and the employee should conclude an employment contract, having regard to the balance between its contractual terms and conditions and the employee's real working conditions (Article 3.2).

336. While there was no actual law comprehensively regulating differential treatment based on employment status other than the anti-discrimination provisions of Articles 3 and 4 of the LSA (*see* Chapter 7, section 2 and 3), there were cases in which claims of unlawful treatment of non-regular employees based on the so-called principle of equal pay for equal (value) work were brought before the courts. However, the courts have denied the legality of such a principle. The *Maruko Keihoki* case[156] was almost the only case in which a claim for damages was granted prior to the enactment of the former Article 20 of the LCA (*see* below,

155. Council Directive 97/81/EC, clauses 4 and 5; Council Directive 1999/70/EC, clauses 4, 6 and 7.
156. The *Ueda* Branch, the Nagano District Court in 1996, RH, No. 690, p. 32.

enacted in the 2012 revision and replaced in 2018). In this case, twenty-eight married women who had worked for the defendant company for between 6 and 27 years under repeatedly renewed two-month contracts and were engaged in the same duties for the same working hours and days as regular employees, claimed wages equal to those of regular employees. The decision attracted attention because it ruled that the wage difference that violated the principle of equal treatment underlying the principle of equal pay for equal work was a violation of public order and good morals and allowed the claim for the portion of wages that was less than 80% of the wages of regular employees.

337. This case shows that there is a rather peculiar Japanese practice regarding non-regular employees, where there are employees who are called 'part-timers' but who do the same or almost the same work and working hours as full-time employees in the same establishment. These are employees who simply do not have the status of regular full-time employees in that company. However, the court was criticized for its weak reasoning and for allowing the company to use its discretion in determining the difference up to 80%. After the *Maruko Keihoki* decision, the courts made no attempt to reconcile the different treatment of non-regular and regular employees with the requirements of equality, simply denying that the principle of equal pay for work of equal value existed as a general norm governing labour relation. Although the court recognized that their jobs were the same and that their jobs could be even more intensive than their regular counterparts, the court held that the employer remained free to employ these non-regular employees under a separate wage scheme that was different from that of the regular employees.[157]

338. The situation drastically changed in 2012 when the LCA was amended to provide that where working conditions differ between indefinite-term employees and fixed-term employees employed by the same employer, the difference should not be unreasonable having regard to the difference in job content, responsibility, duty content and the extent of changes in duty (Article 20). This provision purported to interfere with the freedom of contract, as fixed-term employees often face difficulties in negotiating working conditions for fear of the employer's refusal to renew the contract. Although this provision does not necessarily establish the general principle of equal treatment for equal work, it played a significant role and led to a large accumulation of case law, including seven Supreme Court decisions in just seven years or so, until it was removed and is now replaced by Article 8 of the PFEA, enacted in 2018.

339. Thus, currently, the laws that legally address the vulnerability of non-regular employees are; the LCA with respect to employment security for fixed-term employment (*see* Part 1, Chapter 1, section 2), the PFEA with respect to correcting differences in the treatment of part-time and fixed-term employees, and the WDA with respect to dispatched workers.

---

157. The *Nihon Yubin Teiso* case, the Osaka District Court in 2002, RH, No. 830, p. 22.

340. The PFEA provides for a prohibition of unreasonable differences in treatment (Article 8) and a prohibition of discriminatory treatment (Article 9), which replace and extend the former Article 20 of the LCA in order to cover not only fixed-term employees but also part-time employees. The prohibition of discriminatory treatment (Article 9) is positioned as a rule requiring equal treatment of regular and non-regular employees on the premises performing the same work. On the other hand, the prohibition of unreasonable differences in treatment (Article 8) is positioned as a rule that requires balancing the difference in treatment between regular and non-regular employees who perform different work. In the latter case, the central issue is the framework for assessing the unreasonableness of the difference in treatment.

341. Article 8 of the PFEA provides that 'unreasonableness' should be assessed for each of the basic wage, bonus and other treatments, and that unreasonableness should be considered by taking into account the nature and purpose of each treatment separately. However, case law has held that when several wage items are interrelated, the interrelationship should also be considered.[158] The 'treatment' is defined by administrative interpretation to include all types of wages, education and training, welfare facilities, rest, holidays, paid leave, health and safety, accident compensation, dismissal, and all other forms of treatment.

342. The way to assess 'unreasonableness' according to the nature and purpose of the treatment should be based on three factors to be considered: (1) job description, (2) the extent of the change of the nature of the job and assignment, and (3) other circumstances. These considerations are extremely abstract, it is necessary to refer to the precedents formed around the former Article 20 of the LCA, which was the predecessor of Article 8 of the PFEA.

343. Among these factors, (1) the job description refers to the nature of the work (type of work, core duties) and the level of responsibility associated with that work (scope and degree of authority granted and exercised in the performance of the work), and (2) the scope of the change refers not only to the current job but also to future prospects, including changes in position such as transfers and promotions, and the extent of those changes. In addition, (3) other circumstances include the process and results of labour-management consultation and collective bargaining,[159] and the fact that the employee is rehired after retirement.[160] There are several court decisions that consider the existence of an examination system that allows non-regular employees to be converted into regular employees as an element that negates unreasonableness.

344. These three factors were simply juxtaposed in the previous Article 20 of the LCA, but now Article 8 of the PFEA requires consideration of 'what is deemed appropriate in light of the nature of the treatment and the purpose for which the

158. The *Nagasawa Un-yu* case, the Supreme Court in 2018, Minshu, Vol. 72, No. 2, p. 202.
159. The *Hamakyo Rex* case, Supreme Court, in 2018, Minshu, Vol. 72, No. 2, p. 88.
160. The *Nagasawa Un-yu* case, the Supreme Court in 2018, Minshu, Vol. 72, No. 2, p. 202.

treatment is provided' among these factors. This is a framework for identifying the treatment's nature and purpose, and then selecting appropriate judgment factors. Therefore, in interpreting the unreasonableness of the article, it is important to identify the nature and purpose of the treatment in question.

345. However, the nature and purpose of such treatment are not easy to identify when it is of a mixed nature or determined by fundamentally different principles. Recognition should not be based on the name of the treatment or the subjective intention or perception of the employer, but rather on a substantive judgment based on specific payment standards and actual conditions.[161] Unlike allowances and benefits, differences in treatment such as base pay, bonuses, and retirement benefits, which are composite in nature and closely related to long-term careers, are generally not found to be unreasonable. In two of the Supreme Court decisions issued in October 2020, the unreasonableness of bonuses and retirement benefits, which had been partially approved at the High Court level, was denied in both cases.[162]

346. The term 'deemed unreasonable' does not refer to a lack of 'reasonableness', but rather to whether the difference in treatment 'can be judged to be unreasonable' under the case law.[163] It could be said that the Supreme Court has established a modest standard of judgment that does not find unlawful those ranges that are not reasonable, but not unreasonable, from the perspective that labour-management negotiations should be the principle for setting working conditions and the employer's business judgment should be respected.

347. In the absence of a provision directly affecting a contract like Article 13 of LSA in the PFEA, Article 8 of PFEA cannot be considered to directly regulate a contract's content following its invalidity (no supplementary effect).[164] Therefore, the main remedy is to compensate for the damage caused by the establishment of a tort.

348. In contrast, the prohibition of discriminatory treatment in Article 9 of the PFEA has been referred to as the equal treatment provision because it requires equal treatment of regular and non-regular employees on the basis that they are in the same circumstances for the same period of time. Because the effect of the equal treatment requirement is clear when applying this provision, it is important to interpret the requirements in terms of the same job description and scope of change. With respect to part-time/fixed-term employees whose job content is the same as that of regular employees and who should be treated in the same manner as regular employees (in light of business practices and other circumstances, the job content

161. Labour Policy Council Report, 'On Legislation Concerning Equal Pay for Equal Work' (9 June 2017).

162. The *Osaka Ikayakka Daigaku (Osaka Medical and Pharmaceutical University [former Osaka Medical College])* case, Supreme Court, in 2020, Shumin, No. 264, p. 63 and the *Metro Commerce* case, Supreme Court, in 2002, Minshu Vol. 74, No. 7, p. 1901.

163. The *Hamakyo Rex* case, Supreme Court, in 2018, Minshu, Vol. 72, No. 2, p. 88.

164. *Ibid.*

and assignment are expected to change to the same extent as that of regular employees throughout the period until the employment relationship with the employer concerned ends), the employer shall not discriminate against such part-time/fixed-term employees on the basis of being part-time/fixed-term employees (Article 9). With respect to the extent of the change in job description and assignment, the comparison with regular employees is limited to the duration of the contract, unless the statutory renewal under Article 19 of the LCA is applied to fixed-term employees, and the scope for recognition of this is considered to be quite narrow.

349. In case of violation of Article 9, unlike Article 8, the PFEA provides the basis for administrative supervision and guidance. The PLB with jurisdiction over the establishment is required to collect reports and provide advice, guidance and recommendations to the employer, and if the employer does not follow the recommendations of the Minister of Health, Labour and Welfare, the name of the employer may be made public (Article 18. 2). Penalties (fines) are also provided for refusal to collect reports or false reports.

350. With regard to fixed-term and part-time employees, to whom Articles 8 and 9 above do not apply, employers are only required to endeavour to set wages taking into account the balance with regular employees (Article 10). The PFEA also requires employers to provide part-time/fixed-term employees with the same opportunities for education and training as those required for the work performed by regular employees (Article 11). Employers must also ensure that part-time/fixed-term employees are given the opportunity to use the employer's facilities as a fringe benefit (Article 12). It should also be noted that the PFEA also requires employers to take prescribed measures to promote the conversion of part-time employees into full-time employees and vice versa, regarding their actual working situation (Article 13).

351. With regard to dispatched workers, the WDA similarly prohibits unreasonable differentials and disadvantageous treatment in comparison with the corresponding conditions of regular workers employed by the relevant client (Article 30. 3(1)(2). *see* Part 1, Chapter 1, section 2, VI).

Part II. Collective Labour Relations and Dispute Resolution

Chapter 1. Trade Union Rights

§1. Constitutional Rights

352. Article 28 of the Constitution guarantees the right of workers to organize, bargain and act collectively. This constitutional provision can be construed in the following ways:

1. The nation must not suppress or restrict workers' freedom to organize, bargain and act collectively. Thus, as long as the organization of a trade union, collective bargaining, dispute acts, or other union activities remain within the limits of propriety in their nature, they will be immune from any criminal and civil liability. These effects are confirmed by Article 1(2) and Article 8 of the TUA of 1949. Any legislation or administrative action which restricts, without just cause, freedom to organize and to bargain collectively or act will also be unconstitutional and void.
2. The nation has a political obligation to provide legislative systems which promote collective bargaining. It is understood that the enactment of laws such as TUA and the LRAA of 1946 is based on this obligation. The creation of the normative effect of collective agreements, the system of relief from unfair labour practice and other legal innovations resulted from it.[165]
3. It is generally agreed that Article 28 also directly regulates the labour–management relationship. Even if Article 28 is not so interpreted, it should be understood that Article 28 has established the public policy of respecting workers' rights to organize, to bargain collectively with employers or to engage in collective action against employers. Therefore, an employer's action which infringes these rights will be void, in violation of public policy (Civil Code, Article 90), and will be illegal and therefore may constitute a tort (Civil Code, Article 709).

353. The rights proclaimed under Article 28 are composed of the right to organize, the right to collective bargaining and the right to collective action. The meaning and effect of each right is as follows:

165. Sugeno & Yamakawa, *supra*, p. 37.

1. The right to organize is defined as the right to form or join a workers' organization. A contract which makes it a condition of employment that the worker must not join or must withdraw from a trade union will be void in violation of this right. Dismissals, disciplinary actions or other disadvantageous actions which are taken against an employee who has organized or joined a trade union will be void and may constitute a tort. However, it has generally been decided that a request for enjoinment or removal of an employer's action obstructive to the right to organize may not be granted on the basis of Article 28.[166]
2. The right to collective bargaining is defined as a guarantee to workers that they will be able to bargain collectively with their employer. Where an employer refuses a trade union's request for collective bargaining without just cause, the union may apply to the court for a declaratory judgment affirming its bargaining status.[167]
3. The right to collective action is classified into the right to industrial action such as strike and the right to union activities (i.e., the right to collective actions other than industrial action). As far as this right is concerned, immunity from civil and criminal liability is the most important effect of its exercise. Dismissals, disciplinary actions or other disadvantageous actions which are taken against employees who have participated in a proper industrial action or other union activities will be illegal and void and may constitute a tort.

354. One of the theoretical issues concerning Article 28 of the Constitution is how to understand the relationship between that article and the unfair labour practice system. The unfair labour practice system is provided for by Article 7 of the TUA. Under Article 7, the employer shall not be allowed to carry out the following practices: (1) to treat a worker in a disadvantageous manner by reason of his or her trade union membership or union activities or for having filed a complaint with the LRC, (2) to make it a condition of employment that the worker must not join or must withdraw from a trade union, (3) to refuse to bargain collectively with the representative of the workers without proper reasons, or (4) to control or interfere with the formation or management of a trade union. An aggrieved worker or union can file a complaint with the LRC, an administrative committee, for a remedial order. There are three different views concerning the relationship between Article 28 of the Constitution and the unfair labour practice system. The first view is that the system is intended to realize the constitutional guarantee of the right to organization and collective bargaining and action. This view regards unfair labour practices as a conduct infringing the right to organize and to participate in collective bargaining and action. The right to unfair labour practice relief is merely part of the rights guaranteed by Article 28. The second view is that the system is meant to establish public order for fair industrial relations under the constitutional guarantee of the right to organize and participate in collective bargaining and action. The third view is that the purpose of the system is to make effective collective bargaining possible. This

---

166. The *Tomita Kiki Seisakusho* case, the Yokkaichi Branch of the Tsu District Court in 1973, RKS, No. 807, p. 3.
167. The *Kokutetsu* case, the Supreme Court in 1991, RH, No. 589, p. 6.

view stresses that the administrative relief for unfair labour practices is not merely the confirmation of the contents of Article 28 but the special administrative system created according to the policy expressed by Article 28. The Supreme Court seems to take the second view because it has stated that the purpose of the present relief system is to restore promptly and maintain the normal order of collective labour relations.[168]

§2. The Concept of Trade Unions

355. Under the TUA, a trade union can be freely organized without obtaining a licence from or submitting a notice to public offices. However, it should satisfy certain requirements in order to enjoy the rights provided under TUA. In order to enjoy all these rights, a union must be what is called a 'statutorily qualified union' which satisfies all the requirements of Article 2 and has a constitution containing provisions prescribed by Article 5(2) stated below. Thus, these unions enjoy (a) immunity from civil and criminal liability, (b) a normative effect for their collective agreements, the automatic extension of the terms of their collective agreements applying to other workers in workplaces, (c) the status of a juridical personality, remedies for unfair labour practices, the right to petition for the extension of the terms of their collective agreements applying to workers in the same geographical area, and the capacity to nominate worker commissioners to the LRC. A workers' organization that does not satisfy the requirements of Article 2 is not entitled to the rights listed above. Also, a 'statutorily unqualified union' or 'bona fide union' which only satisfies the requirements of Article 2 but does not have such a constitution cannot enjoy those rights listed above at (c). However, in practice, the distinction between a 'statutorily qualified union' and a 'bona fide union' is not very significant because LRC always advises and allows the particular union to correct the defects in its constitution in the course of screening a union's qualifications.[169] Even if a workers' organization may not satisfy the requirements of the first or second proviso (i.e., no membership admission of managerial personnel and no financial assistance from an employer) of Article 2, it may enjoy constitutional rights such as immunity from civil and criminal liability and courts' remedies against disadvantageous treatment on the grounds of union membership and proper union activities (*see* section 1). However, the law prohibits certain categories of public employees from forming workers' organizations; police officers, maritime safety officers, prison officers and firemen (the National Civil Service Act, Article 108/2(5); the Local Civil Service Act, Article 52(5)).

356. Requirements for a bona fide union provided under the TUA, Article 2 are as follows:

1. Composition: the organization concerned must 'be composed mainly of workers'. The 'workers' are defined as 'those who live by their wages, salaries or

168. The *Daiichi Hato Taxi* case, the Supreme Court in 1977, SMS, Vol. 31, No. 1, p. 93.
169. Sugeno & Yamakawa, *supra*, p. 937.

other remuneration similar thereto regardless of the kind of occupation' (Article 4). The phrase 'those who live by their wages' does not mean those who actually depend on their wages but means those who normally live on wages. Thus, it covers those who are not working but are unemployed. The definition of 'workers' in TUA is wider than that in the LSA. The difference in the definition of these two laws is a reflection of the difference in their purposes (*see* Chapter 2). Therefore, even if particular persons work under contracts other than employment contracts, they are 'workers' as defined by TUA if it is considered that they cannot bargain on an equal footing with the other party to their contracts without collective bargaining.[170] As a result, it has been interpreted that the definition of 'workers' in TUA includes workers who manufacture sandals on a piece-work basis within their own homes, musicians who are free to appear on the stage of other TV stations, and professional baseball players (For the recent Supreme Court cases, *see* section 33-2).

The phrase 'be composed mainly of' means that workers are a major part of the members of the organization concerned and that they lead the operation and management of the organization concerned.

2. Independence: the organization concerned must be 'autonomously formed by workers'. The word 'autonomously' has been interpreted to mean 'independent from employers'. There are two different views on the meaning of 'independence'. One is to understand it as a substantial situation of the organization concerned. If the formation or operation of an organization is substantially controlled by an employer, the organization has no 'independence' and therefore may not be protected under TUA.[171] The other view is to understand 'independence' as that of organizational structure. Therefore, for example, a union whose officers are designated by supervisors or managers is not 'independent from an employer'.[172] The latter view should be more persuasive because it is very difficult to judge whether an organization is substantially controlled by an employer. Separately, the law denies the 'independence' of an organization in two specific cases:
   a. where an organization admits to membership 'those who represent the interests of the employer' (Article 2, the first proviso). Those include persons who have direct authority with respect to hiring, firing, promotions or transfers; persons who have access to confidential information relating to the employer's labour relations policies so that their official duties and responsibilities directly conflict with their loyalties and responsibilities as a member of the trade union concerned; other persons who represent the interests of the employers;
   b. where an organization receives the employer's financial support in defraying its operational expenditures (Article 2, the second proviso). However, the proviso excludes the following cases from 'the employer's financial support': where the employer permits workers to confer or negotiate with

170. 1 Tokyo Daigaku Rodohokenkyukai, *Chushaku Rodokumiaiho* 230 (Yuhikaku 1980).
171. S. Nishitani, *Rodoho* 598 (Nippon Hyoronsha 2020). The *Zen-Daiei-Roso* case, the Yokohama District Court in 1989, RH, No. 557, p. 73.
172. Sugeno & Yamakawa, *supra*, p. 947.

the employer during working hours without loss of time or pay; where the employer contributes to public welfare funds or welfare and other funds which are actually used for payment to prevent or relieve economic misfortunes or accidents; where the employer furnishes minimum office space to the organization;
3. Purpose: the main purpose of the organization concerned must be 'maintaining and improving working conditions and raising the economic status of the workers'. An organization whose objectives are confined to mutual aid or other welfare or are principally politically or socially oriented is not protected under TUA (Article 2, the third and fourth proviso), although it is permissible for trade unions to engage in political or mutual aid activities;
4. Organizations or federations thereof: what is protected as a trade union under TUA must be an 'organization or federation of organizations'. For the purpose of being an 'organization', the organization concerned must not only be composed of two or more persons but also have a constitution and a structure for operation such as union officials because it must be considered to exist for a period of time. For example, the Tokyo High Court denied that a group of workers which demanded a wage increase from the employer was not a trade union because it had no constitution and no provision regarding its representatives and executive organ.[173] On the other hand, where the number of members of such an organization is reduced to one due to the employer's destructive conduct, it does not lose union status since there is a possibility that the membership will increase.[174]

357. To be a 'statutorily qualified union' it is necessary for the organization concerned, in addition to satisfying the above-stated four requirements for a 'bona fide union', to have a constitution containing the following provisions prescribed by Article 5(2). This requirement is meant to effectuate the democratic administration of trade unions:

1. the name and the address of its main office;
2. all members of the union other than a federation shall have the right to participate in all union affairs and the right to equal treatment;
3. nobody shall be refused membership of the union because of his or her race, religion, sex, social status or family origin;
4. in the case of a local union, the officers shall be elected by direct secret ballot of the members, and in the case of a federation or a trade union having national scope, the officers shall be elected by direct secret ballot either of the members of the local unions or of delegates elected by direct secret ballot of the members of the local unions;
5. a general meeting shall be held at least once a year;
6. a financial report together with certification of its accuracy by a professionally competent auditor appointed by the members shall be released to the members at least once a year;

173. The *Asahi Shinbun* case, the Tokyo High Court in 1978, RH, No. 294, p. 45.
174. Sugeno & Yamakawa, *supra*, p. 950.

7. no strike action shall be started without a majority decision made by direct secret ballot either of the members or of delegates elected by direct secret ballot of the members;
8. no constitution shall be revised without the agreement of a majority of the members in a direct secret ballot or, in the case of a federation or a national union, of the delegates elected by a direct secret ballot of all the members.

§3. Union Membership

358. Unions are voluntary associations formed by workers. It is generally considered that it is necessary for a worker to conclude a membership contract with a union in order to be its member. Therefore, to obtain membership in the union, a worker should apply to it for membership. The question is whether the union has complete freedom to decide on admission to membership. It is generally considered that the unions may prescribe the qualifications for union membership on the basis of its voluntary nature. Therefore, unions may restrict their membership to a certain industry, establishment, enterprise, type of work or type of position. Therefore, it is generally considered that a union constitution restricting membership to regular workers and excluding part-timers or temporary workers is valid. A union constitution excluding managerial employees from its membership is also valid.[175] However, taking account of the above-mentioned special protections granted by TUA, refusal of admission to membership on certain grounds is considered to be unlawful. For example, refusal of admission to membership on the grounds of race, religion, sex, social status or family origin is unlawful. There is a case where a court held that a union's refusal to admit a worker to membership was unlawful because there was no reason to believe that he would be detrimental to the union.[176] However, it is generally considered that there is no legal obligation on the union to admit a worker to its membership and therefore, even if the union has refused to admit the worker to its membership, he or she may only claim damages on the basis of a tort action.[177]

359. Because a union is basically of a voluntary nature, workers are free to resign from their union. Accordingly, provisions of a union constitution requiring prior approval of such resignations by executive committees or general meetings have been held to be void.[178] On the other hand, as far as procedures of resignation are concerned, they are valid as long as they are provided for in the union constitution and do not constitute a substantial obstacle to the members' resignation.[179]

360. As already seen in §1, Article 28 of the Constitution guarantees the right of workers to organize. This right is not equal to simple freedom to associate. In fact,

175. The *Zen-Daiei-Roso* case, the Yokohama District Court in 1989, RH, No. 557, p. 73.
176. The *Toho Aen* case, the Tokyo District Court in 1956, RMS, Vol. 7, No. 4, p. 462.
177. The *Zen-Daiei-Roso* case, *supra.*
178. The *Nihon Kokan* case, the Supreme Court in 1989, RH, No. 553, p. 6.
179. The *Zentei Kobeko Shibu* case, the Kobe District Court in 1988, RH, No. 547, p. 74.

the Constitution separately provides for people's right to associate in Article 21. The right of organization has been regarded as one of the fundamental human rights peculiar to the new type of constitutions which came into being after World War II and which were modelled on the Weimar Constitution in Germany – the so-called constitutions of the 'social welfare state'. Thus, the right of organization provided by Article 28 has been construed as a positive right to organize. It does not, therefore, include a right not to organize. This relationship between the right of organization and the right of association is important to understand the judicial decisions concerning the effectiveness of union-shop agreements.

361. A union-shop agreement means an agreement by which the union obligates an employer to dismiss any employees who have not joined or have been expelled or resigned from the union. Union-shop agreements are very popular in Japan, especially among unions in large companies, because most unions are enterprise unions (*see* Chapter 3, section 2). As of 201, 69.8% of unions have union-shop agreements.[180] Other union security agreements, such as closed-shop agreements and agency-shop agreements, are almost unheard of. Because of the construction of the Constitution, Article 28, it has been considered that the right to organize is superior to the freedom not to associate so that a union-shop agreement can be effectively concluded between the union and the employer if such a union represents the majority of the workers in the particular establishment.[181] As a result, the courts have held that the employer may dismiss the employee for non-membership in accordance with such a union-shop agreement without abusing his or her right to dismiss.[182] The courts, however, have restricted the legal application of a union-shop agreement to some extent. Thus, the Supreme Court has ruled that a stipulation of a union-shop agreement which entitled an employer to dismiss an employee on the grounds of non-membership of a particular union was made ineffective by Article 90 of Civil Code (voidance in violation of public policy), applied against those employees who had become members of another union or organized their own union, and that therefore the dismissal of such employees was void unless there was any other rational reason justifying it.[183] In addition, in a case in which an employer dismissed an employee who had been expelled from his union in violation of the union's constitution, the Supreme Court held that the dismissal was void. The Court reasoned that the union-shop agreement could not impose any obligation upon the employer to dismiss the employee in a case in which the expulsion from the union was void because of the violation of the union's constitution and that as a result, the dismissal constituted an abuse of the employer's right to dismiss because the employer had no reason to dismiss him.[184] A result of this ruling is that the employer will be obliged to pay the employee's wages payable but for dismissal. However,

180. Ministry of Health, Labour and Welfare, *Roushi Kankei Sogo Chousa* (Comprehensive Survey on Industrial Relations), 2021.
181. TUL, the proviso to Art. 7.
182. The *Nihon Shokuen Seizo* case, the Supreme Court in 1975, SMS, Vol. 22, No. 4, p. 456.
183. The *Mitsui Unyu* case, the Supreme Court in 1989, RH, No. 552, p. 6; the *Nihon Kokan* case, the Supreme Court in 1989, RH, No. 553, p. 6.
184. The *Nihon Shokuen* case, *supra*.

this result was justifiable because the employer should have been aware of the financial risk when he made the union-shop agreement.[185]

§4. Disciplinary Power of Unions

362. When a worker joins a union, he or she will have rights and duties as a member of the union. Those rights and duties are basically provided for in the union's constitution. There is no statutory provision concerning the legal nature of union constitutions. However, although there is some disagreement as to whether the Constitution should be treated as a contract or legal norm, it is generally considered that it has binding force unless it violates public policy or good morals (Civil Code, Article 90), laws or ordinances. This is justified on the grounds that Article 28 of the Constitution as well as TUA provide union protection and promote the union. Union constitutions are always important in deciding what sort of rights and obligations exist between the union and its members. They often play an important role in determining the effectiveness of a union's disciplinary actions against its members.

363. Most union constitutions have a provision concerning disciplinary matters including causes for disciplinary action, measures of disciplinary action and disciplinary procedures. There are some disagreements as to why the union has disciplinary power against its members. One view is that the union – as a voluntary organization – acquires the power when a worker makes a membership contract with it. The second view is that the union's disciplinary power derives from Article 28 of the Constitution. The Supreme Court has stated:

> the power of the union to take disciplinary action against its members differs from that of other ordinary organizations and derives from Article 28 of the Constitution as part of the union's right of organization as long as it is necessary and reasonable for the union to do so.[186]

However, there is a third view, an influential academic view, that the union's authority to discipline its members is based on the contract of affiliation and is reinforced in some respects and regulated in other respects by the special treatment accorded to unions by the Constitution and the TUA.[187]

364. Most union constitutions provide for the following as causes for disciplinary action against union members: serious violation of the constitution and directives and serious disregard to union policy and decisions. As measures for of disciplinary action, they provide for expulsion, suspension of membership rights, fines, censure or warnings. Most union constitutions also provide for the procedural

185. The *Seishinkai Yamamoto Byoin* case, the Supreme Court in 1984, RH, No. 427, p. 17.
186. The *Mitsui Bibai Tanko* case, the Supreme Court in 1968, *Saikosaibansho Keijijiken Saibanreishu* (SKS), Vol. 22, No. 13, p. 1425.
187. Sugeno & Yamakawa, *supra*, p. 978.

requirements such as an accused member's opportunity of defence, decision of expulsion to be made in the union's general meeting or delegates' meeting, the vote for decision to be conducted by secret ballot. Where a disciplinary action taken against a member for some justifiable cause is too harsh according to the common sense of society, it will be void as it shall be considered to be an abuse of the union's disciplinary powers.[188] Such disciplinary action may also constitute a tort.[189] The courts have also made the expulsion of union members void on the following procedural grounds: violation of the union constitution's requirement of a secret ballot;[190] disregard of the member's right according to the union constitution to defend himself before an inquiry committee;[191] the notice of the general meeting for the discussion of the expulsion being sent to the members three days later than required by the union constitution.[192]

365. It is often rather difficult to decide whether a disciplinary action against a member is justifiable or not because it may infringe upon the member's political freedom, right to free speech or right to union activities. The courts have held that disciplinary action taken against a member for his or her following conduct is void: standing as a candidate for a city assembly despite the union's decision to uniformly support another candidate,[193] supporting a candidate for the Diet authorized by a political party despite the union's decision to support uniformly another candidate authorized by a different party,[194] criticizing the union's decision to collect extra union dues in order to support a candidate for the Diet,[195] distributing handbills which criticize the union executives without involving slanderous, defamatory or false remarks,[196] disobeying the union's illegal instruction, etc.[197] Here, it is important to strike an adequate balance in each case between the effectuation of the union's right to organize and the employee's constitutional rights such as freedom of expression.

---

188. The *Zennissan Jidosha Roso* case, the Yokohama District Court in 1987, RH, No. 505, p. 31.
189. The *Shimotsui Dentetsu* case, the Hiroshima High Court, the Okayama Branch in 1989, RMS, Vol. 40, Nos 4–5, p. 610.
190. The *Kokusai Kogyo* case, the Tokyo District Court in 1956, RMS, Vol. 7, No. 4, p. 660.
191. The *Nogami Dentetsu Roso* case, the Wakayama District Court in 1957, RMS, Vol. 8, No. 5, p. 542.
192. The *Yamanashi Kashikiri Jidosha* case, the Tokyo High Court in 1981, *Hanrei Times* (HT), No. 442, p. 142.
193. The *Mitsui Bibai Tanko* case, the Supreme Court in 1968, SKS, Vol. 22, No. 13, p. 1425.
194. The *Nakasato Kogyojo* case, the Supreme Court in 1969, *Saikosaibansho Saibanshu Minji* (SSM), No. 95, p. 257.
195. The *Doro Hiroshima Chihon* case, the Hiroshima District Court in 1973, HJ, No. 733, p. 35.
196. The *Showa Lock Roso* case, the Osaka District in 1981, RH, No. 357, p. 18.
197. The *Kokuro Hiroshima Chihon* case, the Supreme Court in 1975, RHS, No. 901, p. 25.

Chapter 2. The Trade Unions and Employers' Associations

§1. The Trade Unions

366. As seen in Chapter 3, section 2, most Japanese unions are enterprise unions. The unionization rate was estimated at 17.7% as of 2023. This current figure is considerably low compared with 55.8% around 1950.[198] The decrease in the unionization rate has been caused by a decrease in the proportion of secondary industry, advances in technical innovation, an increase in the number of peripheral workers and changes in workers' values. Most Japanese enterprise unions have, in fact, excluded peripheral or non-regular workers from their membership. It is also true that the unions' attitude, which makes much of the principle of equality among members and leans towards collectivism, is disliked by younger workers aspiring to individualism and freedom. Besides enterprise unions, there are a small number of regional or national general unions which cover workers in diverse small enterprises. Such 'community unions' are very active in organizing dispatched workers as well as part-time workers. Sometimes unorganized workers join the 'community unions' after they are discharged. Labour disputes between such unions and employers have been increasing.

367. Most enterprise unions are affiliated with industrial federations. These industrial federations and some of the more important enterprise unions are affiliated with the national centres: *Rengo*, *Zenroren* and *Zenrokyo*. However, union federations and national centres do not have strong decision-making power since their decisions often do not have the power to effectively bind their member unions. Even though the union federations or their officials sometimes participate in negotiations between their member unions and employers, the collective agreement will usually be concluded between the member union and the employer. In practice, union federations and national centres draw up general policies and coordinate and assist member unions in negotiations and consultation with employers. Also, Rengo, the largest national centre, often participates in the process of making labour policies through recommending candidates for members of the Labour Policy Council, a tripartite council that makes policy proposals for labour matters including legislation.

368. Enterprise unions generally have resolution organs, executive organs and auditing organs. The resolution organ is called a 'general meeting' or 'grand meeting'. Such a meeting generally decides the following matters: policies regarding activities, budget, appointment of executives, amendment of constitution or general principles, ratification of collective agreements, disciplinary matters, industrial actions, etc. Most union constitutions provide that a regular general meeting will be held once a year but an extra general meeting may be held under certain conditions. Many union constitutions provide that a quorum for a general meeting is one-third of the total union members and that a resolution shall require a majority of votes of members present by a secret ballot. Many unions have an interim resolution organ,

198. Ministry of Health, Labour and Welfare, *Rodo-Kumiai Kiso Chosa* (Basic Surveys on Trade Unions), 2013.

a so-called central committee which sometimes has authority to act for a general meeting until the latter is held. However, an interim resolution organ sometimes has an authority to decide only on limited matters. The executive organ is one which executes matters decided by resolution organs and represents the union to outsiders. It is generally called an executive committee, which consists of a president, vice-president, chief secretary and other committee members. The auditing organ is one which audits execution of union business. However, although unions do not have a legal obligation to set up an auditing organ, most unions have such an organ. Many unions set up an election committee, disciplinary committee or other committees.

369. Unions are financed by union dues collected from their members. Union dues are classified into general dues and extra dues. General dues are used for financing the ordinary union budget. The amount of a member's general dues per month is about one or two per cent of his or her monthly wages. The extra dues are used for financing specific union activities such as political activity and supporting other unions. The Supreme Court has held that members are not obliged to pay extra union dues to directly finance political activities but are obliged to pay them to assist other members who are subject to the employer's disciplinary action because of their participation in political strikes.[199] Besides general and extra union dues, special dues are regularly collected from members to make a fund which will be reserved to finance industrial action in the future.

370. Where a union has the status of a juridical personality or incorporated entity, it owns, of course, its property.[200] In comparison, there is some disagreement as to whether union property is owned by the union or in proportional shares by its individual members, in cases where a union does not have a juridical personality although it has a substance of union organization. In fact, many unions do not have the status of a juridical personality because they are not required to do so in order to enjoy legal protection in labour relations. The Supreme Court has held that a union which does not have the status of a juridical personality belongs to all the members in 'communal ownership' as opposed to simple co-ownership.[201] Therefore, whether or not a union has the status of a juridical personality, union members have no individual share of the union property even when they leave the union. There is a debate whether this principle applies when one union is split into two or more groups that have a substance of union organization.

371. The union will be dissolved upon the occurrence of circumstances requiring dissolution as provided for in its union constitution or when the resolution for dissolution is adopted at its general meeting by a plurality of three-fourths or more of the members or the affiliated unions (TUA, Article 10). Where a union has the status of a juridical personality, the assets will revert to the persons designated in the union constitution or the union's endowment. If there is no such person or no method by which such a person is to be determined specified therein, the assets may

199. The *Kokuro Hiroshima Chihon* case, the Supreme Court in 1975, RH, No. 240, p. 24.
200. The *Kokuro Oita Chihon* case, the Supreme Court in 1974, SMS, Vol. 28, No. 6, p. 1382.
201. The *Shinagawa Shirorenga* case, the Supreme Court in 1957, SMS, Vol. 11, No. 12, p. 1943.

be disposed for objects similar to those of the union with the permission of the competent authorities and by a resolution of a general meeting. If the assets may not be disposed of in the above-stated manner, they will revert to the National Treasury (TUA Articles 13 et seq.). Where a union does not have the status of a juridical personality, its assets belong to its members in 'communal ownership' and, according to the Supreme Court's decision, the abolishment of this 'communal ownership' requires the consent of all the members.[202]

§2. The Employers' Associations

372. Currently, there are three employers' associations; the Federation of Economic Organization (*Keidanren*), the Japan Association of Corporate Executives (*Keizaidoyukai*), and the Japan Chambers of Commerce and Industry (*Shokokaigisho*). Formerly, there was the Japan Federation of Employers Association (*Nikkeiren*), which represented the interests of larger companies in the field of labour relations. However, in 2002, *Nikkeiren* was merged with *Keidanren*, and its activities are carried out as one of the functions of *Keidanren*. *Shokokaigisho* represents the opinions of its members, medium- and small- enterprises in particular, on important government policies and provides information and advice on labour relations for these enterprises. However, *Keidanren* and *Shokokaigisho* do not have a significant role in deciding working conditions and industrial relations in individual companies because collective bargaining takes place almost exclusively between individual enterprises and enterprise unions. Meanwhile, *Keizaidoyukai* represents the interests of business in general but is not involved in labour relations. At any rate, employers in Japan enjoy only the freedom of association while workers enjoy the right of organization, and therefore, unlike the trade unions, the employers' associations are not specially protected by law. Representatives of some of these employer organizations participate in the Labour Policy Council, as in the case of Rengo.

202. *Ibid.*

Chapter 3. The Workers' Participation in the Enterprise

§1. Different Forms of Workers' Participation

373. As mentioned before, collective bargaining mostly takes place at enterprise level, industrial relations within an enterprise being the most important part of the Japanese industrial relations system. There is no doubt that collective bargaining is a very important form of workers' participation in the company's decision-making process. However, at enterprise level, there are various important forms of workers' participation other than collective bargaining. These are: the statutory system of workers' participation in the form of employees' representatives and voluntary systems of workers' participation in the form of joint labour-management consultation, the workshop meeting system (*shokuba kondankai*), the grievance procedures system, the suggestion system, the self-reporting system, etc.

§2. Employees' Representative System (Jugyoin Daihyo Sei)

374. There are many statutory provisions which require the employer to acquire the consent of the employees' representatives. The employees' representative means here, in principle, either the trade union, where there exists a trade union organized by a majority of employees at the workplace concerned, or the representative of a majority of the employees, where there does not exist a trade union organized by a majority of employees. The form of participation of this representative which these provisions require can be classified into conclusion of an agreement with the employer, submission of opinion to the employer and recommendation of committee members to the employer. With regard to these three different forms of participation of employees' representative, the main provisions will be seen below.

375. The main provisions requiring a written agreement between an employer and an employees' representative (the so-called worker-management agreement) are those concerning the calculation of working hours outside the premises (*see* Part I, Chapter 3, section 1), the introduction of flexible working hours (*see* Part I, Chapter 3, section 2), overtime work (*see* Part I, Chapter 3, section 4), planned annual paid holidays (*see* Part I, Chapter 3, section 7) and the exception to the regulations concerning wage payments (*see* Part I, Chapter 4, section 4). Other provisions include those worker-management agreements required for specifying workers who cannot take childcare leave (CFLA, Article 6), for workers' savings entrusted to the employer by the employees (LSA, Article 18), for excepting from the employer's obligation to take the statutorily required measures to preserve retirement allowances, for specifying a certain amount of money to ensure payment of retirement allowances (Enforcement Ordinance of the SWPA, Articles 4 and 5), for employment adjustment measures that enable employers to apply for government subsidies (Enforcement Ordinance of the EIA, Article 102-3) and so on. The main provisions requiring employers to hear the opinion of employees' representatives are those concerning drawing up a *shugyo-kisoku* (*see* Chapter 6, section 6) and drawing up a safety and health improvement plan (Industrial Safety and Health Act, Article 78).

The main provisions requiring an employees' representative to make a recommendation to the employer are also found in the Enforcement Ordinance of SWPA the Industrial Safety and Health Act of 1972 and the Act on Special Measures for Improvement of Working Time Arrangements (formerly the Promotion of Shorter Working Hours Act of 1992). The Industrial Safety and Health Act requires the employer to establish a safety committee and a health committee (or a safety and health committee in lieu of these two separate committees) for each workplace in a certain industry and of a certain size. For one-half of the members other than a chairperson, the employer must designate those persons recommended by the employees' representative (Articles 17–19). However, these committees are merely advisory bodies and their resolutions are not binding upon the employers. The Act on Special Measures for Improvement of Working Time Arrangements requires the employer to make a good-faith effort to establish a committee for the improvement of working time arrangements (Article 6). The employer must designate those persons recommended by the employees' representative as one-half of the members of the committee. In contrast to the safety and health committees, this committee's resolutions have certain legal effects. Namely, they will be treated as written agreements between the employer and the employees' representative with regard to the calculation of working hours outside the premises, the introduction of flexible working hours, overtime work, planned annual paid holidays, etc. (Article 7). Article 38.4 of LSA provides for a similar type of committee (the so-called worker-management committee) which determines to adopt discretionary work arrangement (*see* Part I, Chapter 3, section 2). Employees' representative systems other than the worker-management committee are not standing committees in nature and there are no precise regulations concerning the method of selecting committee members, their term of service, guarantee of their status, etc. There is some demand for enacting a law to establish a standing organ of employees' representatives in the enterprise and to regulate their selection, term of service, status guarantee, etc., having regard to the rapid decrease in union membership.

§3. Joint Labour–Management Consultation System (Roshi Kyogi Sei)

376. A survey in 2018[203] found that many of the surveyed establishments employing thirty or more workers had a workshop meeting system (52.7%) and a grievance procedure system (57.8%). It also found that 37.1% of these establishments had joint labour–management consultation systems: 83.9% of the organized establishments and 16.8% of the unorganized establishments.

377. Working hours, holidays and vacation (86.0%), health and safety (77.3%), wages and retirement allowance (69.9%) and mandatory retirement system and continuing employment after retirement age (65.2%) were most often discussed in joint labour–management consultation committees.

203. Ministry of Health, Labour and Welfare, Heisei 30 Nen *Roshi Communication Chosa* (2018 Survey on Communication between Employees and Employers), 2018.

378. Since a joint labour–management consultation discusses matters concerning working conditions as well as matters related to business management, a question arises which system is more often utilized to discuss major matters at the workplace. According to the 2022 survey of companies that employ thirty or more workers, matters relating to wages and retirement allowances are more often discussed in collective bargaining (57.3%) than in joint labour–management consultation (37.6%). On the other hand, matters relating to hiring plan and personnel management such as termination, transfer, performance evaluation and promotion are more often discussed in joint labour–management consultation (47.2%) than in collective bargaining (32.1%). Matters relating to working hours, leaves and holidays are almost equally discussed in collective bargaining (42.5%) than in joint labour–management consultation (43.1%). This suggests there is a tendency that matters more closely related to managerial policies (hiring plan and personnel management such as termination, transfer, performance evaluation and promotion are such matters) are more often discussed in joint labour–management consultation, which has less adversarial nature than collective bargaining in that strikes are not supposed to be carried out and more frank exchange of views and information is expected in the process of joint labour–management consultation.

379. The 2022 survey mentioned above found that 49.8% of surveyed unions regarded collective bargaining as the most important means of resolving the future problems of industrial relations in contrast with joint labour–management consultation (43.3%). However, it should be noted that in large companies employing 5,000 or more workers, joint labour–management consultation is regarded more important (52.3%) than collective bargaining (39.4%). On the other hand, in small companies employing 30 to 99 workers, surveyed unions' view is opposite (collective bargaining is 64.8%; joint labour–management consultation 23.8%). This indicates that joint labour–management consultation is more rooted in large companies, in which union organization rate is usually high and the relationship between the union and employer is usually more stable. .

Chapter 4. Collective Bargaining

§1. Introduction

380. As already mentioned most unions in Japan are enterprise unions. However, an enterprise union is sometimes composed of plural child or local unions (establishment unions) in each establishment of the enterprises. Most unions are affiliated with industrial federations or other types of federation. According to the 2022 survey, 85.4% of unions had collective bargaining by themselves; 11.8% had collective bargaining together with their parent unions organized in the same enterprises; 3.2% had collective bargaining together with industrial federations with which they were affiliated, and 1.1% had collective bargaining together with area organizations of the unions with which they were affiliated.[204]

§2. Parties to Collective Bargaining

381. The unions which satisfy the requirements provided for under TUA, Article 2 are entitled to be the 'party' to collective bargaining. This entitlement is regardless of the size of the union. Theoretically, even a union with only two members is entitled to bargain. Where there are a number of unions in a plant, the employer has to bargain with them. The employer may not refuse to have collective bargaining with a minority union because of its size. Since the exclusive representation system as in the United States does not exist in Japan, such Japanese system is called 'plural representation system'. A federation of unions which satisfies the requirements of Article 2 has its own right to bargain collectively with the employers with whom its member unions are entitled to collective bargaining if it has power to control their member union. However, the federation's right to collective bargaining is limited to matters common to its member unions and those concerning negotiation procedures and the like. If the federation union is particularly given the right to bargain on matters on which the member unions have the right to bargain, it can require the employers to collectively bargain with them. However, in such a case, the employer may require it to adjust negotiating authority with its member union in order to avoid duplicitous negotiations. The employer sometimes negotiates with the majority enterprise union to insert a 'single bargaining representative' clause in the collective agreement. This clause means that the employer does not have collective bargaining with a union other than that union. However, this infringes on other unions' right to collective bargaining and therefore is void.[205] Even a branch union (e.g., an establishment union), if it satisfies the requirements of Article 2, has its own right to collective bargaining with the employer independently of its parent union (an enterprise union) collectively. However, its collective bargaining right is subject to the enterprise union's power to control and cannot be exercised in conflict with

---

204. Ministry of Health, Labour and Welfare, *Reiwa 4 Nen Roushi kan no Kosho nni Kansuru jittai chosa* (2022 Survey on Collective Bargaining), 2022.

205. The *Takikawa Kagaku* case, the Sapporo District Court in 1949, *Rodokankei Minjijiken Saibanreishu*, No. 6, p. 137.

the enterprise union's right to collective bargaining.[206] An employer who has a contract of employment with employees who are members of the union to collective bargaining is the other party to collective bargaining. Where an employer is a corporation, the party to collective bargaining is the corporation itself and not be its organs such as factory or branch managers.[207] As an employers' association does not employ workers, it is qualified as the party to collective bargaining only where its articles provide that it can be the party to collective bargaining for its member employers.[208]

382. The 'negotiators' in collective bargaining should be distinguished from the 'parties' to collective bargaining. They are persons who actually conduct the negotiations.[209] TUA, Article 6 provides that representatives of a union or those to whom authority has been delegated by a union have authority to negotiate with the employer or the employers' organization. Therefore, the president, vice-president or other executive members are entitled to be the negotiators in collective bargaining on behalf of their union. Other persons such as executive members of parent unions can be negotiators if the authority to negotiate is delegated to them by the union. The employer sometimes negotiates with the union to insert into their collective agreement a clause prohibiting the delegation of the negotiation authority to third parties. Such a clause intends to exclude outsiders, especially officials of the federation of unions. The effectiveness of such a clause has not been clarified by judicial cases. However, a presently prevalent view is that a union may voluntarily limit its own negotiating persons to its members and that they are therefore valid.[210] Who should be the negotiators on the employer's side is at his/her discretion. Not only directors or managerial employees but also attorneys such as counsels of the employer can participate in collective bargaining if they are delegated authorities to do so.

§3. Subjects, Forms and Procedures of Collective Bargaining

383. The subject matters of collective bargaining are classified into 'compulsory bargaining matters' and 'voluntary bargaining matters'. Compulsory bargaining matters are the matters over which the employer is legally bound to collectively bargain with the union if the union requires him or her to do so. On the other hand, voluntary bargaining matters are those over which the employers themselves can decide whether they wish to respond to the union's request to bargain. Compulsory bargaining matters are limited to (a) the matters concerning conditions of work and other matters relating to the treatment of workers and (b) those concerning the operation of industrial relations. As a matter of course, the employers must have a

206. The *Oriental Motor case*, the Tokyo High Court in 1987, RH, No. 503, p. 89.
207. The *Tokai Ryokyaku Tetsudo* case, the Osaka District Court in 1989, RH, No. 548, p. 6.
208. K. Yamaguchi, *Rodokumiaiho* 159 (Yuhikaku 2d ed. 1996).
209. Sugeno & Yamakawa, *supra*, p. 1003.
210. Tokyo Daigaku Rodo Ho Kenkyukai, *Chushaku Rodo Kumiai Hu Jo*, Tokyo: Yuhikaku, 1980, p. 296.

power to determine these matters. The matters under (a) include standards or procedures concerning wages, working hours, health and safety, vocational training, welfare, job assignment, discipline, dismissal. Although it is questionable whether individual member's dismissal and work assignments can be the matters under (a) the courts have generally held that they are also compulsory bargaining matters.[211] The matters under (b) include union-shop, check-off, lending of office space as a union office, rules and procedure of collective bargaining, joint labour-management consultation and industrial dispute. Voluntary bargaining matters include those matters which do not come under either (a) or (b). Therefore, matters such as plan of business and production, introduction of new technology, removal, closure or dispersion of factories, or appointment or discharge of corporate executives are usually regarded as voluntary bargaining matters. However, those matters can still be compulsory bargaining matters so long as they have an effect on the employees' employment or working conditions.

384. The employer has the duty to negotiate in good faith with the union. Thus, the employer must not only sit down at the table for negotiation but must also respond to the union's demands in concrete terms. Therefore, for example, the following employer's attitudes do not discharge his or her duty of collective bargaining: response to the union only by telephone, fax and letters;[212] failure to submit to the union any explanation or information materializing in his or her refusal to the union's demands;[213] persistence in his or her counter-proposals without justifiable reasons;[214] refusal to sign a written agreement, without just cause, whose contents have been agreed.[215] At the beginning of collective bargaining, the parties to it, conditions of bargaining such as time, place and negotiators and subject matters must be made clear. Usually, the union first submits a proposal for collective bargaining and then both parties agree on such matters before collective bargaining on subject matters begin. It is illegal for the employer to unilaterally restrict the date, time, place and member of union negotiators, etc. without justifiable reasons.[216] Of course, the employer is not obligated to accept the union's demand. After the employer has bargained in good faith with the union until the impasse, where there is no likelihood of narrowing the gap, the employer can terminate the bargaining.

§4. Remedies

385. When an employer refuses to collectively bargain, the union is entitled to apply to the LRC for administrative remedies (*see* Part II, Chapter 7). There is disagreement among academic views concerning the possibility of the union's petition

211. The *Naragakuen* case, the Supreme Court in 1992, RH, No. 624, p. 9.
212. The *Seiwa Denki Sangyo* case, the Tokyo District Court in 1990, RH, No. 5562, p. 83.
213. The *Otemae Takamatsu Koko* case, the Supreme Court in 1990, RH, No. 600, p. 9.
214. The *Nihon Mail Order* case, the Supreme Court in 1984, HJ, No. 1129, p. 131.
215. The *Osaka Shoken* case, the Tokyo District Court in 1993, RH, No. 626, p. 83.
216. The *Shodai Jidosha Kyoshujo* case, the Tokyo District Court in 1988, RH, No. 516, p. 61.

for a court order requiring the employer to comply with the union's collective bargaining request. Recently, most lower court decisions have rejected the union's petition for such a provisional order on the grounds that the right to collective bargaining under paragraph 2, Article 7 of TUA is not a private right but a public right; that, even if it was a private right, it is impossible to specify how the employer should bargain collectively with the union; that the judicial enforcement for a provisional order requiring the employer to collectively bargain with the union cannot be expected to have a great practical effect.[217] However, an influential academic view has asserted that the union should be able to seek a provisional order declaring its status to bargain over specific subjects on the basis of the requirements of TUA and Article 28 of the Constitution.[218] Accordingly, a high court held that Article 7 has an effect as a private law in that it entitles the union the status to require the employer to collectively bargain with it and therefore that the union can petition the court for a judgment declaring that the union has such a status. This ruling was supported by the Supreme Court.[219]

386. If the right to collective bargaining is one to be protected as a private right, the employer's refusal of collective bargaining may constitute a tort. Indeed, courts have generally held that Article 28 of the Constitution should be construed as a law to establish a public policy requiring the employer to respect the workers' right to collective bargaining. Therefore, the employer's refusal to comply with the union's request for collective bargaining without just cause may constitute a tort.[220]

217. The *Shinbun No Shinbunsha* case, the Tokyo High Court in 1975, Vol. 26, No. 5, p. 723.
218. Sugeno & Yamakawa, *supra*, p. 1029.
219. The *Kokutetsu* case, the Tokyo High Court in 1987, RMS, Vol. 38, No. 1, p. 1; the Supreme Court in 1991, RH. No. 589, p. 6.
220. The *Seiwa Denki Sangyo* case, the Iwaki Branch of the Fukushima District Court in 1989, RMS, Vol. 38, No. 6, p. 1.

Chapter 5. The Collective Agreement

§1. The Significance of the Collective Agreement

387. In Japan, the provisions of TUA give special legal effects to collective agreements, which are concluded in a specific form required by it. Therefore, as seen later, the term 'collective agreement' is not used as meaning a mere agreement between the employer and union in this chapter. Namely, it means an agreement between a union and an employer which is put in writing and is either signed by or with names affixed with seals by both of the parties. Most collective agreements are concluded between the enterprise union and the employer in a specific company (enterprise) because collective bargaining usually takes place between them. This is the case even though the negotiation on wages has been carried out through the method of *Shunto* (*see* Chapter 3, section 2, V).

388. According to a survey conducted in 2017[221] on collective agreements of unions having thirty or more members, 94.7% of those unions had collective agreements. More than 50% of those collective agreements stipulated the following items: personnel actions such as dismissal and disciplinary action, wages and working hours. . It is to be noted that an agreement made through collective bargaining or joint labour-management consultation between the employer and the union is often imported into the shugyo-kisoku (work rules) instead of resulting in a formal collective agreement. The items regarding management such as introduction of new technology an downsizing, closing or transfer of workplaces are stipulated only in 21.3% of collective agreements.

§2. Formation of the Collective Agreement

389. Those who qualify as parties to collective agreements are the same as those for collective bargaining. Therefore, a union such as a branch organization, an enterprise union and a federation of unions which satisfies the requirements provided under Article 2 of TUA qualify. As regards the form of the agreement, Article 14 of TUA provides that collective agreements must be put in writing and be either signed by or with names affixed with seals by both of the parties concerned. There is some disagreement as to what effect is legally given to an oral agreement or an agreement without the parties' signatures or seals. One view considers that such an agreement should have the same effect as a collective agreement. Another view considers that it has an effect merely as an ordinary contract between two parties. The Supreme Court took the second view, holding that an agreement that does not fulfil the requirement under Article 14 does not have special normative effect that the TUA provides.[222] However, there seems to be no reason to deny that it has an effect as an

221. Ministry of Health, Labour and Welfare, *Heise 29 Nen Rosho Kan no Kosho ni Kansuru Jittai Chosa* (Survey on Collective Bargaining), 2017.
222. *Tominami Jidosha Kyoshujo* case, the Supreme Court in 2001, RH, No. 805, p. 23.

ordinary contract if it is considered that TUA gives special normative effects only to the collective agreement which is formed in the prescribed form.

390. A term of validity exceeding three years should not be provided for in a collective agreement. A collective agreement providing for a term of validity exceeding three years is regarded as a collective agreement providing for a term of validity of three years (TUA, Article 15(1) and (2)). However, some collective agreements provide a clause of automatic renewal or automatic extension. A clause of automatic renewal means a provision which makes the collective agreement valid for a similar period of time unless either party gives notice before its expiration to amend or revoke it. In this case, of course, the new period of time must not be over three years. A clause of automatic extension means a provision which extends the term of collective agreement until the parties reach agreement on a new contract or for any other prescribed period. In this case, the prescribed period plus the duration of the original term of collective agreement must not exceed three years.

§3. Legal Effect of the Collective Agreement

I. The Contents of the Collective Agreement

391. As the basic nature of the collective agreement is a contract between the union and the employer, the collective agreement as a whole has a contractual effect on both parties. This contractual effect of the collective agreement is called a 'contract-obligation effect'. In addition, Article 16 of the TUA gives a normative effect especially to the standards concerning conditions of work and other matters relating to the treatment of workers provided for in the collective agreement. The part of the collective agreement to which such a normative effect is given is called a 'normative part'. This part includes, for example, provisions concerning wages, working hours, safety and health, workers' accident compensation, discipline, etc. The remaining part is called a 'contract-obligation part'. Aside from this 'normative part', collective agreements usually includes, for example, provisions concerning union membership qualification, granting of facilities to the union, union activities, collective bargaining, the procedure of industrial disputes, joint labour-management consultation, etc. These provisions only have a 'contract-obligation effect'. Therefore, the contents of the collective agreement are usually divided into two parts: the normative part with a normative effect and the contract-obligation part with a contract-obligation effect. Precisely speaking, however, the normative part has a contract-obligation effect as well as a normative effect.

II. Normative Effect

392. Article 16 of the TUA provides that any provision in an individual labour contract contravening the standards concerning conditions of work and other matters relating to the treatment of workers provided for in the collective agreement shall be void and that the invalidated provision shall be governed by the provisions of the standards. It also provides that the same rule shall apply to any part of the collective agreement which is not provided for in the individual labour contract. Therefore, the normative effect of the collective agreement is divided into the effect of compulsorily invalidating any inconsistent part of an individual employment contract, and of directly reforming that part.[223]

393. The normative part which has a normative effect is the part providing for the 'standards' concerning conditions of work and other matters relating to the treatment of workers. The term 'standards' has not been construed in a strictly literal sense. A typical example is the majority view on the effect of union consultation clauses or union consent clauses which require the employer to consult with or obtain consent from the union prior to the transfer, discipline or dismissal of workers. Although there have been a small number of cases in which consultation or consent clauses are held not to constitute a normative part because they provide only for a decision-making procedure, the majority of courts' decisions have indicated that they have normative effects because they provide for the standards concerning treatment. Accordingly, the majority of courts' decisions have made the transfer, discipline or dismissal of workers in contravention of consultation or consent clauses void. However, this legal consequence may be led to by the principle of abuse of a right even if those clauses do not have normative effects because they do not provide for the standards concerning treatment. It has often been disputed whether an employer contravenes consultation or consent clauses. The courts have held that there is no contravention of such clauses where the union did not respond to the employer's proposal for consultation or where the union refused to give consent to the employer after a sufficient consultation.

394. It has been discussed whether the provision of better working conditions in the individual contract should be interpreted as 'contravening' the standards of the collective agreement or not. In other words, it has been questioned whether a collective agreement can impose disadvantages on workers. The Supreme Court has recently made it clear that it takes an affirmative view on this principle. It stated as follows:

> Having regard to the process and circumstances under which the collective agreement concerned was concluded, the financial conditions of the company and the rationality of standards as a whole provided by the collective agreement, it cannot be said that the collective agreement at issue was concluded in deviating from the union's expected purpose, for example, that it was concluded in order to treat specific or part of the member workers specially disadvantageously. Therefore, there is no reason to deny its normative effect.[224]

395. Accordingly, the union can, in principle, impose disadvantages on its members by concluding a collective agreement with the employer. However, as stated by the above rulings of the Supreme Court, its normative effect may be denied for

223. Sugeno & Yamakawa, *supra*, p. 1043.
224. The *Asahi Kaijokasai Hoken (Ishido)* case, the Supreme Court in 1997, RH, No. 713, p. 27.

an exceptional substantive reason as a deviation from the union's expected purpose. For example, in the *Tomotetsudo* case where the union concluded a collective agreement reducing by 30% the wages of all employees aged 56 or older who had not accepted the company's proposal for their early retirement, the Hiroshima High Court denied the normative effect of that agreement on the grounds that such a big reduction of wages of only those aged employees did not have no sense of reasonableness.[225] Besides, the normative effect may also be denied for serious defects in the union's process of making its collective agreement. For example, in the *Nakane Seisakujo* case where the union concluded a collective agreement reducing the amount of older employees' retirement to a great extent without properly getting from its members an authority to conclude it, the Tokyo High denied the normative effect of that agreement on the grounds of the procedural defects.[226] Apart from the question as to whether a collective agreement can impose disadvantages on workers, there have been cases where courts denied the normative effect of collective agreements with regard to certain matters simply because the union did not have the power to decide on such matters. For example, courts held that the union could not conclude a collective agreement which entitled an employer to terminate individual union members' employment and to dispose of their accrued wages or retirement allowance.[227] Another court held that the union could not conclude a collective agreement on compulsory retirement age which enabled the employer to terminate the contract of an elderly worker who had been employed over the age of the previous compulsory retirement age.[228]

III. General Binding Effect

396. The coverage of the normative effect of a collective agreement is limited to the working conditions and other matters relating to the treatment of members of the union that concludes the agreement. However, the TUA provides for two kinds of extension of the effect of collective agreements. One is the general binding effect in the workplace (Article 17) and the other is that in the locality (Article 18). The first is automatically recognized when three-quarters of 'the workers of a similar kind regularly employed' in a plant or workplace come under the application of a collective agreement and the effect of the agreement is extended to cover the remaining workers of a same kind employed in the plant or workplace. The second is recognized by the decision of the Minister of Health, Labour and Welfare or the Governor of the Prefecture to extend the effect of an agreement which applies to the majority of similar workers in a certain locality to the remaining workers of the same kind in the same locality and their employers. The decision of the Minister of Health, Labour and Welfare or the Governor is taken at the request of one or both

225. The *Tomotetsuso* case, the Hiroshima High Court in 2004, RH, No. 879, p. 82.
226. The *Nakane Seisakujo* case, the Tokyo High Court in 2000, RH, No. 789, p. 6. The appeal was rejected by the Supreme Court in the same year (RH, No. 797, p. 12).
227. The *Hong Kong Shanghai Bank* case, the Supreme Court in 1989, RH, No. 546, p. 6; the *Nippei Isamisangyo* case, the Tokyo District Court in 1956, RMS, Vol. 7, No. 1, p. 231.
228. The *Hokko Taxi* case, the Osaka District Court in 1980, RH, No. 356, p. 9.

of the parties to the collective agreement which is to be extended, and in accordance with the resolution of the LRC. The Commission may amend any of the provisions in the agreement which it finds inappropriate before extending the resolution. Although this general binding effect in the locality has rarely been used because enterprise collective agreements predominate in Japan, there have been a few cases in recent years in which the general binding effect is granted.[229]

397. With regard to the general binding effect in the plant, it has been disputed whether a collective agreement can extend disadvantages to unorganized workers or the workers of other unions. In the *Asahi Kasaikaijo Hoken (Takada)* case, the Supreme Court gave an affirmative answer to this question in a case of unorganized workers. However, the Court stated that the extension of the normative effect would be denied if there were any special reasons for which that it was considerably unreasonable for that agreement to be applied to those unorganized workers, having regard to the degree and contents of the disadvantages, the process of concluding that agreement and other factors including whether those workers have been given opportunities to become members of that union. Indeed, the Court denied the extension of the normative effect of that agreement in this case on the grounds that the plaintiff employee suffered from unreasonably heavy disadvantages and had been excluded from membership of that union.[230] Since the equal rights of minority and majority unions to engage in collective bargaining under Article 28 of the Constitution, it must be said that the normative effect of the majority union cannot extend to members of the minority union,[231] no matter whether the minority union has not yet obtained a collective agreement or not.

398. As far as the general binding effect in the workplace is concerned, another question is what the phrase 'workers of the same kind' means. It is generally considered that whether one is a 'worker of the same kind' should be determined by what persons are subject to the collective agreement. Thus, where a collective agreement applies to administrative or clerical workers as well as production workers, these workers are 'workers of the same kind'. However, managers and supervisors who, pursuant to the TUA, Article 2, paragraph 1, are not covered by a collective agreement, will not be 'workers of the same kind'. There is some disagreement among courts as to whether workers employed under fixed-term contracts or part-time workers are 'workers of the same kind' as regular workers covered by a collective agreement. Some courts consider that it depends upon their duties,[232] the form of their work and the like while others consider that they are not 'workers of the same kind' because the union does not recognize their membership qualification.[233]

229. *See* the website of the Ministry of Health, Labour and Welfare, 'Cases where the Minister of Health, Labour and Welfare Determined Regarding the General Binding Effect of Collective Agreements in localities', 2021 and 2023.
230. The *Asahi Kasaikaijo Hoken (Takada)* case, the Supreme Court in 1996, RH, No. 691, p. 16.
231. *Daiki Kotsu* Case, the Tokyo District Court in 1995, RH, No. 680, p. 34.
232. The *Nihon Yushi* case, the Tokyo District Court in 1949, *Rodokankei Minjijiken Saibanreishu*, No. 6, p. 162.
233. The *Hino Jidosha Kogyo* case, the Tokyo High Court in 1981, RMS, Vol. 32, No. 3–4, p. 437.

399. Special attention should be paid to the consultation or consent clauses. If it is construed that such clauses constitute a contract-obligation part, then it does not have the general binding effect. On the contrary, if it is construed, as a majority of courts' decisions have shown, that they constitute a normative part, then consultation or consent clauses of a majority union organizing three-quarters of workers may apply to the remaining workers of the same kind in the same workplace. However, courts generally deny such application.[234] In other words, it can be said that those normative parts which do not have the effect of compulsorily invalidating any inconsistent part of an individual employment contract do not have the general binding effect. This is reasonable in view of the fact that the union's duty of representation of all employees in the plant has not been recognized in Japan.

IV. Contract-Obligation Effects

400. All the provisions of a collective agreement have an obligatory effect (so-called contract-obligation effect as mentioned above) in the sense that the collective agreement is an agreement between private parties and as such has the same effect as an ordinary contract, giving rights and obligations respectively to both of the parties to the contract. In other words, the provisions which constitute a normative part also have a contract-obligation effect. An obligation which a normative part of the collective agreement imposes on the employer is often called an 'obligation of execution'. An 'obligation of execution' may be regarded as just one of the contract-obligation effects of a collective agreement. However, its importance is emphasized by the fact that it enables the union to request the courts to issue a temporary order or decision declaring the existence of the employer's obligation to provide the working conditions laid down in the collective agreements. The union does not need to get the agreement of all its members to be able to assert its rights deriving from the collective agreement before the courts. The union can sue the employer in its own name without the agreement of individual members.

401. The effect of the check-off agreement between a union and an employer has been a controversial subject. It is an agreement under which the employer deducts union dues directly from their wages and then transfers them to the union. There has been a question as to whether the check-off is subject to the principle of the LSA, Article 24 that wages must be paid in full directly to the workers (*see* Part I, Chapter 4, section 5). The Supreme Court has answered in the affirmative.[235] Accordingly, a check-off agreement between an employer and a minority union is, in principle, not effective because Article 24 provides that any deduction from wages may be permitted in cases otherwise provided for by law or ordinance or in cases where there exists a written agreement with a trade union organized by a majority of the workers at the workplace or with a person representing a majority of the workers. Majority of unions in a particular workplace are effective. There has also been a question as to whether individual union members can require the

234. The *Hitachi Medico* case, the Tokyo High Court in 1980, RH, No. 354, p. 35.
235. The *Saiseikai Chuobyoin* case, the Supreme Court in 1989, SMS, Vol. 43, No. 12, p. 1786.

employer to stop deducting their union dues from their wages according to the check-off agreement. Some theorists assert that this cannot be so. According to them, as the deduction of union dues from wages falls under the standards concerning matters relating to the treatment of workers, the check-off agreement has a normative effect and therefore is binding on individual union members. However, the Supreme Court has held that, in order to deduct their union dues from their wages, it is necessary for the employer to have the consent of individual union members in addition to the check-off agreement with their union.[236]

V. Peace Obligation

402. It has been held that there is a peace obligation on the parties not to resort to dispute acts such as strikes and lock-outs during the life of the collective agreement in order to change matters contained in it. The courts have held that a peace obligation is implied in every collective agreement[237] and therefore that the parties always have such an obligation even if there is no written clause about it. The party who violates this obligation is obliged to pay compensatory damages. There is however a difference of opinions among academics regarding the scope of damages. The majority hold the opinion that it must be the entire loss caused by a violation of the peace obligation. There is also the question of whether a provisional disposition order may be granted to restrain its violation. While there are cases where the courts issued a provisional disposition order,[238] there are cases as well where the courts did not recognize the employer's right to claim for an injunction as the right to be protected by a provisional disposition order[239] or where the courts did not recognize the necessity for issuing a provisional disposition order.[240] Another question is whether the employer can take disciplinary action against an employee who participated in an industrial action violating the peace obligation. The Supreme Court has denied the legal effect of such disciplinary action on the grounds that the employee's participation in a dispute act violating a peace obligation constituted only a breach of his employment contract and not an infringement of workplace discipline.[241]

§4. Termination of Collective Agreements

403. A collective agreement with a term of validity, as seen above, will automatically terminate on the expiry of its term. On the other hand, a collective agreement without a term of validity may be terminated by either party by giving notice to the other party in writing either signed by or with name affixed with seal by the

236. The *Esso Sekiyu* case, the Supreme Court in 1993, RH, No. 650, p. 6; the *Nestle Japan* case, the Supreme Court in 1995, RH, No. 670, p. 10.
237. The *Konan Bus* case, the Supreme Court in 1968, SMS, Vol. 22, No. 13, p. 3194.
238. The *Kyoto Station Hotel* case, the Kyoto District Court in 1960, RMS, Vol. 11, No. 2, p. 354.
239. The *Nihon Shintaku Ginko* case, the Tokyo District Court in 1960, RMS, Vol. 11, No. 3, p. 674.
240. The *Northwest Air* case, the Tokyo High Court in 1973, RH, No. 193, p. 24.
241. The *Konan Bus* case, *supra.*

party giving notice at least ninety days before its termination (TUA, Article 15). A collective agreement can, of course, be terminated by an agreement between both parties. The question has been raised as to whether either party may unilaterally terminate a particular part of a collective agreement without a term of validity by giving ninety days' notice. Academic views generally deny this in principle. The Tokyo High Court has recently held that either party can terminate a particular part of a collective agreement by giving ninety days' notice if the part is separable from the other parts and if the parties could expect at the time of the conclusion of the collective agreement that the part may be separately dealt with in the future.[242] Besides, there are various causes of termination of a collective agreement such as the disappearance of parties, the formation of an inconsistent collective agreement, the achievement of its objects, and the like. On the other hand, the union's amalgamation with another union or the company's merger with another company will not automatically terminate their collective agreement.

404. When a collective agreement terminates, the contract-obligation part will lose its legal foundation and, therefore, clauses providing rights and obligations between the union and the employer will lose its binding effects. What about the effects of the normative part? It is difficult to say that even after a collective agreement expires, the normative effects will remain because, unlike Germany, there is no such legal provision for this. However, it is not realistic for existing conditions of work provided for in the collective agreement to suddenly disappear or change at the termination of a collective agreement. There are two persuasive legal theories which affirm the continuity of the conditions of work provided for in a collective agreement after its termination. One is a view that the contents of the previous collective agreement have been imported into individual employment contracts and remain as the contents of these contracts. Another is a view that the parties to an employment contract usually intend to maintain the previous conditions of work provided in the previous collective agreement till some new agreement is made between them. In a case where employees claimed retirement allowance after the termination of a collective agreement providing for it, the Supreme Court stated that the amount of retirement allowance should be 'determined by a reasonable interpretation of their employment contracts, the *shugyo-kisoku* or others'. In that case, as the *shugyo-kisoku* provided that the retirement allowance was regulated by the collective agreement, the Court held that the contents of that agreement were imported into the *shugyo-kisoku* and remained as the standards to determine retirement allowance.[243] In any event, the contents of the employment contract may be modified when the employer and the union conclude a new collective agreement or when the employer changes the working conditions through the reasonable change of *shugyo-kisoku* according to the requirement of Article 10 of the LCA (*see* Chapter 6, section 6).

242. The *Sony* case, the Tokyo High Court in 1994, RH, No. 675, p. 67.
243. The *Hong Kong Shanghai Bank* case, the Supreme Court in 1989, RH, No. 546, p. 6.

Chapter 6. Dispute Acts and Other Collective Actions

§1. The Notion of Dispute Acts and Other Collective Actions

405. Article 28 of the Constitution guarantees the 'right to act collectively' for all workers. Both in actual industrial relations and in labour law theory the term 'dispute act' is frequently used to mean a variety of union actions for strike purposes. The LRAA gives the following definitions of 'labour dispute' and 'dispute act'. 'Labour dispute' means, 'a disagreement over claims arising between the parties concerned with labour relations regarding labour relations and resulting in either the occurrence of an act of dispute or in conditions where there is the danger of an act of dispute occurring' (LRAA, Article 6). Here, the term 'Labour relations' means collective labour relations. 'Dispute acts' means, 'strikes, slow-downs, lockouts and other acts and counteracts hampering the normal course of work in an enterprise and performed by the parties concerned with labour relations with the object of attaining their respective claims' (Article 7).

406. Although these definitions are given in order to specify the necessary conditions for the initiation of the dispute settlement procedures provided by the LRAA, they have also been relied on for the interpretation of the law which deals with the legal effect of dispute acts. Through the constitutional guarantee of the right to act collectively and the rather broad definition of a dispute act in the LRAA, there is a remarkable tendency in Japanese industrial relations to admit the legality of a variety of actions taken by the unions which hamper the normal course of business. However, a more restrictive view on the concept of dispute acts has been asserted by some influential theorists.[244] It is their view that the central act of the dispute acts is a strike and that the concept of dispute acts should be restricted to strikes and slow-downs (i.e., total or partial refusal to work) and acts to maintain and support them (e.g., picketing, sit-down, etc.). Also, because the constitutional guarantee of the right to act collectively only applies to workers, the employer's right to lock out has been very extensively restricted – especially when compared with the extensive legal recognition granted to dispute acts by the unions.

§2. Proper Dispute Acts

407. As a result of the constitutional guarantee of the right to act collectively, a legal indemnity (exemption from legal liability) is recognized (Articles 1(2) and 8 of TUA) – both in civil and criminal law – for trade union activities. In order to be given indemnity, the act must be carried out by a trade union, be carried out in a proper way, be of a proper type and have a lawful purpose.

244. T. Shimoi, *Roshikankeiho* 169 (Yuhikaku 1995); Sugeno & Yamakawa, *supra*, p. 1078.

I. Acts by Bona Fide Unions

408. The act should be carried out by a bona fide union. For their dispute acts to be protected or given indemnity, unions need not be registered or qualified under the TUA (*see* Part II, Chapter 1, section 2) although they should be bona fide unions. Workers' organizations which confine themselves principally to backing political or social movements, providing mutual aid, or doing other welfare work are not entitled to indemnity. Workers' groups which are not organized in the sense of having their own rules and representatives are not granted legal indemnity for their actions either. The same is true of a group within a union which engages in dispute acts without official authorization from the union or in violation of the union's policy (unauthorized or so-called wild-cat strikes). Thus, 'wild-cat' strikes are not protected in usual cases.

II. The Purpose of the Dispute Acts

409. Article 2 of the TUA provides that the trade union's main purpose should be to maintain and improve working conditions and raise the economic status of the workers. Therefore, dispute acts which intend to pursue these purposes are in principle proper dispute acts. However, since Article 28 of the Constitution is construed to guarantee dispute rights as a means to make the collective bargaining process substantially function,[245] these purposes should be restricted to those which are attainable through the collective bargaining process. Accordingly, dispute acts aimed at demonstrating workers' particular political opinions are improper because such a purpose is not generally attainable by collective bargaining.[246] A so-called sympathy strike is also generally considered to be improper. A 'sympathy strike' is defined as one in which workers do not present any demands to their own employer with regard to their own labour relations but only seek to support the demands of other workers who have an existing dispute with those workers' employer. As most unions are enterprise unions, this type of strike rarely occurs. However, in a case in which an industrial federation of enterprise unions directed its member unions to participate in a 'sympathy strike' to support an existing strike between one of their member union (*Kishima* company union) and an employer (*Kishima* company), a court held that the strike was improper because the dispute was limited to the *Kishima* company and the *Kishima* union.[247] On the other hand, even where a union carries out a dispute act in putting forward an unrealistic economic demand, the dispute act is held to be proper unless the union intends to adhere to it.[248] Similarly, even where a union carries out a dispute act in demanding the discharge of a

245. Sugeno & Yamakawa, *supra*, p. 1081.
246. The *Mitsubishi Juko* case, the Supreme Court in 1982, RH, No. 618, p. 14.
247. The *Kishima Tanko Roso* case, the Tokyo District Court in 1975, RMS, Vol. 26, No. 5, p. 870. *See* Sugeno & Yamakawa, *supra*, p. 1083.
248. The *Wako Junyaku Kogyo* case, the Kobe District Court in 1950, RMS, Vol. 1, No. 4, p. 505.

company executive or to prevent rationalization of a company or closure of a factory, the dispute act is held to be proper if its real purpose is to attain improvement of its members' working conditions.[249]

III. Proper Ways of Dispute Acts

410. Since the right to dispute acts is guaranteed to make the collective bargaining process substantially function, it is not proper for the union to start dispute acts before the employer responds to its demands.[250] However, a dispute act is generally considered to be proper if the union's purpose is to protest an employer's unfair labour practices or to stop an employer from violating a collective agreement or law.[251] On the other hand, dispute acts without giving notice to the employer are not always considered to be improper. Moreover, if there is a collective agreement or labour relations custom requiring the union to give notice of dispute acts, the union which conducted a dispute act in violation of it cannot be immune to civil liability. In fact, the 2020 survey found that 49.7% of the unions had an obligation to give notice of dispute acts under a collective agreement or labour relations custom.[252]

IV. Proper Dispute Acts

411. Section 2 Article 1, TUA, declares that in no event shall acts of violence be construed as proper acts for trade unions. On the other hand, the same article of the TUA lays down a criminal indemnity. This superficial contradiction is generally solved by interpreting it to mean that there is criminal indemnity for those criminal acts which would possibly amount to threats, coercion or trespass in ordinary civil life but which are usually accepted by trade unionists as ordinary acts in the course of industrial relations when they are demanding to negotiate, trying to persuade strike-breakers and so on. In any case, the law allows criminal and civil indemnity for 'proper dispute acts', a phrase which is regarded as including a variety of acts and not just strikes or slow-downs. Thus, what constitutes a proper act of dispute should be considered separately for each category of act which is regularly used in Japanese industrial relations.

§3. Different Types of Dispute Acts and Other Collective Actions

I. Strikes

412. Japan has rather smaller numbers of working days lost and of workers involved in work stoppage than other major industrialized countries (*see* Tables 15

249. The *Ohama Tanko* case, the Supreme Court in 1949, SKS, Vol. 3, No. 5, p. 592; the *Tokyo Shibaura Denki* case, the Yokohama District Court in 1949, *Rosaishi*, No. 7, p. 303.
250. The *Fuji Bunka Kogyo* case, the Urawa District Court in 1960, RMS, Vol. 11, No. 2, p. 280.
251. The *Meiji Nyugyo* case, the Tokyo District Court in 1969, RMS, Vol. 20, No. 5, p. 1415.
252. Ministry of Health, Labour and Welfare, *Reiwa 2nen Dantaikoshoto nikansuru Jittaichosa* (Survey on Collective Bargaining and other matters), 2020.

and 16). Table 15 clearly shows that dispute acts have decreased rapidly since 1975 when they were induced greatly by the first oil crisis. The number of working days lost in 1975 was 8,016,000 but was only 3,652 in 2023. One of the characteristics of dispute acts in Japan is that they last for a very short time, e.g., one or two hours. The short duration of strikes reflects a relatively small number of working days lost in Japan. Another characteristic is that the number of workers involved is rather disproportionate to the number of stoppages (*see* Table 16). Because most unions are enterprise unions, the number of workers involved is usually very small.

413. A strike is regarded as a proper type of dispute act because workers only collectively refuse to work. Workers' collective refusal to do overtime or holiday work is also regarded as a proper dispute act. Partial strikes as well as all-out strikes are regarded as a proper type of dispute act. Moreover, unions have often used a 'nomination strike' in which a few members or sometimes even only one member are nominated to be strikers or a striker. A nomination strike has also been regarded as a proper dispute act.[253] There were some cases in which, in order to demand that an employer cancel his or her order of transferring its member employees to different workplaces, the union nominated those employees as strikers. The courts have generally held that such nomination strikes were not improper if those employees only refused to work in the workplace to which they were transferred.[254] A rolling strike, a limited-duration strike, a slow-down and a concerted annual leave action in which workers simultaneously take annual leave are also not regarded as being improper since they are basically a collective action to refuse to work.

Table 15 Stoppages in Progress 1975–2023 in Japan

Year	*Stoppages*	*Working Days Lost (Thousands)*	*Workers Involved (Thousands)*
1975	7,574	8,016	4,614
1985	4,230	264	1,355
1995	685	77	222
2005	129	6	27
2015	99	14	23
2023	75	4	8

Sources: Ministry of Labour (Health, Labour and Welfare), *Rodo Sougi Jittai Chosa* (Survey on Labour Disputes).

253. The *Nihon Kayaku* case, the Hiroshima High Court in 1960, RMS, Vol. 10, No. 3, p. 531.
254. The *Shinko Service* case, the Tokyo District Court in 1987, RH, No. 498, p. 13. Recently, a lower court decision held that a strike of university professors to refuse to teach classes for which the time schedule was unilaterally changed by the university was held to be improper. *Kansai Gaigo Daigaku* case, Osaka High Court in 2021, *Roso Keizai Hanrei Sokuho* No. 2444, p. 3.

Table 16 Labour Disputes in Major Industrialized Countries in 2022

Countries	*Labour Disputes*	*Working Days Lost (Thousands)*	*Workers Involved (Thousands)*
USA	23	2,195	121
Germany	1,532	267	285
UK	749	2,518	93
Australia (2019)	147	64	53

Source: JILPT, Databook of International Labour Statistics, 2024.

II. Picketing

414. Picketing is one of the main measures of dispute acts of union members on strike to watch others (their members, non-member workers, the employer and customers of the employer), and persuade them not to obstruct the strike. Picketing is generally carried out in order to prevent the employer or non-union members from breaking the strike, to prevent suppliers or customers from bringing materials in or taking products out of the company's premises. The Supreme Court has generally given indemnity of civil liability to picketing involving only peaceful persuasion by speech.[255] Therefore, union drivers sitting down in front of a garage to prevent non-union drivers from running taxis was held to be improper.[256] Although the Supreme Court has stated that criminal liability for picketing should be determined from the standpoint of the entire legal order, it has limited a proper type of picketing basically only to persuasion by speech.[257]

III. Occupation of Workplace or Facilities and Boycotts

415. There are many other types of dispute acts whose propriety was disputed before the court. Since most unions are enterprise unions, strikers tend to stay in their workplaces, to occupy enterprise facilities and to obstruct the employer's operation during the strike. The courts have generally held that strikers' occupation of the workplace does not lose indemnity of civil and criminal liability if the occupation of the workplace is only partial and does not prevent others from entering that workplace to work.[258] During a strike, members of taxi drivers' unions sometimes take wheels or tachometers off taxis or remove certificates of car inspection

255. The *Asahi Shinbun* case, the Supreme Court in 1952, SMS, Vol. 6, No. 9, p. 857.
256. The *Mikuni Hire* case, the Supreme Court in 1992, RH, No. 619, p. 8.
257. The *National Railway Kurume Station* case, the Supreme Court in 1973, SKS, Vol. 27, No. 3, p. 418.
258. The *Gunma Chuo Bus* case, the Maebashi District Court in 1954, RMS, Vol. 5, No. 4, p. 369.

or engine keys in order to prevent non-union drivers from running taxis. These practices are not regarded as proper dispute acts because they constitute an obstruction of the employer's exercise of ownership.[259] Boycotting is the practice of union members on strike of appealing to customers and the public not to buy products of the employer. It is generally considered that boycotting as a means of dispute acts to effectuate the union's strike is a proper dispute act unless it involves violence, threats or defamatory statements.[260] There was a case in which the court held that union officials or members request that the customers or financial institutions stop the employer's unfair labour practice and to otherwise stop their business with the employer was not improper (namely, illegal) conduct when such a request was made peacefully and did not involve any threat or unjust psychological pressure.[261]

IV. Putting Up Posters, Wearing Ribbons, Etc.

416. Putting up posters on the walls and windows of the company premises and wearing ribbons, arm bands, and head-bands with the union's demands or other slogans written on them are all actions which are quite frequently resorted to during labour disputes. Of course, such activities were originally a source of propaganda for the union and a means of communicating information to union members, non-union workers, customers and the general public about the position of the union and the situation which gave rise to the dispute. Therefore, according to the above-mentioned restrictive view on the concept of dispute acts, these cannot constitute dispute acts but merely are other collective actions. Unions sometimes put an enormous number – often hundreds and sometimes thousands – of rather shabby and poorly-made posters in a disorderly fashion on company buildings. In some cases, the company has had to employ special workers to clean the building because the posters were put back repeatedly as soon as they had been taken away and the excess paste was left all over the walls. The wearing of arm bands or ribbons disturbs the normal course of business when the appearance of the employees is important – especially in the service industries. They are not dispute acts by nature but often function as dispute acts. Even if they cannot constitute dispute activities, there is a possibility that indemnity may still be given to them if they are a proper union activity because indemnity is not limited to dispute acts but given to a proper collective action in general under Article 28 of the Constitution.

417. As regards the legality of putting up posters, in criminal cases, the courts usually have taken into account the degree of excessiveness; namely, the number of posters, their quality and the method of pasting them. Accordingly, in some cases, it was held that putting up numerous posters over and over again, thus making the building very dirty and extremely hard to clean, was considered the crime of destroying the function of buildings.[262] Even in civil cases, many courts once held

259. The *Meiwa Taxi* case, the Kanazawa Branch, the Nagoya High Court in 1986, RH, No. 477, p. 62.
260. The *Fukui Shinbun* case, the Fukui District Court in 1968, RMS, Vol. 19, No. 3, p. 714.
261. The *Nishinari Godoroso* case, the Osaka District Court in 1992, RH, No. 620, p. 60.
262. The *Kanazawa Taxi* case, the Supreme Court in 1968, SKS, Vol. 22, No. 1, p. 23.

that putting up posters on company properties without the employer's consent is not necessarily improper and that the legality of pasting posters should be determined by comparison of the necessity of the union's pasting posters and the degree of obstruction to the employer's control of his or her facilities and the operation of his or her business. However, the Supreme Court later took a more restrictive view of the legality of pasting posters in the *Kokutetsu Sapporo Station* case:[263]

> The use of the enterprise's facilities without permission in union activities is not a proper union activity because it violates the employer's right to use and control the facilities in order to maintain a good and proper work environment and carry on business in an orderly fashion. The only exception to this rule is where there are special circumstances under which the employer's refusal to permit the union to use the facilities constitutes an abusive exercise of his right. Although there has been much criticism against this ruling, the Supreme Court has reiterated this view since this case.

418. The courts once held that, although wearing ribbons constituted union activity during working hours, it was a proper activity if it did not disturb the normal course of the employer's business.[264] However, the courts later held that wearing ribbons disturbs workplace discipline and violates the employees' obligation to concentrate on their duties, and therefore it is not proper even if it does not disturb the normal course of the employer's business.[265] In the *Hotel Okura* case where union member employees wore a ribbon for about five days as a strategy to put pressure on their employer, the Supreme Court held that this activity was not a proper union activity in view of the fact that it was conducted during working hours at a prestigious hotel by union members including those who directly deal with hotel guests, in violation of the hotel employees' dress code.[266]

419. Recently, unions often utilize social network services (SNS) such as YouTube and X as a means of collective action to criticize or provide information on employers for general citizens through the Internet. Lower courts tend to rely on a framework similar to the rule on defamation under tort law, under which such union activities are protected if the contents of publicized information are true, or if there is a sufficient reason for believing it is true, taking into consideration the manner in which such information is disclosed.

§4. Legal Effects of Dispute Acts

I. Civil Indemnity

420. Article 8 of the TUA provides that 'no employer shall claim indemnity from a trade union or its members for the damage caused by strikes or other dispute

263. The *Kokutetsu Sapporo Station* case, the Supreme Court in 1979, SMS, Vol. 33, No. 6, p. 647.
264. The *Nada Yubinkyoku* case, the Kobe District Court in 1967, RMS, Vol. 18, No. 2, p. 302.
265. The *Nada Yubinkyoku (Appeal)* case, the Osaka High Court in 1976, RMS, Vol. 27, No. 1, p. 18.
266. The *Taisei Kanko* case, the Supreme Court in 1982, SMS, Vol. 36, No. 4, p. 659.

acts which are proper'. Although this provision does not refer to collective actions such as union activities other than dispute acts, it has been interpreted to refer to union activities as well as dispute acts because Article 28 of the Constitution guarantees collective actions in general. TUA, Article 8, only mentions the exemption from liability against the employer; the courts hold that, because of the constitutional guarantee of the right to act collectively, the legal indemnity of the union and its members applies to everybody affected by the act of dispute,[267] although it is a different question whether union conduct is aimed at putting pressure on third parties such as a secondary employer. Thus, any damage caused by the lawful dispute acts is recoverable only if the customer claims for it against the employer. With the exception of a few theorists, it is generally accepted that the employer is liable to the customers for such damage if he or she was forced to breach the contract by a dispute act. As an employer, he or she is responsible for the actions of his or her employees.[268] The minority view is that the act of dispute should be regarded as an 'act of God' since it is legally guaranteed and the employer can do nothing about it.[269]

421. The exemption from civil liability is so comprehensive that it includes breach of contract by individual union members. In other words, union members have no responsibility at all as regards breach of contract and they are free not only from the responsibility to pay damages but also from any responsibility in connection with the reason for their conduct, as long as the union's collective action is proper and entitled to immunity. In this sense, they are completely exempted from any contractual responsibility whatsoever. The exemption also includes the tort liability of the union, as well as of the union leaders, in terms of tort. They are completely free from any responsibility for the damage caused by dispute acts in so far as they are proper in the sense described above.

422. Such broad exemption from legal liability, covering union members as well as their leaders, causes difficult problems as to who should be responsible, and to what degree, if the dispute act turns out to be illegal. However, it is impossible to deny that as far as the union's dispute acts are improper and illegal the union member's failure to work during those dispute acts constitutes a breach of his or her employment contract. The courts also generally hold that the Civil Code, Articles 44 and 715 concerning a tort should apply to the union as well as to its individual members for their illegal dispute acts.[270] Article 44, which is currently contained in the Act on General Incorporated Associations and General Incorporated Foundations (Article 78), provided that a legal entity is liable to make compensation for damage done to other persons by its directors or other representatives in the performance of their duties. Article 715 also provides that a person who employs another to carry out an undertaking is bound to make compensation for damage

267. The *Ojiseishi* case, the Muroran Branch, the Sapporo District Court in 1967, RMS, Vol. 19, No. 1, p. 295.
268. The *OS Eigagekijo* case, the Osaka District Court in 1948, *Rosaishi*, No. 1, p. 152.
269. K. Ishikawa, *Rodoho* (Tokyo, Yuhikaku, 1978), p. 58.
270. The *Misuzu Tofu* case, the Nagano District Court in 1967, RMS, Vol. 18, No. 2, p. 237; the *Shosen* case, the Tokyo District Court in 1992, RMS, Vol. 43, No. 2–3, p. 540.

done to a third person by the employee in the course of the execution of the undertaking. Accordingly, if union officials or members participate in an improper (illegal) strike, slow-down and the like, the union is subject to vicarious liability under tort law.

423. In many cases, an employer takes disciplinary action against individual members participating in illegal dispute acts partly because the court action to sue the union and its members for damages on the basis of a contract or a tort is time consuming and partly because it is rather difficult for the employer to prove the causal relationship and the amount of damages. In practice, an employer has more often taken disciplinary action against union officials because this can damage the union power most effectively. The courts generally hold that an employer is entitled to take disciplinary action against union officials directing or participating in deciding to carry out illegal dispute acts.[271] However, the legal effectiveness will depend upon the degree of responsibility of each union member for damaging the enterprise order. If a certain disciplinary action is judged to be too severe against a member's responsibility, it will be held to be void.

II. Criminal Indemnity

424. Article 1, section 2 of the TUA states that 'the provisions of Article 35 of the Criminal Code shall apply to collective bargaining and other acts of trade unions which are appropriate'. Article 35 of the Criminal Code establishes the immunity of acts which are done with the authorization of the law or as a legitimate business activity even though these acts may, per se, constitute a certain type of crime; for example, the execution of a convicted criminal in prison is not regarded as murder or homicide and an operation by a qualified surgeon never constitutes the crime of injury or violence. Thus, the proper acts of trade unions are regarded as legally authorized acts even if they actually constitute a certain type of crime. However, the real meaning and scope of application of this provision is rather confusing. Also, a proviso in Article 1, section 2 of the TUA provides that 'in no event shall acts of violence be construed as appropriate acts of trade unions', it is questionable as to what kind of crime could ever be called 'appropriate'.

III. Dispute Acts and Wages

425. Because of the legal nature of the act of dispute in Japan, all acts of dispute are conducted without terminating the employment contract. In spite of the continuance of the contract it is agreed in principle that union members will not receive their wages during a strike, since they do not perform work. Of course, difficult problems often arise with regard to the amount of wages lost during a strike. For example, it was disputed whether an employer may deduct family allowances from the wages of strikers where such allowances are not calculated strictly based on the

271. The *Zentei Tohoku Chihon* case, the Supreme Court in 1978, SMS, Vol. 32, No. 5, p. 1030.

days they worked. In one case, the Supreme Court once held that the employer may not deduct the family allowance from the wages of strikers..[272] The reasoning behind such decisions is that there are certain parts of the wages which are, in their nature, not directly connected with the daily work, and as such should not be deducted just because the employee did not work on a certain day – regardless of the reason for his or her absence, strike or sickness. However, it is not very easy in practice to distinguish between those parts of the wages which are connected with daily work and those parts which are not. Accordingly, the view which has recently become more prevalent is one that it should be determined by interpretation of a particular employment contract whether or not certain parts of wages may be deducted. The Supreme Court has rejected the view that wages by nature consist of deductible part and non-deductible part and held that the family allowance should be reduced because of the strike since there was a labour-relation practice in that workplace which allowed the reduction of family allowances as a result of a strike.[273]

426. In the case of partial strikes and other dispute acts in which all or some union members come to work and eventually do at least part of the work expected, the problem of how much the employer should pay is a fairly pressing one. Where union members who had been ordered by their employer to go on a business trip or to perform outside work refused that order and were engaged in internal work as a dispute act of the union, then the employer need not pay their wages during the period of those orders because their engagement in internal work does not constitute performance in accordance with the tenor and purport of their obligation under their employment contracts.[274]

427. When a partial strike as described above is conducted, the question arises as to whether the employer has to pay wages to the union members who did not in fact participate in the strike even if their work could not be performed because of the strike. The courts have generally applied Article 536 of the Civil Code to such cases. This article provides that if performance becomes impossible for any reason for which neither of the parties is responsible, the obligor is not entitled to counter performance but that if the impossibility of performance was brought about by any cause for which the obligee is responsible, the obligor shall not lose his right to demand counter performance. Accordingly, where it became impossible or worthless in the common sense of society for an employer to engage non-participants in their work, the employer need not pay wages because their performance is regarded as impossible for reasons which neither of the parties was responsible for.[275] This is also the case with the suspension allowance under Article 26 of the LSA, since the suspension of work for union members who do not engage in the partial strike is not caused by the employer.[276] On the other hand, while the employer is not

272. The *Meiji Seimei* case, the Supreme Court in 1965, SMS, Vol. 19, No. 5, p. 52.
273. The *Mitsubishi Juko* case, the Supreme Court in 1981, SMS, Vol. 35, No. 6, p. 1028.
274. The *Suido Kiko* case, the Supreme Court in 1985, RH, No. 449, p. 49.
275. The *Northwest Air* case, the Supreme Court in 1987, SMS, Vol. 41, No. 5, p. 1350.
276. *Ibid.*

required to pay wages to employees who are not organized by the union and unable to work because of the union's strike under Article 536 of the Civil Code, the employer still has to pay the suspension allowance under Article 26 of the LSA.[277]

§5. Lock-Outs

428. Whether the employers' right to lock out is recognized or not becomes an important issue in Japan, as the Constitution guarantees the right to act collectively only to workers. The majority of theorists admit the right of employers to lock workers out for 'balance' or 'fairness' between employer and worker. The Supreme Court upheld the majority's view in the *Marushima Suimon* case as follows:

> It is unreasonable not to allow the employer to resort to any dispute acts in labour disputes and only to allow him or her to take countermeasures as recognized in civil law principles. In a particular labour dispute, where the power balance between workers and their employer collapses because of the workers' dispute acts and therefore the employer is subjected to extraordinarily disadvantageous pressures, the employer can prevent such pressures and take defensive measures which are relevant to restore the power balance in light of the fairness principle. They will be approved as an employer's proper dispute acts.[278]

429. According to the Supreme Court's decision in the *Marushima Suimon* case, whether a particular lock-out is a proper dispute act or not depends upon whether it is regarded as a proper measure of defence against the union's dispute acts from the viewpoint of equality in labour-management relations, having regard to circumstances such as the attitude taken in the relevant labour-management negotiations, their progress, the forms of dispute acts engaged in by the union, and the extent of their impact upon the employer. Therefore, offensive or aggressive lock-outs which are initiated by the employer without receiving damages by the union's dispute act, are generally not regarded as proper dispute acts and even defensive or protective lock-outs will be regarded as improper dispute acts after the power balance between the union and the employer is restored in light of the fairness principle.[279] There are only a few cases where a lock-out was held to be proper. For example, it was so held in the *Marushima Suimon* case in which the union resorted to slow-downs, putting up posters on the walls and windows of the company buildings, demonstration marching and criticizing company directors over loudspeakers on the company premises.

430. The legal effects of a lock-out are not just limited to wage claims, but also involve the possibility of the expulsion of workers from the company's premises.

277. The *Meisei Denki* case, the Maebashi District Court in 1963, RMS, Vol. 14, No. 6, p. 1419.
278. The *Marushima Suimon* case, the Supreme Court in 1975, SMS, Vol. 29, No. 4, p. 481.
279. The *Daiichi Kogata Hire* case, the Supreme Court in 1977, RH, No. 278, p. 61.

The question is whether the employer can actually turn out workers who are sitting-in on the premises, and most courts have answered in the affirmative.[280] However, in any case, the employer has the legal right, based on his property rights, to expel anyone who enters and stays on the company premises against his will. Even during a strike by a union, an employer is free to conduct business operations.[281] This is the case even during his or her lock-out. Therefore, the employer is entitled to continue to conduct business operations using supervisors, non-union employees or strike replacements. However, where there is a so-called scab-prohibition agreement between a union and an employer which prohibits the employer from hiring replacements for strikers, the union is entitled to claim damages for his or her violation or to prevent him or her from hiring strike replacements for strikers.

§6. Restriction and Prohibition of Dispute Acts

I. Prohibition of Dispute Acts which Endanger Human Life

431. Article 36 of the LRAA prohibits 'any act which hampers or causes a stoppage in the maintenance or normal operation of safety procedures in factories, mines and other places of employment'. This is interpreted as meaning that the law prohibits any act, which endangers human life in the workplace, but not those acts which merely destroy the property of the company. The latter are also regarded as being illegal if they take the form of positive destruction, although they are not prohibited by Article 36. Negative acts which may eventually cause the destruction of the property (such as refusing to do maintenance work) are not necessarily illegal because in such cases the employer can and may take the steps required to avoid destruction as long as the unions do not obstruct him.

II. Restriction of Dispute Acts in Public Welfare Business

432. Article 37 of the LRAA requires the parties concerned in a case involving public welfare business to give notice of any acts of dispute to the LRC and the Ministry of Health, Labour and Welfare or the Prefectural Governor at least ten days before the day on which the dispute act is scheduled to begin. Public welfare business is defined by Article 8 as work which provides services essential to the daily life of the general public: transportation, post and telecommunications, the supply of water, gas or electricity, medical treatment, public health work and any other work designated by the Prime Minister with the approval of the Diet as work which, if stopped for a period of more than one year, would seriously affect the national

280. The *Omikenshi* case, the Hikone Branch, the *Otsu* District Court in 1954, RMS, Vol. 5, No. 3, p. 318.
281. The *Mikuni Hire* case, the Supreme Court in 1992, RH, No. 619, p. 8.

economy or endanger the daily life of the general public. The employer, his organization, the unions or any other person who is responsible for an act of dispute without giving ten days' notice will face a maximum fine of one hundred thousand yen.

III. Emergency Adjustment and Dispute Acts

433. The Prime Minister may decide to prevent a stoppage by announcing an emergency adjustment when he or she deems that a stoppage would pose a serious threat to the national economy or the daily life of the nation, for example if it is in public welfare work or because of the scale of the dispute or the special nature of the work. The Prime Minister must ask the opinion of the CLRC before he or she makes his or her decision; and when he or she has decided, he or she will publish his or her decision – with his or her reasons – and notify the Commission of it. After the publication of a decision to make an emergency adjustment the parties are forbidden to engage in any act of dispute for fifty days from the day of publication (LRAA, Article 38). The Commission will try to settle the dispute within these fifty days (*see* Part II, Chapter 8). This Emergency Adjustment took place only once in 1952.

IV. Prohibition of Dispute Acts in the Public Sector

434. In the public sector, any act which hampers the normal course of operations in government's and local governments' enterprise or the public service of the government and the local governments is completely prohibited and not entitled to civil or criminal immunity. This prohibition of dispute acts in the public sector is extremely strict and very broad in two senses. First, all kinds of dispute acts, including those which are small-scale and fairly harmless, are prohibited if they hamper the normal course of operations in the public sector. Second this covers the whole range of both enterprises (of railway and bus services, electricity, gas, water supply) operated by local governments and government enterprises (including the National Forests, the government Printing Office and the Mint Bureau) and all categories of civil servants (including simple clerks and even janitors insofar as they are employed by the government or the local governments). The prohibition of the civil servants' dispute acts originated in the Government Order No. 201 (in 1948) and was replaced by the National Civil Service Act as amended in 1948, the Public Corporation and Government Enterprise Labour Relations Act (in 1949 and later amended and renamed as the Act on Labour Relations of Administrative Executive Institutions), the Local Civil Service Act (in 1950) and the Local Public Enterprise Labour Relations Act (LPELRA) (in 1952). The Supreme Court once made a restrictive interpretation of such statutes that prohibit the dispute acts of the civil servants and public employees in light of the Article 28 of the Constitution.[282]

282. The *Tokyo Chuyu* case, the Supreme Court in 1967, SKS, Vol. 20, No. 8, p. 901; The *Tokyoso* case, the Supreme Court in 1969, SKS, Vol. 23, No. 5, p. 305.

However, the Court has taken less restrictive view that indiscriminate and complete prohibition is constitutional on the grounds that civil servants and public employees must have their working conditions directly or indirectly set by the Diet or local legislatures and that therefore they occupy a special status pursuant to the financial democracy which is contained in the fundamental principle of parliamentary democracy.[283] In any event, after 1982, the National Railways, the Telegraph and Telephone Public Corporation, the Tobacco Monopoly Public Corporation and Alcohol Monopoly Enterprise, the Post Office were privatized and the employees of these enterprises became free from the prohibition of striking.

435. In this connection, it should be pointed out that, as to certain kinds of civil servants, the law restricts the right to organization and to collective bargaining as well. Police officers, prison officers, officers of the Maritime Safety Agency, firemen and officers of the Defense Agency are prohibited from organizing and collective bargaining. Other national and local civil servants have the right to organize and, although the right to conclude collective bargaining agreements are not included, the right to bargain collectively to a certain extent. Employees of public enterprises and Administrative Executive Institutions have many of the rights under the TUA, although there are certain exceptions such as the prohibition of dispute acts and the prohibition of the expenditure that is impermissible under local ordinances (Local Enterprise Labour Relations Act, Article 10).

283. The *Zennorin Keishokuho* case, the Supreme Court in 1973, SKS, Vol. 27, No. 4, p. 547. The *Nagoya Chuyu* case, the Supreme Court in 1977, SKS, Vol. 31, No. 3, p. 182.

Chapter 7. Unfair Labour Practices and Administrative Relief

§1. The Unfair Labour Practice System

436. Article 7 of the TUA, prohibits five categories of employers' acts as an unfair labour practice:

1. disadvantageous treatment of a worker by reason of his or her membership or activities (paragraph 1);
2. retaliatory disadvantageous treatment of a worker for having filed a complaint with the LRC for an unfair labour practice, for having requested the CLRC to review a LRC's order, or for having presented evidence or spoken at LRC's proceedings (paragraph 4);
3. contractual agreement conditioning employment upon the employee's not joining a union (paragraph 1);
4. refusal to bargain with a union (paragraph 2);
5. domination or interference with the formation or management of a union (paragraph 3).

437. As a remedy for unfair labour practice, LRCs will give a remedial order in favour of an aggrieved worker or union in a quasi-judicial administrative procedure. The Japanese unfair labour practices system was introduced by the American Occupation Forces using as a model the Wagner Act of 1935. The protection of the unions and the promotion of their bargaining power is the fundamental purpose of the American system. However, the function of the system has taken a different form in Japan. First, the Japanese system is regarded as having its legal foundations in the constitutional guarantee of the worker's right to organize. Thus, in Japan, it is generally agreed that there is no possibility of accepting a notion such as that of an unfair labour practice by a union, introduced in the United States by the Taft–Hartley Act of 1947. Second, the Japanese administrative organs – LRCs – are fairly different from their American counterparts – the National Labour Relations Board (NLRB). LRCs are composed of members representing employers' interests, those representing employees' interests and those representing public interests. Their procedures are closer to the procedures of conventional civil courts than the procedures of the American Boards. Also, Japanese courts have concurrent jurisdiction over unfair labour practice cases so long as the cases are related to right disputes under civil law, whereas the unfair labour practice disputes are basically pre-empted by the NLRB.

§2. The Concept of an 'Employer' under the Unfair Labour Practices System

438. The term 'employer' under the unfair labour practices system means the party to industrial relations in which collective bargaining should function. Therefore, although there is no provision defining the term 'employer' in the TUA, it is considered to include more than the normal meaning of the term under contract law, i.e., an employer who has a contract of employment with a worker. First, a person (or an organization that has a juridical personality) who was a party to an employment contract with workers may come under the term 'employer'. For example, a person who refused to have collective bargaining with a union, which represented workers dismissed by him, was held to be an employer. It is also the case even if the worker became a member of the union after his dismissal.[284] Second, a person who will most probably be a party to an employment contract with workers may come under the term 'employer'. For example, a person who refused to have collective bargaining with a union of seasonal workers who had not yet concluded employment contracts with him was also held to be an employer on the grounds that employment contracts between that person and those workers have been repeatedly concluded and will be concluded in a short time without special circumstances.[285] Similarly, a person who refused to re-employ seasonal workers whose contracts had once been terminated was held to be an employer on the grounds that those workers were usually re-employed at their request.[286]

439. The term 'employer' is construed even to include a person who is not a party to an employment contract with workers but is in a substantially similar position in relation to them. There are various cases in which a person has been held to be an employer in this sense. First, there are cases in which a party to a contract for work or a contract of commission with workers was held to be an employer. For example, a TV broadcasting company which had a freelance performance contract with a group of orchestra musicians was held to be an employer with regard to those musicians on the grounds that the contract intended to ensure a complement of the musicians indispensable to the company's broadcasts, that the contract obliged the musicians to perform at the request of the company, that it could not deny that the company had a basic right to oversee the musicians' performance, and that the performance fees could be regarded as compensation for work.[287] Second, there are cases where a company was held to be an employer of workers who were, as a formality, employed by another company. For example, where a company directed and supervised the subcontractor's workers at its workplace and where those workers used the company's equipment and were engaged in the same work as the company's employees and where the subcontract fees were allocated to those workers in proportion to their work performance, the company was held to be an employer of those workers.[288] Similarly, a company operating a cabaret which had a contract for work with the leader of a music band composed of several musicians was held to be an employer on the grounds that those musicians constituted an important component of the company's enterprise and performed during the time instructed by the company at the cabaret under its general direction and supervision.[289] These two

284. The *Nihonkokan Turumi* case, the Supreme Court in 1986, RH, No. 484, p. 21.
285. The *Tosashimizu Katuobushi Suisankakogyo Kyodokumiai* case, the Takamatsu High Court in 1971, RMS, Vol. 22, No. 3, p. 536.
286. The *Manza Io* case, the Tokyo District Court in 1953, RMS, Vol. 4, No. 6, p. 549.
287. The *Chubunihon Hoso* case, the Supreme Court in 1976, SMS, Vol. 30, No. 4, p. 437.
288. The *Yukenkogyo* case, the Supreme Court in 1976, SMS, Vol. 30, No. 4, p. 409.
289. The *Hanshinkanko* case, the Supreme Court in 1987, RH, No. 492, p. 6.

cases can be seen as cases in which another company or person had no substantial existence as an employer with regard to the workers concerned.

440. On the other hand, it is more difficult to decide whether a company is an employer with regard to workers who are employed by another company or person where the latter company or person has a substantial existence as an employer. In the *Asahi Broadcasting Company* case where the company refused to have collective bargaining with a union of workers who were employed by its subcontracting companies, the Supreme Court overruled the decision of the Tokyo High Court that *Asahi* was not an employer who was obliged to have collective bargaining with the union unless there was an exceptional reason because the subcontracting companies were employers who were so obliged when they were parties to an employment contract and determined the basic working conditions. In this case, the subcontracting companies dispatched their own employees to the places where *Asahi* required them to do so. These dispatched employees were engaged in making TV films together with *Asahi*'s own employees. They worked with machines supplied by *Asahi* according to the instruction of the schedule prearranged by *Asahi*. The directors employed by *Asahi* directed the dispatched employees as to how to work and changed the working time and recess fixed under the schedule. The Supreme Court held that where a client company controlled and determined part of the basic working conditions of workers of subcontracting companies substantially as much as the subcontracting companies who had the employment contract with the workers, the client company would be the employer under the TUA, Article 7 as regards the matters with which the client company can control as much as the subcontracting companies. In this case, the Court stated that *Asahi* had substantially determined the allocation of working time, the way of working, working environment, etc., with regard to the employees dispatched from the subcontractors and therefore that that company was the employer under the TUA, Article 7. Third, where there is a parent and child relationship between two companies, LRCs have sometimes found that the parent company is an employer with regard to the employees of its child company which has been wound up and accordingly they have ordered it to reinstate and to provide back-pay for the discharged employees.

441. Another question is whose conduct is regarded as the conduct of an employer. This is not the issue of the 'employer' but the scope of the employer's liability regarding the conduct of other persons related to the employer. The conduct of the president (i.e., representative) of the company or the members of the board of management (i.e., directors) are regarded as the employer's conduct as a matter of course. The conduct of persons who represent the interests of the employer (e.g., factory managers, department managers etc.) is also regarded as the employer's conduct unless there are special circumstances where their conduct is purely personal.[290] The conduct of the employees who are not in positions representative of the employer's interest but are in positions close to them, will also be attributed to the employer if such employees engage in the conduct in the implementation of

290. The *Kojin Pulp* case, the Tokyo High Court in 1970, RMS, Vol. 21, No. 5, p. 1229.

the employer's intent.[291] On the other hand, the conduct of employees in lower positions (e.g., assistant section chiefs, chief employees, foremen, etc.) is not regarded as the employer's conduct unless it complies with the employer's intention.[292]

§3. Intent for an Unfair Labour Practice

442. There is disagreement over the need for anti-union intent for unfair labour practice as a requirement for finding the employer's liability. Majority views require anti-union intent to be shown for all types of unfair labour practice, but some theorists consider that it should be shown in cases of disadvantageous treatment towards union members (provided by paragraphs 1 and 4 in Article 7) but not in cases of the employer's domination and interference with trade unions. Some theorists consider that anti-union intent need not be shown for all types of unfair labour practices. This disagreement is somewhat related to the words of statutory provisions, that is, paragraphs 1 and 4 of the TUA, Article 7 have the phrase 'by reason of' or 'for' while paragraphs 2 (concerning an employer's refusal to have collective bargaining) and 3 (concerning an employer's control or interference with a union's affairs) do not have it. However, the most important cause of disagreement among theorists is differences in understanding the reason why the TUA provides a remedial system for unfair labour practice. In fact, there once was a case in which the Supreme Court seems to have taken the view that no anti-union intent is required for the types of unfair labour practices provided for by paragraph 3.[293] However, the prevailing judicial view at present supports the above majority view that anti-union intent to be shown for unfair labour practice falls in disadvantageous treatment (paragraphs 1 and 4) as well as paragraph 3 (domination and interference), while the employer's intent needs not be found in the refusal to bargain cases

443. A more practical problem regarding intention in Article 7, paragraph 1 is the issue of mixed motives. There is a difference of judicial opinion on whether an employee or his or her union can prevail even when the employer's legitimate business reason for the employee's dismissal is proved at the same time as a union related reason is proved. Some courts take the view that where there is a reasonable causal relationship between anti-union intention and dismissal, the dismissal constitutes an unfair labour practice even if there exists another legitimate reason for it.[294] This view seems to have been the most prevailing one among LRCs decisions. A judge writing in an academic capacity has stated that differential treatment constitutes an unfair labour practice where it can be said that it would not have occurred but for union activity.[295] This 'but for' test has been adopted by some courts. Yet,

291. *JR Tokai* case, the Supreme Court in 2008, RH, No. 929, p. 5.
292. Koichiro Yamaguchi, *Rodokumiaiho* 78 (Yuhikaku 2nd ed. 1986).
293. The *Yamaoka Naiinenki* case, the Supreme Court in 1954, SMS, Vol. 8, No. 5, p. 990.
294. The *Star Taxi* case, the Fukuoka District Court in 1964, RMS, Vol. 15, No. 8, p. 258.
295. K. Tanabe, *Rodofunso To Saiban*, Tokyo: Kobundo, 1965, pp. 358–359.

many courts have applied a 'dominant motive' test. The test is that the anti-union motive must be shown to have been the dominant one for disadvantageous treatment.[296]

§4. Different Types of Unfair Labour Practice

I. Disadvantageous Treatment

444. As for disadvantageous treatment in violation of Article 7, paragraph 1 of the TUA, the question arises as to what constitutes disadvantageous treatment. Disadvantageous treatment includes not only treatment involving disadvantages in employment relations but also treatment involving disadvantages regarding union activity or private life. Therefore, for example, the transfer of a union member to a new location, which compels him or her to leave his or her family behind, constitutes a disadvantageous treatment. Even the promotion of a union member to a managerial position constitutes disadvantageous treatment if he or she automatically loses union-membership by reason of his or her engagement in such a position. On the other hand, the Supreme Court held that refusal to hire shall not constitute disadvantageous treatment under Article 7, paragraph 1 of the TUA, except when the refusal to hire is substantially equal to the disadvantageous treatment in the existing employment relationship.[297] In determining whether an employer engaged in the disadvantageous treatment as an unfair labour practice, one of the most important tasks for the LRCs is to find the employer's intent for an unfair labour practice (*see* section 3).

II. Conclusion of 'Yellow Dog' Contracts

445. It is an unfair labour practice for an employer 'to make it a condition of employment that the worker must not join or must withdraw from a trade union'. That condition need not further indicate that the worker will be dismissed if he or she joins or does not withdraw from a union.[298] It is also an unfair labour practice to make it a condition of employment that the worker must not join a particular union or form a union.

III. Refusal to Engage in Collective Bargaining

446. It is an unfair labour practice for an employer 'to refuse to bargain collectively with the representative of the workers employed by him or her without proper reasons'. There are two types of refusal; refusal to engage in collective bargaining itself without proper reasons and to engage in collective bargaining without good

296. The *Tokyo Shoketsu Kinzoku* case, the Supreme Court in 1998, RH, No. 740, p. 22.
297. *JR (refusal to hire)* case, the Supreme Court in 2003, SMS, Vol. 51, No. 11, p. 2335.
298. The *Leader Kikai* case, the Tokyo District Court in 1966, RMS, Vol. 17, No. 4, p. 1004.

faith. The former type of refusal to bargain may be questioned where the employer refuses to bargain with a union by insisting, for example, that he or she is not the employer of workers represented by the union; that the subject matters about which the union demands to bargain with him or her are not compulsory subject matters; that certain procedural matters must be discussed before collective bargaining can start. Typical cases of collective bargaining without good faith are where an employer responds to a union only by telephone or fails to submit to a union any explanation at the time of refusing its demand (*see* Part II, Chapter 4).

IV. Control or Interference

447. It is an unfair labour practice for an employer to control or interfere with the formation or management of a trade union by workers or to give financial support in defraying the union's operational expenditures. There is a wide range of an employer's conduct falling under the phrase 'control or interfere with the formation or management of a trade union'. It includes, for example, an employer's interference with a union election, obstruction to a union meeting, subsidizing anti-union workers' groups, persuasion of workers to withdraw from the membership of a union, unilateral cancellation of check-off agreements, manipulation to split a union and spying on union activities. An employer's conduct of 'control and interference' may constitute an unfair labour practice irrespective of whether the union activity has actually been obstructed. Since an employer's conduct aiming to weaken unions generally falls under the phrase 'control or interfere with the formation or management of a trade union', the employers' disadvantageous treatment against union members (under paragraph 1, Article 7) or refusal to engage in collective bargaining (under paragraph 2, Article 7) often falls under 'control or interference' (under paragraph 3, Article 7).

448. A difficult question concerning an employer's conduct of 'control and interference' is how to strike a balance between the prohibition of unfair labour practice and the employer's freedom of speech. An employer may express his or her policy on business operation and call on employees (including union members) for their cooperation. However, if in his or her speech the employer makes some remarks implying any form of reprisal towards union members or in such a manner as to disturb the union activities considerably, the speech will constitute a conduct of 'control and interference'. In determining if his or her remarks constitutes an unfair labour practice, the courts generally take account of the contents of his or her speech, time and place of the speech, the situation regarding labour relations, the influence of the speech (e.g., a large decrease in union membership after the speech), and other circumstances.[299]

449. Paragraph 3, Article 7 of the TUA provides that it is a conduct of 'control and interference' for an employer to give financial support in defraying the trade union's operational expenditures. However, the same paragraph adjusts this with the

299. The *Prima Ham* case, the Supreme Court in 1982, RKS, No. 1134, p. 5.

necessity of such financial support to the union. Thus, it further provides that the employer may permit workers to confer or negotiate with the employer during working hours without loss of time or pay, that the employer may contribute towards public welfare funds or welfare and other funds which are actually used for payments to prevent or relieve economic misfortunes or accident and that the employer may furnish the union with minimum office space. Moreover, it is generally understood that an employer is allowed to give financial support or to provide facilities as long as this does not substantially damage the union's independence. For example, in a case in which an employer agreed with a union to pay a small amount of bonus twice a year to its union official for engaging only in union business, a district court held that it did not constitute an unfair labour practice and that therefore the employer could not refuse to pay it.[300]

450. Another problem concerning an employer's conduct of 'control or interference' is whether it is an unfair labour practice for an employer not to permit a union to use his or her premises or facilities for union activities. As stated before, the Supreme Court has held that the employer's refusal to permit the union to use his or her premises does not constitute an unfair labour practice unless it constitutes the abuse of the employer's property right (*see* Part II, Chapter 6, section 3, IV). The courts generally do not easily recognize the abuse of the employer's right to control his or her premises. However, there are exceptional cases where the Supreme Court held that cancellation or refusal to grant a union the use of the company's facilities for its union activities constituted an unfair labour practice. In those cases, the employer continued to grant another union the use of them[301] or there was a longstanding practice under which the employer had permitted the union to use them except under special circumstances.[302]

451. Since an employer's conduct aiming to weaken unions generally constitutes an unfair labour practice of 'control or interference', even a conduct based on his or her right may constitute such a practice. For example, although the employer is entitled to terminate the collective agreement without a term of validity by giving ninety days' notice to the union, such termination will constitute an unfair labour practice if it is found that the employer has done so by deliberately choosing the timing so as to hit the union badly.[303]

§5. Existence of Plural Unions and Unfair Labour Practice

452. In Japan, there are cases where plural unions exist in one company. In such cases, employers often prefer one of such plural unions that is less adversarial in labour relations. Then, it is often questioned whether an employer's different treatment of different unions constitutes an unfair labour practice. The TUA does not

300. The *Kohoku Taxi* case, the Osaka District Court in 1982, RKS, No. 1117, p. 8.
301. The *Nissan Jidosha* case, the Supreme Court in 1987, HJ, No. 1247, p. 131.
302. The *Sogo Hanamaki Byoin* case, the Supreme Court in 1985, RKS, No. 1236, p. 3.
303. The *Suruga Ginko* case, the Tokyo High Court in 1990, RH, No. 583, p. 25.

adopt the exclusive representation system such as exists in the United States. Therefore, each different union in a company is entitled to engage in collective bargaining with the employer. According to the Supreme Court's decision in the *Nissan Jidosha* case, the employer is obliged to engage in collective bargaining in good faith with each of those unions. Not only at the time of collective bargaining but also at any other time, the employer has to observe neutrality towards each union and to recognize and respect the unions equally and must not discriminate against them because of their character, inclination and previous policy.[304] For example, in the *Nihon Mail Order* case, in a bargaining process, the employer proposed to two unions, as a condition of an increase in bonus, that they should cooperate to improve productivity. The majority union accepted that proposal but the minority union, which are more adversarial, did not. As a result, the members of the minority union were paid less than those of the majority union. The Supreme Court held that it was an unfair labour practice for the employer to have made and adhered to an unreasonable proposal with the intention of weakening the minority union. In this case, the employer did not explain the meaning of its request that employees should cooperate to improve productivity, and the union had a good reason to suspect the request would be used to suppress the union's demand. Similarly, in the *Nissan Jidosha* case *supra.*, the Supreme Court held that it was an unfair labour practice for the employer to have excluded the members of the minority union from all opportunities to earn overtime wages with an intent to weaken the union's organizing on the pretext of the minority union's general policy of opposing a scheduled overtime work.

453. It is often very difficult to prove discrimination against the members of a union in evaluating their job performance for the purposes of wage raises, bonuses, promotions, etc. Therefore, the LRCs have adopted a method, the so-called mass observation method in order to simplify examination in such cases. According to that method, the Commissions first determine from the data presented by the complaining union whether the average evaluation rate of their members is generally lower than that of the members of other unions or non-union members in the same company. For this purpose, comparisons are made for the employees with the same years of service, the same educational background, and the same types of occupations. Once a prima facie case of discrimination has been established by this method, the employer has to rebut it by proving that individual evaluations of individual members of the complaining union have been made on the fair ratings of their performance or job-related attitudes.[305] Recently, against the background of the progress of merit- or performance- based evaluation, the CLRC slightly modified this method through requiring the complaining union to show some evidence that the performance of the union members as a whole is not inferior to that of the members of the other union.

---

304. The *Nissan Jidosha* case, the Supreme Court in 1985, SMS, Vol. 39, No. 3, p. 730.
305. The *Beniya Shoji* case, the Supreme Court in 1986, RH, No. 467, p. 6.

§6. THE LABOUR RELATIONS COMMISSIONS

454. The LRCs are tripartite administrative agencies, consisting of the Prefectural Labour Relations Commissions (PLRCs) and the CLRC. Both bodies consist of equal numbers of members representing employers, workers and the public interest. The members representing employers are appointed on the recommendation of an employers' association, the members representing workers on the recommendation of labour unions, and the members representing the public interest from the panel of scholars and men of experience with approval of both of the other members of the Commission. Their status is in principle part-time public official. Most representatives of the public interest, who are exclusively given power to make a decision on unfair labour practice, are professors of law or labour economics, lawyers or people from similar professions. The complaint is initiated and pursued by the workers, their union or both, throughout the whole LRC proceedings. When a complaint is filed with a PLRC within one year of the conduct which is alleged to be an unfair labour practice, the PLRC will open an investigation and, if it is deemed necessary, will hold a hearing (TUA, Article 27-7). The LRCs may demand, with the sanction of a fine against default, the attendance of or the presentation of reports, books or documents from the employer, the employers' organization, the unions or others who may be involved (TUA, Article 22). However, in practice, this order has seldom been made because it must be based on the resolution of the Commission. Thus, two new procedures were introduced in the 2004 amendment to the TUA. First, the LRC may, if necessary, order parties to the proceedings or witnesses to give testimony (Article 27-7, paragraph 1, item 1). Second, the LRC may order submission of documents or other objects to persons who possess them, if it is difficult to find necessary facts without such objects (Article 27-7, paragraph 1, item 2). After the hearing, members representing the public interest of the PLRC will meet in order to make a decision about the complaint. However, prior to this meeting, the members representing the public interest have to ask the opinions of the members representing labour and management respectively who have attended the hearings.

455. Complaints may be disposed of on the basis of an agreement between the parties at any of the above stages of the procedure. There are two different types of agreed settlement: that based on a recommendation, made formally, by the Chairman of the PLRC and the other made without such a recommendation. The second type, an informal settlement, is usually carried out in the form of withdrawal of the complaint. According to national statistics, a large number of unfair labour practice cases brought against employers are disposed of informally. In 2022, for example, approximately 21.0% of the total number of applications to the PLRC were disposed of by full or partial remedial orders, about 15.1% were dismissed, about 12.3% were withdrawn, and about 51.6% were disposed of by agreement between the parties (Table 17).

Table 17 Disposition of Unfair Labour Practice Complaints in the PLRC (Percentage in Parentheses)

	2019	*2020*	*2021*	*2022*
Withdrawals	32(11.4)	28(11.4)	55(21.3)	31(12.3)
Agreement	140(49.8)	129(52.7)	122(47.3)	130(51.6)
Dismissal	38(13.5)	29(11.8)	35(13.6)	38(15.1)
Remedial order	71(25.3)	48(19.6)	46(17.8)	53(21.0)

Source: Central Labour Relations Commission, *Rodo Iinkai Nenpo* (Annual Report of the Labour Relations Commissions), No. 77.

456. A party which is dissatisfied with the order of the PLRC may, within fifteen days of receiving the order, file a request for a review by the CLRC. Where the dissatisfied party does not elect to request a review of the order of the PLRC or where the CLRC issues a reviewal order, the dissatisfied party may petition an appropriate district court for judicial review of the PLRC's or CLRC's order within thirty days (when a union or a worker files a petition, this period is extended to six months) of the date of issue of the order (Article 27–19). In a case where the employer files such a petition, the court with which the petition is filed may, at the request of the PLRC or, as the case may be, of the CLRC, issue an emergency order, known as *kinkyu-meirei*, requiring the employer to comply in full or in part with the order, pending final judgment by the court (Article 27–20).

457. Where an employer has violated the *kinkyu-meirei*, he or she will be liable to a non-penal fine not exceeding JPY 500,000 (in cases where the said order demands affirmative action, and where the number of the non-compliance days from the day following the date of order exceeds five days, the amount obtained by multiplying one hundred thousand yen by the number of days exceeding five shall be added). The same rule applies in cases where an employer has violated the order of the LRC which has become irrevocable because he or she did not file a petition for judicial review (Article 32). The employer cannot appeal against the *kinkyu-meirei* but may only request the court to cancel or modify it. Where an employer has violated an order of the LRC after all or a part of the order has been upheld and finalized by an irrevocable judgment of the court, he or she will be liable to imprisonment not exceeding one year, to a fine not exceeding JPY 1,000,000 or both.

458. Where the district court receives a petition for cancellation of the LRC's order, it may itself establish the facts independently of the findings of the LRC. Unlike the National Labour Relations Act (NLRA) in the United States, the substantial evidence rule does not exist here. The court can also review thoroughly whether the LRC's interpretation and application of Article 7 of the TUA is appropriate or not because the LRC does not have discretion over what constitutes an unfair labour practice.[306] The LRC has only discretion to determine what remedy should be given to a union and its members for an unfair labour practice. Therefore, the courts should respect this discretionary authority of the LRC. However, remedial orders should be designed to promptly restore orderly and normal collective labour relations by directly correcting the situation created by the employer's acts of unfair labour practice.[307] Where the LRC has exercised its discretionary authority beyond this limitation or in an arbitrary manner, the court can repudiate the LRC's remedial orders.

§7. Administrative Remedies and Judicial Remedies

459. Typical contents of the LRC's remedial orders are reinstatement and back-pay orders in cases of dismissal, orders of collective bargaining in good faith in cases of refusal to engage in collective bargaining and cease/desist orders in cases of 'control and interference'. These orders are often accompanied with orders of posting notices. The order of posting a notice is an order to require an employer to put up a notice in which he or she states that it has been found by the LRC to have committed an unfair labour practice and that he or she would not repeat any similar act in the future. The LRCs sometimes ordered an employer to post a notice stating that he or she 'deeply regrets' or 'apologizes' what he or she has done, and 'vows' not to repeat any similar act. Therefore, it has been disputed whether an order of posting such a notice infringes an employer's freedom of conscience, provided for by Article 19 of the Constitution. The Supreme Court has, however, held that it does not do so because those expressions were used to emphasize non-repetition of any similar act of unfair labour practice and not to force the employer to manifest his or her mind.[308]

460. The LRCs do not necessarily deduct from the back-pay the dismissed worker's interim earnings from other employment between the time of dismissal and the time of reinstatement. The Supreme Court held in the *Dainihato Taxi* case that an award of back-pay is not only purported to relieve employees of monetary losses arising from dismissal but is also intended to reduce the discouraging effect on union activity and therefore that interim earnings should not automatically be deducted. The Court continued to hold that if the LRC failed to give reasonable consideration to both purposes of the award, its decision would go beyond the limits of its discretion and would be illegal.[309]

461. The LRCs sometimes make a remedial order on the condition that the complainant do some action specified thereby. For instance, an LRC orders the employer to reinstate the complaining worker with back-pay on the condition that the worker submit to the employer a document stating that he or she would not use violence in

306. The *Kotobuki Kenchiku Kenkyujo* case, the Supreme Court in 1978, RH, No. 312, p. 54.
307. The *Dainihato Taxi* case, the Supreme Court in 1977, SMS, Vol. 31, No. 1, p. 93.
308. The *Roseikai Takatsu Chuobyoin* case, the Supreme Court in 1990, RH, No. 584, p. 38.
309. The *Dainihato Taxi* case, the Supreme Court in 1977, SMS, Vol. 31, No. 1, p. 93.

the workplace any more. This sort of remedial order has generally been accepted as a suitable means to normalize future labour relations.[310]

462. Some attention will be paid to judicial remedies made for an unfair labour practice because the union or its members can also bring an action in the courts directly. As stated above, the pre-emption by the LRCs does not exist in Japan. Typical judicial remedies available to them are formal judgments declaring his or her contractual status or provisional dispositions in cases of dismissal, provisional dispositions affirming the union's status as the party to collective bargaining and orders of paying damages on the grounds of a tort in cases of refusal to engage in collective bargaining and the employer's control of and interference with unions.

463. There are many cases where the company continues business in some form after a resolution of voluntary liquidation. In these cases, the LRC may order a previous employer or new employer that is substantially equivalent to the previous employer ('alter ego'), or both, to employ or re-employ the dismissed employees with back-pay.[311] In order to oppress or extinguish union activities, the company sometimes closes that part of its business premises where there is a lot of union activity and dismisses all the employees there, but continues to own the other part of its business. In such cases ('false dissolution'), the LRC usually orders the company to employ the dismissed employees in the remaining part of the business premises or to employ them in their previous workplaces if the company re-opens business there.[312] Moreover, there were cases in which, although the company decided to go into voluntary liquidation on the basis of anti-union *animus*, it is likely to re-open its business. In such cases, the LRC ordered the company under a process of liquidation to re-employ the dismissed employees first if it re-opens its business.[313] These remedial orders contrast with judicial decisions which generally deny that the company's resolution is void. For example, in the *Sankyo Shiki* case, the Tokyo High Court stated that Article 22 of the Constitution guarantees every person's freedom to choose his or her occupation. The abolition of a company and the resolution to liquidate a company is free because it falls under the freedom to choose one's occupation. Therefore, the court held that this freedom should not be restricted even if the company's liquidation is motivated by a desire to destroy a union.[314] However, there are cases in which a court applied the doctrine of piercing the corporate veil of juridical personality (*hojinkaku-hinin*) and held that the parent company would be the employer in the subsidiary's employment contracts with certain employees who were dismissed following the sham dissolution.[315]

310. The *Nobeoka Yubinkyoku* case, the Tokyo High Court in 1978, RMS, Vol. 29, No. 2, p. 262.
311. The *Jiritsukeizai Tokushinsha* case in 1961, *Meireishu*, No. 24-5, p. 46.
312. The *Shinnihon Kanko Kogyo* case in 1976, *Meireishu*, No. 34-5, p. 225.
313. The *Sanei Kogyo* case in 1975, *Meireishu*, No. 55, p. 579.
314. The *Sankyo Shiki Seisakujo* case, the Tokyo High Court in 1962, RMS, Vol. 13, No. 6, p. 1172.
315. The *Funai Denki* case, the *Tokushima* District Court, RH, No. 232, p. 24.

Chapter 8. Resolution of Labour Disputes

§1. Categories of Labour Disputes

464. Conflicts in labour relations or labour disputes are divided into several categories in industrialized countries, and for each category dispute settlement procedures are designed which take into account their different natures. Individual disputes versus collective disputes, disputes of vested rights versus disputes of interest and economic disputes versus political disputes are the most popular distinctions. There distinctions are theoretically recognized in Japan too, but are not very meaningful in the actual situation. There is no clear-cut distinction between individual and collective conflicts, since Japan does not have labour court system and both of them are handled by the ordinary courts. Connected with this is the fact that the distinction between conflicts of rights and conflicts of interest is never very clear because the courts often give rulings on questions of appropriateness: for instance, the appropriateness of the company collective dismissals or good-faith attitude in bargaining sessions. These problems are handled in substance during the bargaining between the parties, but they may become issues to be decided by the Courts if the unions ever claim that their right to organize and to bargain collectively is being challenged; since of course the rights to organize and to bargain are guaranteed as legal rights by the Constitution. The appropriateness of dismissals is a matter which is suitable for bargaining between the parties, but at the same time it could become a legal issue if the workers claim that the employer has abused his right to dismiss the employees. Individual grievances about dismissal, transfer, job assignment, the grading of individuals on particular wage grades and so on can be legal issues as well as issues for bargaining, depending on how the worker chooses to raise the problem.

465. The reasons for this confusing situation are rather complicated. The most important factor is the Japanese neglect of the binding character of a contract. In Japanese society in general, people do not pay much attention to written contracts and rely rather on the personal relationship of mutual trust. The parties to a contract think that written documents do not count for much if the mutual trust between them is lost. Whenever problems arise, they will try to settle them by negotiation on the basis of personal understanding. Clear-cut decisions based on certain universal standards are not at all popular in Japanese society. In individual relations also the pariies seem to follow this pattern. Another factor is the underdevelopment of some distinct dispute settlement procedures designed to deal with certain categories of dispute in the industrial relations system. There are various procedure's such as bargaining, consultation and grievance procedures, which have been formally set up by the unions and management. But these formal procedures introduced in accordance with the Western model often exist only in the official documents such as collective agreements, and in actual industrial relations informal procedures of a more personal nature prevail.

§2. Role of the Courts

466. In Japan, there is no labour court or tribunal to deal with labour disputes irrespective of whether they are collective or individual.[316] Therefore, an employee or a union, which wishes to seek legal relief, should go to an ordinary court. There are fifty District Courts (main offices) having territorial jurisdiction over their respective judicial districts, the area of which is almost identical with that of each prefecture. The District Courts have jurisdiction over civil and criminal cases for the first instance, although family affairs and juvenile delinquency cases are exclusively dealt with by the Family Courts which are established in the same places at which the District Courts are located. There are 438 Summary Courts, which have jurisdiction over civil cases involving claims not exceeding 1,400,000 yen and criminal cases relating to light offences. The District Courts also have appellate jurisdiction over appeals lodged against judgments of the Summary Courts in civil cases. Several proceedings for summary disposition of civil cases and criminal cases are available in the Summary Courts. The High Courts are located in eight major cities: Tokyo, Osaka, Nagoya, Hiroshima, Fukuoka, Sendai, Sapporo and Takamatsu. They have jurisdiction over appeals filed against judgments rendered by District Courts or Family Courts. In 2023, there are about 2,100 judges and 850 assistant judges for these lower courts. The Supreme Court is the highest court and is composed of the Chief Justice and fourteen Justices and one of its functions is to deal with appeals filed against judgments rendered by the High Courts.[317]

467. The number of civil cases is rather small. The District Courts received 126,664 applications in civil cases in 2022. As far as labour cases are concerned, however, the number of cases has considerably increased. In 1991, the District Courts received only 662 applications for formal judgments under ordinary civil procedure. However, especially after the Labour Tribunal System began its operation in 2008, the number of individual labour cases has considerably increased as written below. In 2023, there were 3,763 applications for formal judgments and 3,473 applications for Labour Tribunal orders. Those 3,763 applications for formal judgments were classified into 1,067 claims for affirmation of the existence of an employment contract, 3,607 claims for wages, 1,539 claims for damages, and 592 other claims.[318] Those 3,473 applications for Labour Tribunal awards were classified into 1,658 claims for the matter regarding the existence of an employment contract, 66 claims for other non-monetary matters, 1,282 claims regarding wages, 64 claims regarding retirement allowances, and 403 other monetary claims.

468. However, there is no doubt that the above number of applications is still apparently very small when compared with the situation in other countries. This seems mainly due to the inaccessibility of the courts. The average duration of district court proceedings in formal civil trials concerning labour disputes was about

316. Introduction of the Labour Tribunal System in 2004 did not establish labour court, but created a new procedure for individual labour cases in ordinary district courts.
317. Website 'Courts in Japan' (2023).
318. *Hoso Jiho*, Vol. 76, No. 8, pp. 60–64 (2024).

17.2 months in 2022. On the other hand, the average duration of the Labour Tribunal proceeding is fairly short, i.e., 90.3 days in 2022. This appears to be the reason why the Labour Tribunal cases have increased rapidly. The average duration of the proceedings in provisional disposition orders is unknown but most cases are presumed to be less than half a year. A survey shows that the reasons why people do not want to go to court are that doing so is 'too costly' (64.6%), 'too time-consuming' (54.0%) and also dislike of 'the win-or-lose' solution (26.3%).[319] This shows that people often prefer conciliation or mediation to litigation. Even in cases of labour litigation, the proportion settled by agreement is rather high. In 2022, that proportion was 52.82% of applications for formal judgments. As regards the Labour Tribunal cases, about 70% of the cases are resolved by mediation before the Tribunal renders its awards. Probably the shortage of lawyers was another important reason for people's reluctance to go to court. In 1995, there were only 15,517 lawyers in Japan. Both the Government and the Japan Bar Association have recently started grappling with reform of the judicial systems. As a result of the judicial reform, the number of lawyers in Japan has been increasing. As of April 2024, the number of lawyers admitted to the Japan Federation of Bar Associations reached 45,826.

469. The high proportion of labour litigation cases settled by agreement is also caused by the very nature of labour disputes. The fact is that the courts are only supposed to deal with disputes of vested rights, but labour disputes often simply cannot be distinguished either as disputes of vested rights or as disputes of interest. The same dispute can be regarded both as one of rights and as one of interest. For instance, when a dispute arises about a wage claim by the union, and there is a relevant collective agreement, the union's demands could be settled by interpreting the appropriate provisions. However, it is often the case that the interpretation of the provision is not really the issue, but that the union's real interest is in the amount of wages to be paid in the future. Quite a few bargaining issues can be claimed as legal rights because of the peculiar legal construction of the right to organize in Japan. Thus, the courts are frequently required to settle cases by conciliation rather than by decision; not only because of the general preference of the Japanese for settling disputes by reconciliation, but also because of the very nature of industrial disputes.

§3. Alternative Resolution of Individual Disputes

I. Background

470. Besides the court system, there are several alternative systems of labour disputes resolution which are available to individual employees. Such alternative resolution systems have recently gained more and more attention. This is because the number of individual labour disputes over dismissals and deterioration of working conditions occurred mainly due to drastic changes in the employment situation

319. M. Kato, *The Role of Law and Lawyers in Japan and the United States*, 1987 Brigham Young U.L. Rev. 627, at 674 (1987).

and labour-management relations mainly due to the collapse of the bubbling economy along with the rapid globalization of market economies in 1990s. However, as seen above, court proceedings are expensive, are not very accessible and are very time-consuming. Moreover, there are still other reasons to consider that the present court system is not quite adequate to deal with individual employment disputes. For example, judges do not have expertise in industrial relations; court hearings are so adversarial as to easily destroy the employment relationship; the employee's burden of proof is rather heavy.

II. ADR Systems – Administrative in Nature

471. There are two different alternative dispute resolution (ADR) systems presently available for individual disputes; one is administrative and the other is judicial in their nature. The former is advice, guidance or conciliation through Labour Bureau, PLRCs and prefectural bureaus of labour affairs. In Part I, Chapter 6, section 6, we have already discussed the advice, guidance or recommendations of the PLB under EEOA. The LSIOs under the supervision of the PLB may, of course, receive an employee's report on violation of the LSA or of an ordinance issued pursuant to the law. In 2212, LSIOs received 19,937 reports form employees on such violation. Violations that were found based on such reports were related to the provisions concerning payment of wages (78.4%), dismissal (9.6%), working hours (2.3%), health and safety (4.0%) and minimum wages (5.7%).[320] LSIOs deal only with reports on violation of LSA, other related statutes and their ordinances and do not deal with disputes on contractual matters.

472. However, under the 1998 amendment of LSA, the PLB became entitled to deal with individual labour disputes on working conditions except for those concerned with collective matters or those concerned with equal employment opportunity law. Furthermore, the Act on Promoting the Resolution of Individual Labour Disputes (APRILD) of 2001 gives the power to deal with contractual matters. Under APRILD, the prefectural Labour Director may give necessary advice or guidance to the parties to the individual labour dispute where he is requested by one or both parties to do so. If the Director finds it necessary, he/she has to hear the opinions of experts in labour issues. An employer is prohibited from dismissing or otherwise treating an employee disadvantageously by reason of having requested such assistance (Article 4). Where one or both parties to an individual labour dispute petition for conciliation with regard to the disputes, the Director has to have the Dispute Adjustment Commission conduct conciliation if he considers it necessary (Article 5). The Commission is established at the Prefectural Labour Office (Article 6). It must be composed of no fewer than three persons and no more than thirty-six persons (Article 7). APRILD also provides that local municipal entities have to endeavour to foster the provision if information, consultations, conciliation and other necessary measures to employees, job applicants and employers in order to prevent

320. Ministry of Health, Labour and Welfare, *Rodo Kijun Kantoku Nenpo* (Annual Report on Labour Standards Inspection), 2012.

individual labour disputes from happening and promote the voluntary resolution of individual labour disputes (Article 20). Accordingly, most PLRCs have also started to conciliation of individual labour disputes. In 2023, the PLBs throughout the country received totally 266,162 inquiries on individual labour disputes. Most of those cases were resolved through the assistance of the relevant advising officers at the PLBs and its LSIOs before the PLBs' acceptance of formal application for advice or guidance. The number of formal applications for PL Director's advice or guidance accepted by the PLBs was 8,372. About 12.2% of such formal applications were related to worsening of working conditions, while 11.5% is related to bullying and harassment. It is to be noted that there are different procedures for typical types of harassment such as sexual harassment. The number of requests for conciliation accepted by the PLBs was 3,687. About 21.7% of those requests were related to bullying and harassment and about 21.5% were related to dismissal. In about 74.0% of the conciliated cases, the conciliation proceeding was completed within two months. About 32.9% of those completed cases resulted in agreed settlements.[321]

III. ADR Systems – Judicial in Nature (Labour Tribunal Procedure)

A. *Overview*

473. The APRILD has been quite successful in settling a number of individual labour disputes. However, the final means of resolution of disputes under the APRILD is a conciliation to promote the voluntary resolution of individual labour disputes. Conciliators do not have any authority to examine evidence or to summon witnesses. Accordingly, this way of dispute resolution is not apt for cases in which either party to the disputes is not willing to compromise with the other party. Therefore, around the enactment of APRILD, the need for an easily accessible, less costly and expeditious judicial resolution system of individual labour disputes was recognized and several plans to establish such a system were discussed. Based on the decision by the labour issue branch of the government's Task Force on judicial reform, the LTA was enacted in May 2004 and put into force in April 2006. Labour tribunals were set up in district courts across the country. The coverage of LTA is limited to civil disputes arising between individual employees and business proprietors concerning the presence or otherwise of labour contracts and other matters related to labour relations (Article 1). Accordingly, collective labour disputes, e.g., disputes concerning unfair labour practices, are not covered. Under LTA, sessions for a trial can be held a maximum of three times in principle (Article 15). A dispute which seems unlikely to be disposed within sessions, for example, a complex dispute containing many issues, is regarded as inappropriate for the labour tribunal procedures (Article 24).[322]

321. Minister of Health, Labour and Welfare, *Kobestu Rodo Funso kaiketsu Seido Shikojokyo*, (Report on the Situation of Individual Labour Dispute Resolution Scheme), 2012.

322. As regards the features of the Labour Tribunal System from a comparative viewpoint, *see* Susan Corby & Ryuichi Yamakawa, *Judicial Regimes for Employment Rights Disputes: Comparing Germany, Great Britain and Japan*, 51(5) Industrial Relations Journal 374 (2020).

474. The Labour Tribunal System was established in the district courts with the objective of settling individual labour disputes. A panel consisting of a professional judge acting as the labour tribunal judge (*rōdō shimpan-kan*) and two members with expert knowledge of labour relations, each representing labour and management sides, is allowed to hold up to three hearings (*rōdō shimpan-in*), initially to try to settle each dispute by conciliation (*chôtei*) or resolution through voluntary agreement and, if the conciliation fails, to make a ruling for settlement of the dispute, which is subject to an objection by a party as explained below.

475. The system has seven distinctive features: (1) it is intended to settle individual labour disputes, with no trade union having a standing in the proceedings; (2) it takes place within the civil courts, not the labour courts; (3) it involves participation of labour and management experts in the proceedings; (4) it is designed as a speedy, simple and flexible procedure; (5) it may result in a normal civil proceeding when an objection is filed by a party to the ruling of the tribunal; (6) it is 'non-contentious' in its legal nature and the procedure is not open to the public. In addition, (7) the Labour Tribunal Procedure is not a prerequisite for the ordinary civil action. Thus, complaining party can choose the Labour Tribunal Procedure and ordinary civil procedure, as long as the case can be handled by both procedures.

476. The purpose of the Labour Tribunal System is defined as 'to seek settlement of individual civil law labour disputes between an individual worker and the employer' (LTA Article 1). The law also refers to 'the individual civil labour dispute' which typically arises from an employment contract but is also interpreted to include claims by individual workers based on collective agreements, or the legality of alleged discriminatory treatment because of union membership or union activities. As far as claims by individual workers are concerned, cases of collective dismissals, gender discrimination or changes of work rules, which may relate to a number of workers and can be supported by unions, are to be handled by the Labour Tribunal, although trade unions themselves have no standing in the proceedings as mentioned before.

477. In order for a petition for relief to be accepted, an employment relationship must exist or allegedly exist between the claimant worker and the respondent employer. Strictly speaking, there is no employment contract relationship between a host enterprise and dispatched workers (i.e., those sent to employers by temporary employment agencies), however, some of the provisions of the LSA are applied to their relationship (WDA, Article 44(1)) and some court decisions have recognized the obligations of host enterprises as employers. Thus, their relationship is regarded as one involving 'labour relations' under the LTA and is interpreted as being covered by the system.

478. Employment relations in the public sector are also excluded from the jurisdiction of this system because there is a special system to handle individual disputes in the public sector established in the Administrative Personnel Authority

(*Jinji-in*), which is an independent government agency in charge of personnel management for government employees. It goes without saying that non-Japanese individuals as employees and foreign corporations as employers are subject to the jurisdiction of the Labour Tribunal.

479. Individual civil labour law disputes as described above may be brought as labour tribunal cases before the district court whose jurisdiction covers either (1) the place of residence, business facilities or office of the defendant, (2) the place of present or past work, or (3) a place agreed upon by both parties.

480. Complainants may submit a petition which specifies the facts and reasons for the complaint with (1) disputed issues and relevant material facts, (2) evidence supporting each point, (3) the history of the negotiations and other processes carried out by parties, and (4) the names and addresses of the parties' attorneys, if any. Cases involving foreign individuals or corporations are handled in the same way, except that certain rules of conflicts of law may be applicable or special measures such as taking evidence abroad may become necessary. Parties to a labour tribunal case may be represented by a lawyer (*bengoshi*) or by a non-lawyer with the permission of the court (LTA, Article 4(1) proviso), although permission for non-lawyer representation has rarely been granted.

B. Participation of Labour and Management Experts in the Proceedings

481. Proceedings are carried out by a three-member panel, which consists of a professional judge (tribunal judge) and two members representing the labour and employer sides, respectively. Member candidates are only required by law to be persons of expert knowledge in labour relations (LTA, Article 9(1)), but are in fact appointed by the courts based on recommendations of representatives of labour and employers' organizations.

482. Courts assign non-judicial panel members for each case from the list of appointed candidates, taking into consideration the proper labour-management balance of the members (LTA, Article 10). Proceedings are carried out under the leadership of the tribunal judge, but panel deliberation is to be held privately and decisions are made by a majority vote by all three members on an equal basis (Article 12). Consequently, at least theoretically speaking, unanimous votes by members on both sides could prevail over the minority opinion of a professional judge in rare instances.

483. In principle, the tribunal judge should set up the first hearing session within 40 days of the submission of the complaint. The number of hearing sessions is, as a rule, limited to three (LTA, Article 15(2)). During the first hearing, the panel hears an opening statement from both parties, reviews the evidence as much as possible, confirms the issues in dispute and makes a plan for a future hearing, unless the hearing concludes in the settlement of the dispute (RLT, Articles 21(1), 22(1)). The second session is devoted to the review of evidence and to hearing testimony (LTA,

Article 17) and to the conciliation of the case. For hearing testimony, the panel usually initiate questioning, and the cross-examination style is rarely used. Unless the case is resolved, a third session will be scheduled. In practice, the third session is focused on whether parties agree to the conciliation proposal by the panel in the second session. If the conciliation fails, the panel hands down its ruling, usually an on-the-spot oral ruling.

484. The process of conciliation normally involves the panel meeting with each party in separate alternating sessions (caucusing). If a written agreement is made as the outcome of the conciliation, it will have legal effect as a conciliation agreement according to the provisions of the Civil Conciliation Act (Article 16, as applied by LTA, Article 29) and hence possess the same effect as a settlement in court (*saiban-jo no wakai*) entered into during an ordinary civil action. If the matter cannot be conciliated, the panel closes the hearing and renders an on-the-spot oral ruling or hands down a written ruling at a later date (LTA, Article 19).

C. Ruling (Award)

485. A ruling is made by 'taking into consideration the legal relationship of the parties and the result of the hearings' (LTA, Article 20(1)). The panel may 'confirm the legal rights of the parties, issue an order for monetary payment, delivery of goods or provision of properties, or otherwise appropriate steps to be taken' (LTA, Article 20(2)). The wording of this provision suggests that the panel may hand down a ruling that is of a flexible nature in accordance with the nature of the individual case, not necessarily sticking to a formal legalistic approach. The ruling has the same legal effect as a settlement in court if no challenge is raised through an objection of either party within two weeks after the ruling has been delivered to the parties (LTA, Article 21(1)).

486. The panel may close the proceedings without rendering a ruling whenever it finds it inappropriate to handle the dispute through the labour tribunal due to the nature of the case. When this happens, a formal complaint is deemed to have been brought to the ordinary civil court at the time of filing of the original petition with the labour tribunal (LTA, Article 24(1)(2)). The same is true when either party or both parties raises an objection to the ruling within two weeks. The ruling then automatically loses its effect (LTA, Article 21(3)).

487. In both of the above instances, the case is regarded as being filed as formal litigation under the Code of Civil Procedure (CCP) with the district court where the labour tribunal was formed for the particular case. Thus, the original petition is regarded as a written complaint in the civil action (LTA, Article 22(3)). A labour tribunal case may therefore end up as a formal civil litigation case with all of the procedural guarantees available under the CCP. The promoters of this system of an automatic transfer from the informal tribunal to the civil court expect that consideration of the potential costs of a full-blown civil action eventually might stimulate the preference for an early resolution during the tribunal proceedings. At the same time, it is expected that the tribunal will provide a simple and quick resolution that will potentially reduce the caseload burden of ordinary civil courts. In this sense, it has been pointed out that the system possesses similarities to the development of the court-annexed ADR procedures in the United States.

488. The substantive parts of the Non-Contentious Cases Procedure Act are made applicable to the Labour Tribunal proceedings (LTA, Article 29) because the labour tribunal procedure is structured as 'non-contentious'. In 'non-contentious' judicial proceedings, the court is freed from the ordinary procedural constraints imposed by the CCP. The court is not strictly bound by the claim and arguments presented by the plaintiff. Ex officio gathering of evidence is also allowed. The court is expected to grant the relief it considers most appropriate.

489. Under the LTA, the panel is required to make a ruling based not only on the rights and obligations of the parties but also on the basis of the desirable relationship which has been found through the totality of proceedings before the tribunal (Article 20(1)). The tribunal is therefore given discretion to order a monetary payment and/or delivery of goods or other property or to order anything appropriate for the settlement of the case quite apart from the rules of applicable substantive law (Article 20(2)). In other words, a dispute of rights can be treated like a dispute of interests. As a result, the panel possesses substantial discretion to decide what is appropriate and to make a flexible ruling without being confined solely to the respective rights and duties of the parties under the law. For instance, in dismissal cases in an ordinary civil action under the CCP, the court is bound to declare an illegal dismissal null and void, confirm the existing employment contract and issue an order for the retroactive payment of wages starting from the date of the dismissal and also for reinstatement of the plaintiff to the workplace if demanded by the plaintiff. However, the labour tribunal may issue an order for payment of compensation regardless of the legality of the dismissal in order to settle the case if the panel finds that the dismissed person is unwilling to be reinstated and the employer is not opposed to making a financial settlement. In effect, the labour tribunal may reach a decision creating the same outcome which would have been reached by the parties through amicable settlement.

490. The parties' substantive rights must be guaranteed as long as either party wants to have his/her rights vindicated by the court through the ordinary civil procedure in which the judge is strictly bound by the rules of substantive law. Therefore, the ruling of a labour tribunal binds the parties only when it is accepted by both of them. If one of the parties does not accept it, a formal litigation proceeding must be available to such a party; otherwise, the whole system would become unconstitutional, since it would infringe the party's right to resort to formal court procedure to resolve legal disputes guaranteed under Article 32 of the Constitution.

491. The labour tribunals had accepted 877 complaints in 2006, 1494 in 2007 and 2,052 in 2008. Then, the number of complaints sharply rose to 3,468 in 2009 probably due to the increase of employment disputes resulted from the recession after the Lehman shock. After that, the tribunals have accepted around 3,500 cases per year. Although the number of complaints rose to 3,907 in 2019, it fell down slightly probably under the influence of COVID-19, and is now in the process of recovery (3,473 in 2023). The increase of the cases indicates the steady acceptance of the system in Japan. It is safe to say that the labour tribunal system is now regarded as a main measure of employment dispute resolution together with the ordinary procedure. The number of complaints for ordinary civil procedures is almost similar to that of the Labour Tribunal System as stated below.

The distribution of the cases settled by the tribunals using the different methods are shown in Table 18below.

Table 18 Cases at the Labour Tribunal by Different Means of Disposal

Year	*Number of Cases Disposed*	*Ruling*	*Challenged*	*Conciliation (Chôtei)*	*Article 24*	*Withdrawal*	*Rejected or Transferred*
2006	606	107 17.7%	74 69.2	427 70.5%	19 3.1%	50 8.3%	3 0.5%
2010	3,436	612 17.8%	364 59.5%	2,433 70.8%	121 3.5%	240 7.0%	30 0.9%
2015	3,674	613 16.7%	372 6%	2,497 68.0%	193 5.3%	340 9.3%	31 0.8%
2020	3,755	608 16.2%	352 57.9%	2,559 68.1%	191 5.1%	363 9.7%	34 0.9%
2023	3,248	548 16.9%	266 48.5%	2,235 68.8%	177 5.4%	246 7.6%	42 1.3%

Source: Homu Sho (Ministry of Justice), *Rodo Kankei Minji Gyosei Jiken no Gaiyou* (Summary of Civil and Administrative Labour-related Cases in Judiciary).

492. It is to be noted that about 70% of the cases have been closed by conciliation by mutual agreement. The success rate of conciliation is quite high compared with the success rate of conciliation by the Dispute Adjustment Commissions under the administrative ADR explained before, which is about 30 to 40%. This is probably due to the feature of the Labour Tribunal System that the panel finds facts and notifies certain evaluation of the case when the panel presents its conciliation proposal in such a way as 'Based on the evidence of this case, the dismissal is problematic.' Facing such a disclosure of the case evaluation, the parties can predict the result of the final disposition, i.e., a ruling in the form of award by the panel or even a final judgment by the court if the parties object to the award. Cases in which conciliation efforts have been failed usually result in panel's awards. However, among remaining 30% of the cases where the parties have not agreed to the conciliation proposal and the panel has issued its awards, about 40% of the awards become finalized without being challenged by either party. This means that the parties accept the awards as a ruling of the panel. As a result, more than 80% (70+30×0.4) of the Labour Tribunal cases are disposed in the Labour Tribunal procedure without going to the ordinary civil procedure.

D. Duration of the Proceedings

493. As shown in Table 19, more than 90% of the cases have been terminated within the first three hearing sessions each year since the operation of the Labour Tribunal System started. This shows that the intention of the law to permit the holding of more than three hearings only 'in unusual circumstances' (LTA, Article 15) has been well observed in practice. Moreover, the majority of cases have been terminated before the third session. This is most probably because the cases are often closed by way of conciliation at the first or second sessions. It is often mentioned by attorneys participating in the Labour Tribunal procedure that effective and intensive representation in the first session is crucial, since the second session is often devoted to conciliation.

Table 19 Cases at the Labour Tribunal by Number of Sessions

Year	*Cases Disposed*	*0 Session*	*1 Session*	*2 Sessions*	*3 Sessions*	*4 Sessions*	*More Than 5*
2006	606	32 5.3%	101 16.7%	215 35.5%	245 40.4%	13 2.1%	0
2010	3,436	171 5.0%	910 26.5%	1,289 37.5%	996 29.0%	67 1.9%	3 0.1%
2015	3,674	249 6.8%	1,072 29.2%	1,425 38.8%	887 24.1%	394 1.1%	23 0.1%
2020	3,755	264 7.0%	1,290 34.4%	1,396 37.2%	750 20.0%	52 1.4	3 0.1%
2023	3,248	188 5.8%	1,085 33.4%	1,303 40.1%	635 19.6%	35 1.5%	2 0.1%

Source: Homu Sho (Ministry of Justice), *Rodo Kankei Minji Gyosei Jiken no Gaiyou* (Summary of Civil and Administrative Labour-related Cases in Judiciary).

Table 20 Cases at the Labour Tribunal by Duration of Proceedings

Year	*Cases Disposed*	*Up to*					*More Thanl Year*	*Average by Month*
		1 Month	*2 Months*	*3 Months*	*6 Months*	*One Year*		
2006	606	36 5.9%	192 31.7%	207 34.2%	171 28.2%	0	N.A.	2.4
2010	3,436	141 4.1%	1240 36.1%	1237 36.0%	799 23.3%	10 0.6%	0	2.4

Year	*Cases Disposed*	*Up to*					*More ThanI Year*	*Average by Month*
		1 Month	*2 Months*	*3 Months*	*6 Months*	*One Year*		
2015	3,674	122 3.3%	1,043 28.4%	1,301 35.4%	1,155 31.4%	27 0.8%	1 0.0%	2.74
2020	3,755	82 2.2%	651 17.3%	953 25.4%	1671 44.5%	396 10.5%	2 0.1%	3.6
2023	3,248	107 2.9%	1,350 36.5%	1,363 36.9%	865 23.4%	98 3.0%	3 0.1%	3.0

Source: Homu Sho (Ministry of Justice), *Rodo Kankei Minji Gyosei Jiken no Gaiyou* (Summary of Civil and Administrative Labour-related Cases in Judiciary).

494. As shown in Table 20, more than 90% of the cases are closed within the six months. The average duration of the proceeding at the tribunal has usually been 2.4 to 3.0 months. The exception was 2020, when the average duration of the proceeding was 3.6 months because the courts in Japan were temporarily closed that year due to COVID-19. Although in recent years the average duration of the proceeding has become slightly longer, the proceeding is much shorter in comparison with the duration of ordinary labour law litigation in the district courts and unfair labour practice cases handled by LRCs. The average duration of labour law cases in the ordinary civil courts was 17.9 months in 2023, which has become longer in recent years.

495. The average duration of unfair labour practice cases at the LRCs in the year 2006, when the Labour Tribunal System started, was 1,228 days at the local level (first instance) and 2,137 days at the Central LRC (review) level.[323] Although the average duration of unfair labour practice cases has been rather remarkably reduced within recent years, the average duration of unfair labour practice cases at the local level was still long, i.e., 671 days at the local level and 739 at the Central LRC in 2021.[324]

496. Another fact worth mentioning here is that both plaintiffs and defendants are usually represented by lawyers. Among the cases that were disposed in 2023, 89.0% of plaintiffs and 87.6% of defendants were represented by lawyers. LTA). It is interesting that the rate of settlement by conciliation is much higher in cases where both of the parties were represented by lawyers. In 2023, the rate of settlement by conciliation was 75.8% in cases where both parties were represented by lawyers, in contrast with 33.7% in cases where neither party were represented by lawyers (34.4% where only plaintiffs were represented by lawyers; 54.4% where

323. 61 *Rôdô Iinkai Nempo* [Annual Report of the Labor Relations Commissions] 9, 15 (2006).
324. 77 *Rôdô Iinkai Nempo* [Annual Report of the Labor Relations Commissions] 10, 17 (2023).

only defendants were represented by lawyers). This is probably because lawyers often recommend settlement after the panel discloses its legal evaluation of the case in offering the settlement proposal.

497. As the data of the operation of the Labour Tribunal System indicate, the original intention in introducing the this system to provide a 'speedy and simple procedure' to settle disputes seems so far to have been rather well realized. In the year of 2010 after four years of implementation of the system, a comprehensive academic research on the practice of the system was carried out.[325] It was conducted through hearings of 1,782 persons involved in the procedures of the labour tribunal as parties of the procedure. According to the final report of the survey the system was fairly highly evaluated on account of: (1) speedy solution, (2) professional quality and (3) proper management of the system. However, according to the opinion of the participants of this research project, the result of the survey indicated a couple of rather significant findings such as:

1. Among parties of the procedure the respondents from employer tended to give negative while those from labour side gave positive evaluation of the function of the system.
2. It was noted that there was a striking difference of evaluation between parties from larger enterprises and smaller ones. Particularly those from smaller enterprises with less than 100 evaluated the function of the tribunal negatively in terms of 'understanding of the reality of employment relations', 'adequate interpretation of legal principles', and 'satisfactory solution of the cases'. Professors who conducted the research explain the reason of the second point findings as follows: 'non-judge panelists of the tribunal are appointed from those with experience of either personal management or union leaders of larger enterprises or enterprise unions of larger companies.'

IV. Resolution System Inside Workplaces

498. Besides the above-mentioned public dispute solution systems, there are grievance solution channels inside workplaces. However, special bodies dealing with grievances such as grievance committees are not utilized in workplaces. A survey in 2019 found that 57.8% of workplaces have some sort of schemes for handling employees' grievances. However, only 16.7% of these workplaces have grievance committees, while 81.1% of them have procedures of consultation. . In most cases, grievance committees are established under collective agreements and therefore it is difficult for non-members of unions to resort to them. The same survey found that, of employees who made grievances to the companies, 77.8% made them through their immediate supervisors, 13.6% through their unions.[326] In view

325. Kazuo Sugeno et al., *Rodo shinpan seido no Riyousha Chosa* (Survey of Users of Labour Tribunal System), Yihukaku, 2013.
326. Ministry of Health, Labour and Welfare, *Reiwa 1nen Roshi Communication Chosa* (Survey on Communication between Employees and Employers), 2019.

of the recent increase of workplace dispute as is illustrated the growing number of labour cases in the Labour Tribunal procedure and ordinary civil litigation, it is future challenge for Japan to develop effective dispute resolution system inside workplaces.

§4. Settlement of Collective Disputes

499. In addition to its quasi-judicial function of dealing with unfair labour practice cases, the LRCs have the function of settling industrial disputes by conciliation, mediation or arbitration. A distinguishing feature of industrial dispute settlement in Japan is the almost total lack of, and very minor role played by, private machinery such as private arbitration or mediation – both as regards disputes of interest and as regards disputes of rights. Private arbitration is practically unknown and the mediation or conciliation of an industrial dispute by, for example, someone with political influence, is also very rare. Also, an arbitration agreement of individual labour disputes based is prohibited if such an agreement is concluded before the dispute arises (Supplement Article 4 of the Arbitration Act). The settlement of disputes of interest is almost exclusively handled by the LRC, while the settlement of disputes of vested rights is almost monopolized by the Courts. This monopoly of dispute settlement by government organs like the courts and the LRCs seems to contradict the Japanese preference for reconciliation. However, this can be explained by the virtual impossibility of finding a third party with authority and influence over both parties to the dispute; whereas in traditional Japanese society disputes are often settled by influential people with sufficient authority who can and do appeal to sentiment rather than to any universal norm. In industrial relations, this type of sentimental appeal does not often work, for the parties are likely to be involved in a real confrontation.

500. The LRAA distinguishes three kinds of settlement regarding collective labour disputes: conciliation, mediation and arbitration. In principle these dispute settlement procedures (with the exception of conciliation) can only be brought into use with the consent of both parties to the dispute – unless it is public welfare work or in the public sector, as we shall later see. Conciliation is carried out by a conciliator or conciliators appointed by the Commission. The conciliator's job is to confirm both parties' claims and to try and settle them in the most appropriate way. There is no specialized formal procedure for the conciliator to follow. Mediation is undertaken by a mediation committee consisting of at least one member from each of the three sides (public, labour and employer). The committee may make a proposal to settle the case and, if necessary, publicize it, together with the reasons for it, through the mass media channels of the radio and newspapers. However, under no circumstances can the parties be forced to accept the proposal put forward. Arbitration is handled by a committee of arbitrators appointed by the chairman of the Commission from among the public members, although worker and employer members may still attend the meetings of the committee and express their opinions. An arbitration award issued in writing by the committee is binding on both parties and has the same legal effect as a collective agreement.

501. In spite of the legal distinctions between the three methods the parties still prefer the most informal kind of settlement; that is, conciliation rather than the other more formal and legally binding procedures. Therefore, mediation and arbitration are rather rare (*see* Table 21).

Table 21 Number of Applications for Dispute Adjustment Received by the LRCs

Year	*Conciliation*	*Mediation*	*Arbitration*
2018	236	9	0
2019	202	3	0
2020	226	2	1
2021	232	3	0
2022	172	3	0

Sources: CLRC, *Rodo Iinkai Nenpo* (Annual Report of the LRCs).

502. The LRAA has special provisions concerning adjustment of labour disputes in public welfare work (*see* Part II, Chapter 6, section 6). Before the Prime Minister makes a decision of Emergency Adjustment on a particular labour dispute of public welfare work as the dispute severely hampers national economy or citizens' life, he or she should ask the opinion of the CLRC about it. As soon as such a decision has been reached, the Prime Minister should publicize his or her decision with the reasons for it promptly and notify the Commission (Article 35.2). The Commission should then use its utmost efforts to settle the case through conciliation, mediation or arbitration and, if necessary, by investigation and publicizing the facts of the case and making proposals for a settlement (Article 35.3). The Commission should also give priority to disputes in public welfare work about which a decision of Emergency Adjustment was made. When the Prime Minister's decision is open to public, both parties are prohibited from conducting dispute acts for fifty days. Since the enactment of the LRAA 1n 1946, this Emergency Adjustment was carried out only once in 1952.

Selected Bibliography

Industrial Relations and Social Background (Books and Monographs Only)

Abegglen, J., *Management and Worker: the Japanese Solution*. Tokyo: Sophia/Kodansha International, 1973.

Aoki, M., *Information, Incentives, and Bargaining in Japanese Economy*. Cambridge: Cambridge University Press, 1988.

Aoki, M. and Dore, R.P., *The Japanese Firm – Source of Competitive Strength*. Oxford: Oxford University Press, 1994.

Boyer, R. and Yamada, T. (ed.), *Japanese Capitalism in Crisis: A Regulationist Interpretation*. London: Routledge, 2000.

Cole, R.E., Work, Mobility, and Participation: *A Comparative Study of American and Japanese Industry*. Berkeley: University of California Press, 1979.

Dore, R.P., *British Factory – Japanese Factory*. Berkeley: University of California Press, 1973.

Dore, R.P., *Flexible Rigidities: Industrial Policy and Structural Adjustment in the Japanese Economy, 1970–80*. London: Athlone Press, 1986.

Dore, R.P., *Taking Japan Seriously: A Confucian Perspective on Leading Economic Issues*. Stanford: Stanford University Press, 1987.

Fu, U., *An Emerging Non-Regular Labour Force in Japan*. Routledge, 2012.

Hanami, T., *Labour Relations in Japan Today*. Tokyo: Kodansha International, 1979.

Hart, R.A. and Kawasaki, S., *Work and Pay in Japan*. Cambridge: Cambridge University Press, 1999.

Hasegawa, H. and Hook, G.D. (ed.), *Japanese Business Management*. London: Routledge, 1998.

Hayashi, S., *Culture and Management in Japan*. Tokyo: University of Tokyo Press, 1989.

Imai, K. and Komiya, R. (ed.), *Business Enterprise in Japan*. Cambridge: MIT Press, 1994.

Imai, J., The Transformation of Japanese Employment Relations. Palgrave Macmillan, 2011.

Kawanishi, H., *The Human Face of Industrial Conflict in Post-War Japan*. London: Kegan Paul International, 1999.

Koike, K., *Understanding Industrial Relations in Modern Japan*. London: Macmillan, 1988.

Koike, K., *The Economics of Work in Japan*. Tokyo: LTCB International Library Foundation, 1995.
Kono, T. and Clegg, T.R., *Transformations of Corporate Culture: Experiences of Japanese Enterprise*. Berlin: Walter de Gruyter, 1998.
Marsland, S., *Birth of the Japanese Labor Movement*. Honolulu: Univ. of Hawaii Press, 1989.
Mouer, R. and Kawanishi, H., *A Sociology of Work in Japan*. Cambridge: Cambridge University Press, 2005.
Nakamura, K., *Going Global: Structural Reforms in Japan's Economic and Business Systems*. Tokyo: Japan Times, 1996.
Nakane, C., *Japanese Society*. Berkeley: University of California Press, 1970.
Price, J., *Japan Works: Power and Paradox in Postwar Industrial Relations*. Ithaca: Cornell University Press, 1997.
Shirai, T. (ed.), *Contemporary Industrial Relations in Japan*. Madison: University of Wisconsin Press, 1983.
Sumiya, M., *The Japanese Industrial Relations Reconsidered*. Tokyo: Japan Institute of Labour, 1990.
Tachibanaki, T. and Noda, T., *The Economic Effects of Trade Unions in Japan*. London: Macmillan, 2000.
Tachibanaki, T., *Wage Determination and Distribution in Japan*. Oxford: Claredon Press, 1996.
Tachibanaki, T., *Who Runs Japanese, Business?*, Cheltenham: Edward Elgar, 1998.
Takanashi, A. et al., *Shunto Wage Offensive*. Tokyo: Japan Institute of Labour, 1996.
Takezawa, S., *Japan Work Ways 1960–1976–1990*. Tokyo: Japan Institute of Labour, 1995.
Teranishi, J., *Revolution of the Economic System in Japan*, Cheltenham: Edward Elgar Publishing Limited, 2005.
Vogel, E.F., *Japan As Number One, Lessons For America*. Cambridge: Cambridge University Press, 1988.
Whittaker, D.H., *Small Firms in the Japanese Economy*. Cambridge: Cambridge University Press, 1997.

Law in General

Foote, D. (ed.), *Law in Japan: A Turning Poin*t, University of Washington Press, 2007.
Fujikura, K., *Japanese Law and Legal Theory*. Aldershot: Dartmouth, 1996.
Kojima, T. (ed.), *Perspectives on Civil Justice and ADR: Japan and the U.S.A*. Tokyo: Chuo Univ. Press, 1990.
Luney Jr., P.R. and Takahashi, K. (ed.), *Japanese Constitutional Law*. Tokyo: University of Tokyo Press, 1992.
Oda, Hiroshi, *Japanese Law*. London: Butterworth, 1992.
Ramseyer, J.M. and Nakazato, M., *Japanese Law: An Economic Approach*. Chicago: University of Chicago Press.
Yanagida, Y. et al., *Law and Investment in Japan: Cases and Materials*. Cambridge: Harvard University Press, 1994.

Selected Bibliography

Labour Law

Legislation

Japan Institute for Labour Policy and Training, *Labour Laws of Japan*. https://www.jil.go.jp/english/laws/index.html

Books and monographs

Araki, T., *Labor and Employment Law in Japan*. Tokyo: Japan Institute of Labour, 2002.
Hanami, T., *Labour Law and Industrial Relations in Japan*. Deventer, The Netherlands: Kluwer, 1979.
Hanami, T., *Labour Law and Industrial Relations in Japan* (second & revised edition). Deventer, The Netherlands: Kluwer, 1985.
Hanami, T., *Labor Law and Social Security*. Tokyo: CCH Japan Business Law in Japan, 1988.
Hanami, T., *Managing Japanese Workers*. Tokyo: Japan Institute of Labour, 1991.
Komiya, F., *A Comparative Analysis of the Law on Dismissal in Great Britain, Japan and the USA*. London: London School of Economics, 1986.
Komiya, F., *A Comparative Study of the Law of Dismissal in Japan, Great Britain and United States from the Perspective of Employment Protection (Ph.D. thesis)*. London: London School of Economics, 1997.
Sugeno, K., *Japanese Employment and Labour Law*. Carolina Academic Press, 2002.

Articles

Araki, T., 'Characteristics of Regulations on Dispatched Work (Temporary Work) in Japan', *Japan Labor Bulletin* Vol. 33, No. 8.
Araki, T., 'Modification of Working Conditions Through Dismissal?', *Japan Labor Bulletin* Vol. 34, No. 8.
Araki, T., 'Regulation of Working Hours for White-Collar Workers Engaging in "Discretionary Activities"', *Japan Labor Bulletin*, Vol. 35, No. 7.
Araki, T., 'Changing Japanese Labor Law in Light of Deregulation Drives: A Comparative Analysis', *Japan Labor Bulletin* Vol. 36, No. 5.
Araki, T., 'Recent Legislative Developments in Equal Employment and Harmonisation of Work and Family Life in Japan', *Japan Labor Bulletin* Vol. 37, No. 4.
Araki, T., '1999 Revisions of Employment Security Law and Worker Dispatching Law: Drastic Reforms of Japanese Labor Market Regulations', *Japan Labor Bulletin* Vol. 38, No. 9.
Araki, T., 'Bargaining Decentralization, Workforce Diversification and Challenges Labor Union Face: Focusing on German and Japanese Case', A. Höland et al. (eds.), *Employee Involvement in a Globalising World: Liber Amicorum Manfred Weiss*, Berliner Wissenschafts-Verlag, 2005.
Araki, T., 'Changing Employment Practices, Corporate Governance, and the Role of Labor Law in Japan', *Comparative Labor Law and Policy Journal*, Vol. 28, No. 2, 2007.

Selected Bibliography

Araki, T, 'New Forms of Dispute Resolution: Japan's Labor Tribunal System', K.V.W. Stone and H. Arthurs (eds.), *Rethinking Workplace Regulation: Beyond the Standard Contract of Employment*, Russel Sage Foundation, 2013.

Araki, T., 'The Relationship Between State Law, Collective Agreement, and Individual Contract', G.Kiss (ed.), *Recent Developments in Labour Law*, Akademiai Kiado, 2013.

Araki, T., 'New Labour Policies on Non-standard Employment in Japan: A Focus on the New Regulations on Fixed-term Employment Contracts', M.Henssler and K.Tezuka (eds.), *Aktuelle arbeitsrechtliche Herausforderungen in Japan und Deutchland, [Japanisches Recht, Band 50]*, Carl Heymans Verlag, 2014.

Araki, T., 'Cooperative Versus Conflictual Industrial Relations: Japanese Experience', A. Perulli and T. Treu (eds.), *The Role of the State and Industrial Relations*, Wolters Kluwer, 2019.

Arita, K., 'Legal Regulation of Dismissal in Japan', King's Law Journal, Vol. 33, No.2, 2022.

Asakura, M., 'Discrimination in Employment in Japan', R. Blanpain (ed.), *Discrimination in Employment.* Leuven: Peeters, 1998.

Hanami, T., 'The Characteristics of Labour Disputes in Japan', *Social and Cultural Background of Labour – Management Relations in Asian Countries.* Tokyo: Japan Institute of Labour, 1972.

Hanami, T., 'The Influence of ILO Standards on Law and Practice in Japan', *International Labour Review.* Vol. 120, No. 6 (November–December 1981).

Hanami, T., 'Flexibility and Wages: A Comparative Treatment in Japan', R.Blanpain (ed.), *Flexibility and Wages: A Comparative Treatment*'. Deventer: Kluwer Law and Taxation Publishers, 1990.

Hanami, T., 'Equal Employment Revisited', *Japan Labor Bulletin* Vol. 39, No. 1.

Hanami, T., 'Labor Law Reform for the 21st Century', *Comparative Labor Law and Policy Journal*, Vol. 21, No. 3, 2000.

Hanami, T., 'Deregulation and international regulation: an Asian perspective', R. Blanpain & M. Weiss (eds.), *Changing Industrial Relations and Modernisation of Labour Law-Liber Amicorum in Honour of Professor Marco Biagi*, Kluwer, 2003.

Hanami, T., 'Women's Involvement in Men's Society in Japan', Armin Höland, Christine

Hanami, T., 'Nothing Fails like Failure-Trade Unionism in Japan', *Liber Amicorum Reinhold Fahlbeck*, Juristförlaget I Lund, 2005.

Hanami, T., 'The Changing Labor Market, Industrial Relations and Labor Policy', R. Haak (ed.), *The Changing Structure of Labour in Japan*, Palgrave Macmillan, 2006.

Hanami, T., 'Labor Tribunal System', Taniguchi-Reich-Miyake (ed.), *Civil Procedure in Japan*, Juris Publishing, Inc., 2009.

Hayakawa, C., 'Labor Law and Policy Issues Relating to Foreign Workers in Japan', *Japan Labor Review*, Vol. 7, No.3, 2010.

Ikezoe, H., 'Work-Life Balance in Japan: Outline of Policies, Legal Systems and Actual Situations', *Japan Labor Review*, Vol. 11, No. 1, 2014.

Iki, N., 'The Development of Labor Policy on Women: From the Perspectives of Justice, Effective Use, and Welfare', *Japan Labor Review*, Vol. 10, No. 1, 2013.

Ishida, M., 'Death and Suicide from Overwork: The Japanese Workplace and Labour Law', J. Conaghan et al. (eds.), *Labour Law in An Era of Globalization: Transformative Practices & Possibilities*, Oxford University Press, 2002.

Kanki, C., 'Legal Structure of, and Issues with, Japan's Regional Minimum Wage System: Comparative Study of the UK and French Systems, including the Social Security Systems',

Japan Labor Review Vol. 8, No.2, 2011.

Kanno, T., 'Study on Legal Issues Involving Intermediate Age Brackets: Aiming to Facilitate Work-Life Balance', Japan Labor Review Vol. 13, No. 1, 2016.

Kasagi, E., 'The Reform of the Health Care System for the Elderly People – The Transformation of Health Care System in Japan', Gebauer et al. (eds.), *Alternde Gesellschaften im Recht*, Mohr Siebeck GmbH, 2015.

Kezuka, K., 'Legal Problems Concerning Part-time Work in Japan', *Japan Labor Bulletin* Vol. 39, No. 9, 2011.

Kezuka, K., 'Significance and Tasks involved in Establishment of Labor Tribunal System', *Japan Labor Review*, Vol. 3, No. 1.

Komiya, F., 'The Changing Nature of the Employment Relationship', in R. Blanpain (ed.), *Private Employment Agencies*. The Hague: Kluwer, 1999.

Komiya, F., 'Dismissal Procedures and Termination Benefits in Japan', *Comparative Labor Law Journal* 151 (Winter 1991).

Komiya, F., 'Law of Dismissal and Employment Practice in Japan', *Industrial Relations Journal*, Vol.22, No.1.

Komiya, F., 'Private Employment Agencies in Japan', R.Blanpain (ed.), *Private Employment Agencies*. The Hague: Kluwer, 1999.

Komiya, F., 'Reconsideration on Employment Termination Law in Japan', *Liber Amiorum* Reinhold Fahlbeck, Juristförlaget I Lund, 2005.

Komiya, F., 'Japan', Blanpain, R. & Grant, C. (ed.), *Fixed Term Employment Contracts: A Comparative Study* (Vanden Brode, 2009).

Konishi, Y., 'Legal Benefits System for Retirement Risk in Japan: Basic Structure and Relationship with the Employment System', *Japan Labor Review*, Vol. 9, No.2, 2012.

Kuwamura, Y., 'The Right to Strike: Japan', Bernd Waas (ed.), *The Right to Strike: A Comparative View*, Kluwer Law International, 2014.

Mizushima, I., 'The Legal Issues Surrounding Professionals in Relation to Labor Law', *Japan Labor Review* Vol. 8, No.4, 2011.

Nakagawa, J., 'Does the CRPD Matter? A Comparison of Sheltered Workshop Policies in Japan, Taiwan, and South Korea', R. Sally and K.R. Fisher (eds.), *Research Handbook on Disability Policy*, Edward Elgar Publishing, 2023.

Nakakubo, H., 'Procedures for Resolving Individual Employment Disputes', *Japan Labor Bulletin* Vol. 35, No. 6.

Nakakubo, H., 'Industrial Action and Liability in Japan: A Legal Overview', *Japan Labor Review* Vol. 12, No. 2, 2015.

Nakakubo, H., 'Glass Ceiling or Iron Weight?: Challenges for Female Employees on Their Path to Becoming Managers and Executives in Japan', *Hastings International and Comparative Law Review*, Vol. 32, No. 2, 2016.

Nogawa, S., 'The Great East Japan Earthquake and a Future Vision for Labor Law Japan', *Japan Labor Review* Vol. 9, No.4, 2012.

Obata, F., '*Karojisatsu* – Suicide as a Result of Overwork', *Japan Labor Bulletin* Vol. 39, No. 11.
Ouchi, S., 'Legal Issues Concerning Nominal Supervisors and Managers', *Japan Labor Review*, Vol. 7, No. 4, 2010.
Sugeno, K., 'Flexibility in Working Time in Japan (I & II)', *Japan Labor Bulletin* Vol. 29, No. 6 & 7.
Sugeno, K., 'The Supreme Court's Hitachi Decision on the Duty to Work Overtime Introduction', *Japan Labor Bulletin* Vol. 31, No. 5.
Sugeno, K. and Suwa, Y., 'Trade Union Democracy and Industrial Relations in Japan', *Trade Union Democracy and Industrial Relations*, Deventer: Kluwer Law and Taxation Publishers, 1988.
Sugeno, K., 'Discrimination in Employment: Dynamism and the Limits of Harmonization Law', R. Blanpain (ed.), *Discrimination in Employment*. Leuven: Peeters, 1998.
Sugeno, K., 'A New Law to Protect Whistle-Blowing: Changing Legal Consciousness in Japanese Industrial Society', Armin Höland et al. (eds.), *Employee Involvement in a Globalising World – Liber Amicorum Manfred Weiss*, Berliner Wissenschafts-Verlag, 2005.
Sugeno, K., 'The Birth of Labor Tribunal System in Japan: A Synthesis of Labor-Law Reform and Judicial Reform', *Liber Amicorum Reinhold Fahlbeck*, Juristförlaget I Lund, 2005.
Sugeno, K., 'Judicial Reform and the Reform of the Labor Dispute Resolution System', *Japan Labor Review*, Vol.3, No.1, 2006.
Sugeno, K. and Yamakoshi, K., 'Dismissals in Japan (Part One & Two): How Strict Is Japanese Law on Employers?', *Japan Labor Review*, Vol. 11, No.2 & 4, 2014.
Suwa, Y., 'Unfair Labor Practices Involving JR Firms', *Japan Labor Bulletin* Vol. 28, No. 4.
Suwa, Y., 'Relations of Collective Agreement to Rules of Employment', *Japan Labor Bulletin* Vol. 32, No. 5.
Takeuchi-Okuno, H., 'General Unions and Community Unions, and Japanese Labor Law', *Japan Labor Review* Vol.9, No. 1, 2012.
Takeuchi-Okuno, H., 'Employee Autonomy, Privacy, and Dignity under Technological Oversight', W. F. Matthew and M. Guy (eds.), *Comparative Labor Law*, Elgar, 2015.
Yamada, S., 'Equal Employment Opportunity Act, Having Passed the Quarter-Century Milestone', *Japan Labor Review* Vol. 10, No. 2, 2013.
Yamakawa, R., 'We've Only Just Begun: The Law of Sexual Harassment in Japan', *Hastings International and Comparative Law Review*, Vol. 22, No.3, 1999.
Yamakawa, R., 'New Wine in Old Bottles?: Employee/Independent Contractor Distinction under Japanese Labor Law', *Comparative Labor Law & Policy Journal*, Vol. 21, No. 1, 2001.
Yamakawa, R., 'From Security to Mobility? Changing Aspects of Japanese Dismissal Law', D. Foote (ed.), *Law in Japan: A Turning Poin*t, University of Washington Press, 2007.
Yamakawa, R., 'The Enactment of the Labor Contract Act: Its Significance and Future Issues', *Japan Labor Review*, Vol. 6, No. 2., 2009.

Yamakawa, R., 'Transnational Dimension of Japanese Labor and Employment Laws: New Choice-of-Law Rules and Determination of Geographical Reach', *Comparative Labor Law and Policy Journal*, Vol. 31, No. 2, 2010.
Yamakawa, R., 'Japan's Collective Labor Relations Law in the Public Sector: Constitutional Conflict between Union Rights and Democracy', *Comparative Labor Law and Policy Journal*, Vol. 34, No.2, 2013.
Yamakawa, R., 'Systems and Procedures for Resolving Labor Disputes in Japan', *Comparative Labor Law and Policy Journal*, Vol. 34, No. 3, 2013.
Yamakawa, R., 'Limitations on the Termination of Fixed-term Employment Contracts: Judicially Created Rules and Their Codification in Japanese Law', J. O. Haley, & T. Takenaka (eds.), *Legal Innovations in Asia,* Edward Elgar Publishing, 2014.
Yamakawa, R., 'Chapter 6: Japan', *Resolving Individual Labour Disputes: A Comparative Overview*, E. Minawa, S. Cooney, & C. Fenwick (eds.), International Labour Office, 2016.
Yamakawa, R., 'Innovative Measures for Implementing Labour Laws and Role of Labour Administration: Recent Developments in Japan', J. Heyes & L. Rychly (eds.), *The Governance of Labour Administration*, Edward Elgar Publishing, 2021.
Yonezu, T., 'International Dimensions of National Collective Bargaining', R. Blanpain (ed.), *International Collective Bargaining*. Leuven: Peeters, 1998.

Periodicals

Japan Labor Bulletin, Japan Institute of Labour, Tokyo.
Japan Labour Issues, Japan Labor Review, Japan Institute for Labour Policy and Training, Tokyo.
Japan Labor Review, Japan Institute for Labour Policy and Training, Tokyo.

Selected Bibliography

Table of Statutes

The numbers here refer to paragraph numbers.

Index

The numbers here refer to paragraph numbers.

Index

www.ingramcontent.com/pod-product-compliance
Ingram Content Group UK Ltd.
Pitfield, Milton Keynes, MK11 3LW, UK
UKHW020138290926
15471UKWH00003B/567

9 789403 537191